CHILDREN'S LITERATURE
COMES OF AGE

CHILDREN'S LITERATURE AND CULTURE
VOLUME I
GARLAND REFERENCE LIBRARY OF THE HUMANITIES
VOLUME 1816

CHILDREN'S LITERATURE AND CULTURE

JACK ZIPES, *General Editor*

CHILDREN'S LITERATURE
COMES OF AGE
Toward a New Aesthetic
by Maria Nikolajeva

REDISCOVERIES IN
CHILDREN'S LITERATURE
by Suzanne Rahn

CHILDREN'S LITERATURE COMES OF AGE
TOWARD A NEW AESTHETIC

MARIA NIKOLAJEVA

GARLAND PUBLISHING, INC.
NEW YORK AND LONDON
1996

Library of Congress Cataloging-in-Publication Data

Nikolajeva, Maria
    Children's literature comes of age :   toward a new aesthetic /
Maria Nikolajeva.
        p.   cm. — (Garland reference library of the humanities ; v. 1816.
Children's literature and culture ; v. 1)
    Includes bibliographical references (p.) and index.
    ISBN 0–8153–1556–2 (alk. paper)
    1. Children's literature—History and criticism.   I. Title.   II. Series:
Garland reference library of the humanities ; v. 1816.   III. Series: Children's
literature and culture series ; v. 1.
    PN1009.A1N55   1996
    809'.89282—dc20   95-19560
                                                                      CIP

Cover illustration: Ronia, the Robber's Daughter—a text of many genres.
Illustration by Ilon Wikland. Courtesy of the artist

Printed on acid-free, 250-year-life paper
Manufactured in the United States of America

CONTENTS

CHAPTER 6

CHAPTER 7

General Editor's Preface

Dedicated to furthering original research in children's literature and culture, the Children's Literature and Culture Series will include monographs on individual authors and illustrators, historical examinations of different periods, literary analyses of genres, and comparative studies on literature and the mass media. The series is international in scope and is intended to encourage innovative research in children's literature with a focus on interdisciplinary methodology.

Children's literature and culture are understood in the broadest sense of the term *children* to encompass the period of childhood up through late adolescence. Due to the fact that the notion of childhood has changed so much since the origination of children's literature, this Garland series is particularly concerned with transformations in culture and how they have affected the representation and socialization of children. While the emphasis of the series is on children's literature, all types of studies that deal with children's radio, film, television, and art will be included in an endeavor to grasp the aesthetics and values of children's culture. Not only have there been momentous changes in children's culture in the last fifty years, but there have been radical shifts in the scholarship that deals with these changes. In this regard, the goal of the Children's Literature and Culture Series is to enhance research in this field and, at the same time, point to new directions that bring together the best scholarly work throughout the world.

Jack Zipes

PREFACE

Most of the ideas developed in this book have been tested in essays, articles and reviews published in Swedish and international journals, as well as in papers presented at conferences. This does not, however, mean that my book is a compilation of previously published articles. In fact, I had not realized before I started how much work it takes to turn a number of articles into a book.

There are many theories that have inspired me both in my general approach to children's literature and in concrete evaluation of texts. Above all, I would like to pay tribute to the memory of Yuri Lotman. Although I never attended his classes at Tartu University and had not met him personally before his visit to Stockholm in 1988, I am happy to count myself among his disciples. The scope of ideas expressed in his works and the works of his school, his theories and research models have formed mine, which I am glad to acknowledge. Not least have Lotman's lectures in Stockholm stimulated many valuable reflections. This accounts for the clear semiotic approach in my book.

Like so many studies in humanities, this book is to a very high extent a product of conversations between committed parties and of the afterthoughts which arise after such conversations. Therefore I would like to thank my Swedish and international colleagues for inspiring discussions: Ying Toijer-Nilsson, Rigmor Granlund-Lind, Kristin Hallberg, Boel Westin, Ulf Boethius, Carina Lidström, Andrew Casson, Torsten Rönnerstrand, Gabriella Åhmansson, Jane Johansson and other members of the higher seminar on children's literature at Stockholm University; my colleagues in the International Research Society for Children's Literature, especially Rhonda Bunbury; colleagues and kindred spirits Tony Watkins, Marisol Dorao, William Moebius, Karen Hoyle, Nancy Huse, Sandra Beckett, John Stephens, Janina Orlov, Vincas Auryla, and Kestutis Urba. My very special thanks to Vivi

Edström, the first Scandinavian professor of children's literature, whose inspiration and advice have been indispensable. The Swedish Institute for Children's Books, its Director Sonja Svensson and its marvelous librarians Lena Törnqvist and Cecilia Östlund have been of great assistance, as well as Märta Bergstrand at Stockholm University Library. I would also like to remember all the students who have attended my classes of children's literature at Stockholm University as well as those who came to my lectures in Finland, Britain, Lithuania, the United States and Australia, and who stimulated my thought with their keen questions and their eternal skepticism.

I have received many valuable ideas during the Summer School of Semiotics in Lund in 1992, arranged by the Nordic Association for Semiotic Studies. A Fulbright grant which gave me the privilege to teach and conduct research at the University of Massachusetts, Amherst, was of overall importance for my insight into American children's literature.

Naturally I owe my greatest thanks to all writers who have inspired me not only through their books but also through personal contacts and letters. Nobody is forgotten, but I would like to emphasize the importance of Astrid Lindgren, Gunnel Linde, Maria Gripe, Irmelin Sandman Lilius, Aidan Chambers, Alan Garner, Lloyd Alexander and Norton Juster.

I must also remember the editors of the journals who encouraged me to write for them: Birgitta Fransson of *Opsis Kalopsis*, Lena Kåreland and Eva Nordlinder of *Barnboken*, Pavel Frenkel of *Detskaya Literatura*, Jacques Barchilon of *Marvels and Tales* and Mary Rubio of *Canadian Children's Literature*.

And naturally I remember Jack Zipes, who encouraged me to write the book in the first place and whose comments were the most essential guidelines.

I must also forward my warmest thanks to Charles Rougle, who has polished my English.

Last but not least I express my gratitude toward my family, especially my husband, Staffan Skott, who has patiently read the many versions of this book, and my daughter Julia, born 1982, without whom all my ideas would have remained bare theories.

Maria Nikolajeva
Stockholm

CHILDREN'S LITERATURE
COMES OF AGE

Children's Literature Coming of Age?

By Way of Introduction

The principal difference between research on children's literature and general literary criticism—and this factor is reflected in the way the history of literature is written—is that children's literature has from the very beginning been related to pedagogics. The very emergence of children's literature on a large scale is due to the fact that sometime in the seventeenth century society became conscious of childhood as a special period of life[1] and that children had their own special needs. The notions of childhood and the educational aspects of reading have crucially influenced the evolution of children's literature and have gone hand in hand with pedagogical views of literature as a powerful means for educating children. Children's literature has therefore been studied with a view to the suitability of books for children's reading.

This pedagogical view has led to a certain bias in general histories of children's literature. Using a classification based on country, epoch and the dominant view on childhood, reference sources have included only "suitable" books and simply ignored others. One can see this most clearly in the publishing policies and criticism in countries like the Soviet Union dominated by a single ideology. Histories of children's literature written in this tradition are nothing else than highly manipulated recommendation lists for adults who are to serve as mediators for children. The attitude is reflected in titles like "One Hundred Best Books for Children," "Children's Books Too Good to Miss," and "Best Children's Books of all Times."[2] The selection in these publications is always subjective and depends on the editor's pedagogical preferences.

Another type of history of children's literature, which is quite close to the first, views children's literature in relation to society. The study object of this approach is the triangle Child—Family—School. In this model, works of literature have only a functional, or pragmatic, role in their relation to reality. In reference materials based on this method we encounter chapters like "School," "Family," "Siblings," "Gender Roles," "Death,"

"War," and "Multiculturalism."[3] Even Perry Nodelman, whose approach is generally theoretical, cannot wholly refrain from this topical treatment, and considers books about toys and miniature people as a "subgenre" of children's literature.[4] Issue-oriented handbooks also have practical purposes, as aids to teachers and children's librarians.

There is, however, still another viewpoint or aspect which research on children's literature has quite ignored, and that is to approach children's literature as literature. It is probably only in the past ten years that the literary aspects of children's literature have been noticed and appreciated and subjected to contemporary literary theory and methods. In Sweden Vivi Edström's volume "Form in Children's Books"[5] was the first scholarly endeavor to focus on the literary aspects of children's books. German researchers have produced some noteworthy works,[6] and the Israeli scholar Zohar Shavit's *Poetics of Children's Literature* is a valuable contribution.[7] In North America, Perry Nodelman and Roderick McGillis are undoubtedly among the pioneers in theoretical approaches to children's texts,[8] and in Australia John Stephens has opened new perspectives.[9] Journals like *Children's Literature Association Quarterly* and *Canadian Children's Literature* have recently carried interesting material on various theoretical issues of literature for the young. These attempts notwithstanding, many scholars are reluctant to adopt this new critical view, while others are simply unaware of it.[10]

If children's books are regarded as literature, the scholarly point of departure is the interaction between texts—intertextuality—as well as the inherent features of texts themselves. The goal is to look beyond individual texts or individual *oeuvres* or even countries and nations and to focus instead on tendencies, regularities and their possible explanations. The model may be called historical poetics, and the method has its origins in semiotics.

In Sweden, although children's literature has at long last made its way into general literary history,[11] even today many literary critics do not take children's literature seriously. The reason for this is not only that they lack insight, but also has to do with the self-imposed isolation of children's literature researchers. Many of us still often see the primary subject of our research to be not children's literature but children's *reading*. Most secondary sources on children's literature do not in fact treat children's literature; what they portray instead is the history of childhood reading in a particular country. Because the authors of these studies are interested in the pedagogical aspects of children's literature, what they look for in children's books is subject matter, ideology, and didactic and educational values. You can still read children's book reviews beginning with: "The problem raised in the book is so important that . . . "—meaning that its artistic faults can be forgiven. Instead of encouraging authors to write good books, publishers still encourage competitions on certain issues and subjects. Children's book awards—multicultural book prizes, for example—are often oriented towards issues. The themes of many conferences on children's literature demonstrate the same attitude.

I do not mean that pedagogical aspects of children's literature are of no importance. I could even provocatively suggest that, on the contrary, too little importance is accorded to the pedagogical aspects of adult literature, if by those aspects we mean that the purpose of all literature and art is education in the spirit of humanity. Incidentally, children's reading as well can be studied from a semiotic perspective,[12] but aside from pure communication studies, this has not yet been done on a large scale.

What I mean is that children's literature research has neglected the literary aspects in favor of the pedagogical, while these in fact are closely related. If we consider which books have remained among classical children's literature, we will clearly see that these books possess outstanding literary quality. This is true of both the so-called classics, that is, books which were written for adults and have become a natural part of children's reading, like *Robinson Crusoe*, and of books which were written directly for children, like *Alice in Wonderland*. If we take more recent examples from the turn of the century, we see that today we still read Edith Nesbit and L. M. Montgomery, while many of their contemporaries have become hopelessly obsolete. In Sweden one of the classics still read today is *The Wonderful Adventures of Nils* (1906-1907) by Nobel prize winner Selma Lagerlöf.

Moving still further forward in time we can see what remains of the Swedish socially engaged and problem-oriented children's literature from the 1960s and 1970s. These books came as a reaction to the earlier idyllic children's literature and often discussed social problems without taking literary form into account. Although these books played an important role in society and education and the overall social activity of the 1960s and early 1970s, today they no longer have any social function and most of them are totally unreadable. Examples include teenage novels that produced heated discussion when they were published: *Mia Alone* (1973) by Gunnel Beckman debates abortion; "Peter's Baby" (1971) by Gun Jacobson debates teenage parenthood.[13] These books gave rise to vehement debate when they appeared (*Mia Alone* was also discussed outside Sweden). Today I hear from librarians that young readers will not touch them, and many university students of children's literature have never heard of them. The issues addressed in the books are not as controversial any longer, and their artistic value is conspicuously absent.

A few books from the same period, however, are still read and enjoyed: Maria Gripe's *Hugo and Josephine* books (1961–66) and *Elvis* books (1972–79); *The White Stone* (1964) by Gunnel Linde; *Admission to the Feast* (1969) by Gunnel Beckman. When we read these books today we see in them something different from what we saw then—not the problem, be it divorced parents, a lonely child, fear of death or generation conflict, but a human being, innermost thoughts and feelings, psychological development. We see a depiction of human relations. We see how the authors use the riches of the language and stylistic devices, how they create the time and space of the novel, how they penetrate into their characters. If the book lacks all this we put it aside and say: "obsolete." Something for the history of literature, a period piece, a social phenomenon, but not a living piece of art. Similar examples can be found in other countries than Sweden.

Reading certain children's books from the 1980s and 1990s we see that they sometimes are quite similar to the earlier books in subject matter while their impact on the reader is considerably stronger because of their higher literary quality.

Contemporary writers may not even be aware of the "issue" in their books, gladly emphasized by librarians and teachers. According to Patricia MacLachlan, it was not until she read reviews of her Newbery-winning *Sarah Plain and Tall* (1985) that she realized she had a stepmother in it.[14]

Thus, when we today begin to see children's literature in a broader perspective, it is not only because we have become more clever, but because the object of study, that is, children's literature, has undergone a remarkable change. Today we are slowly but surely becoming aware of a feature thus far entirely ignored by critics, namely that modern children's and juvenile literature has grown more "literary" and artistically elaborate. Early investigations of the literary aspect of children's books, which were made only in a few countries and not before the 1980s, noted first and foremost striking similarities in the form of a constant recurrence of themes, motifs, literary devices and typical characters. This has been the source of the common misunderstanding that, compared to adult literature, children's books are characterized by a simpler narrative structure, poorer language, and inferior artistic resources. A whole theory of the so called "adaptation" in children's literature came into being. This theory has, however, proved untenable. A study of Astrid Lindgren's books, to take one example, has shown that her style, language, word and phrase length, and choice of "difficult" words are much more complicated than in average Swedish adult fiction.

This misunderstanding has encouraged researchers to approach children's literature in a totally different fashion from all other literature.

Up till now, everything new and different in children's books has been treated as "abnormal," while in adult literature critics have always looked for innovation, originality, and experiment in form and content. Not until now have critics started to accept the right of children's literature to be literary, to be part of a *discourse* instead of a mere children's book. Not until now have we realized how rich children's literature was in artistic codes, to use a term from cultural semiotics,[15] nor can anyone today deny that during the last ten or twenty years children's books around the world have become more sophisticated.

This process is probably best observed through genre studies in a diachronic, historical perspective, which reveal that simple structures and superficial renderings of events are replaced by more complicated patterns and deeper psychological insights. The Swedish scholar Ying Toijer-Nilsson has shown this very promptly in her two studies of contemporary historical novels for young readers.[16] I myself have discovered this growing complexity in my studies of fantasy for children.[17] In modern children's literature at large we also see a tendency towards more complex, multi-dimensional texts. Thus many contemporary children's books display an increasing artistic sophistication, a conscious striving to exploit the richness of language, a variety of literary devices and expressive means, patterns from different genres. One common denominator in many such books is a convergence of genres. For many years there were clear dividers between genres and kinds of children's literature. These frontiers were supported by publishers who put distinct labels on their books; in Sweden, books for boys once had green bindings and books for girls red bindings. They were supported by critics who hastened to label books with customer information: adventure, mystery, family story, fairy tale. Even today in many countries children's books carry age recommendations: "7 to 10 years." The same practice in mainstream literature would seem ridiculous; no one would suggest recommending an adult novel "for men between the ages of 35 and 45." These recommendations and genre markers, however, have arisen out of the common prejudice that "children" are a homogeneous group with homogeneous preferences, tastes, interests and previous knowledge.

During the early stages of children's literature this division and classification may have been necessary to establish and confirm children's literature as a special literary system with different levels and structures. Once established, the system started to be questioned by the most radically minded children's writers. Instead of writing *within* a given genre, they began to write *against* the genre, thus changing and renewing it. The rigid system of genres and modes began to disintegrate.

We can take a closer look at one Swedish example from the 1980s, *Ronia, the Robber's Daughter* (1981) by Astrid Lindgren. No ordinary genre category fits this book. As the title suggests, it is related to the robber novel tradition, to the adventure story with the typical features of escape, quest, robinsonade—that is, a real book for boys. But the main character is a girl, and the book often discusses the male and female roles in family and society in a way that would make many feminist authors envious. It is also a typical heroic myth which among other things depicts the miraculous birth of the heroine. It is also a fantasy with supernatural creatures and events that threaten the idyll of childhood. It is also a historical novel which correctly describes medieval customs. It is also a love story with clear allusions to *Romeo and Juliet*. It is also a modern psychological family story of a father's relations with his adolescent daughter. It is a *Bildungsroman* as well, in the best spirit of Goethe, about a young person's breaking away from home, her wandering, trials and final maturation. Thus Astrid Lindgren uses the old time-tested popular forms, but she moulds them into something radically new—a highly literary, complicated novel. Not an adventure story, not a love story, but a novel.

The same is true about the best Swedish junior novel of the past decade, *Johnny My Friend* (1985) by Peter Pohl. It makes use of the superficial traits of a detective story, with a criminal mystery and real and false threads which hold readers in suspense throughout the book. But is also includes features of the traditional school story, the traditional family story, of robinsonade, of fantasy and also of love story. Here again we find a mixture of traditional genres in a multi-dimensional psychological novel which can stand comparison with many books for adults.

In the following chapters I shall follow children's books during the modern period, primarily the twentieth century, as they evolve towards a more complex novel form. This evolution becomes manifest on many different textual levels, in *metastructures* (the relation of the text to both the writer and the reader), in *intertextuality* (the relationship between texts), in *chronotopes* (the sophisticated treatment of space-time relations), and in new experimental forms and narrative techniques.

My intention is not to write a handbook in children's literature, for the approach I want to take differs radically from that of most earlier studies. I focus primarily on general tendencies and questions, rather than on an inventory of writers and texts. My study is based neither on chronology nor on literary genres and modes, but instead examines the different levels in the specific system of children's literature.

I view children's literature as a special semiosphere, or system of signs, which is heavily stratified and emerges and develops in interaction with mainstream literature. The use of a cultural-semiotic model enables me to follow the different processes within the system of children's literature as well as movements between this system and areas beyond.

In chapter one I approach children's literature in different countries as a whole and at the same time attempt to examine possible barriers and boundaries of national literatures due to language, country and cultural community. Here I focus not on particular authors but rather on general tendencies and regularities, and the different forms for the interaction of national literatures are discussed in semiotic terms.

I proceed in chapter two to determine the specific features of children's literature as opposed to adult literature, mainly in two aspects: the communicative (a children's book has two separate addressees, a child and an adult) and the inherent, which implies that children's literature is of a radically different text type than modern adult literature. It is in fact closer to the rigid norms and rules (codes) of folklore or medieval art. This specific text type may be called canonical, or ritual, which explains why children's literature on the whole is less innovative than contemporary adult literature.

The fact that children's literature is mostly based on canon does not mean, however, that it is static. I view the evolution of children's literature in a semiotic light, as a succession of constantly changing codes, an interplay between center and periphery and between culture and noncultural, paracultural and extracultural phenomena. To demonstrate the universal character of the model, in chapter three I illustrate the process with examples from different genres, types of literature and historical periods.

The evolution of modern children's literature leads towards a state in which traditional epic narrative structures are gradually replaced by new structures which, using a term from Mikhail Bakhtin's literary theory, discussed in chapter four, I call polyphonic. The polyphony, or "multivoicedness" of modern children's novels, is manifested through a new type of narrator, in the palimpsestic multilevel text structures, in various experimental forms and advanced narrative techniques. The main feature of the polyphonic children's novel is a convergence of genres which brings children's literature closer to what is generally labelled modern or post-modern literature. Another prominent trait in contemporary literature for children is an extensive introduction of non-literary (TV, video, comics) and paraliterary ("popular fiction") elements.

Among the significant features of modern children's literature is the daring use of time and space relations. In chapter five I treat time and space as an indivisible whole, making use of Mikhail Bakhtin's notion of the chronotope, that is, an entity of time and space as artistically interpreted in fiction. The concept of the chronotope allows me to take a new look at genre, since, according to Bakhtin, chronotope is a genre category, and every genre, type of literature and even particular authors have their specific forms of chronotopes. I demonstrate this very convenient genre approach with an examination of chronotopes in fantasy, in the traditional epic children's novel, the adventure story, books for girls, paraliterature, the modern sophisticated novel, the picturebook, and the historical and retrospective novel. The general tendency of children's literature towards complexity and sophistication is revealed in this investigation. I also propose the notion of the *kenotype* ("new-image") to denote recurrent tokens of our modern time which, unlike archetypes, have no connection with the collective unconscious.

Chapter six takes up the intertextual relations which have assumed increasing importance in modern children's literature. I investigate the use of quotations, allusions, irony and parody within codes for children and adults, open and hidden intertexts, as well as intertextuality within a single *oeuvre* which may provide clues to an interpretation of a difficult, multidimensional text.

Finally, in chapter seven I discuss the relationship among the author, the text and the reader and the problems of realism. For the sake of clarity I analyze novels of metafictional character where the notions of the implied reader and the implied author enable me to highlight the complicated connection between fiction and reality. Both metafiction and polyphony overturn our conventional ideas of realism and allow us to approach the essence of a children's book as a work of art.

The dilemma of children's literature research has recently become the object for debates revolving around the question whether it is at all possible to study children's literature. Particularly the British critic Peter Hunt has questioned most investigative approaches in children's literature and has suggested a change of perspective towards what he calls "childist criticism," apparently in analogy with "feminist criticism."[18] Such a shift would, however, mean that children's literature research would become still more isolated from general literary theory and criticism.

My own investigations convince me that more and more children's books today are approaching the modern (or postmodern) adult novel. Children's literature, which emerged several thousand years later than mainstream literature, is now catching up with it. Unlike Hunt's suggestion, my semiotically inspired model for the examination of children's books as literary phenomena aspires to place the object of study on an equal footing with mainstream literature and to point out the complexity of the modern children's book and the exciting questions this complexity raises.

My study is, of course, not an exhaustive analysis of the phenomenon of children's literature. Such a study demands many years of endeavor on the part of many scholars. Nevertheless, I hope that I have been able to introduce several new perspectives and put children's literature in a new light.

NOTES

1. See Aries, 1962. Nodelman, 1992, has a good bibliography on the history of childhood.
2. Such books continue to appear; see Landsberg, 1988; Hearne, 1990; Saxby, 1991; Nieuwenhuizen, 1992. Among more serious attempts must be mentioned the three *Touchstone* volumes edited by Perry Nodelman (Nodelman, 1985-89).
3. One of the best examples of this attitude is Masha Rudman's issue-approach. See Rudman, 1984.
4. Nodelman, 1992, pp. 198ff.
5. Edström, 1982.
6. See Haas, 1974; Scherf, 1978; Krüger, 1980; Ewers, 1990; Tabbert, 1990; Tabbert, 1991; Ewers, 1992.
7. Shavit, 1986.
8. Perry Nodelman's theoretical essays can be found in *Children's Literature Association Quarterly*; for a more comprehensive view see Nodelman, 1992. Roderick McGillis has published in both *ChLA Quarterly* and *Canadian Children's Literature*; his theoretical volume *Beyond Formalism Again: Literary Theory and Children's Literature* is forthcoming.
9. See Stephens, 1992.
10. The ninth biannual conference of the International Research Society for Children's Literature, held in Salamanca in 1989, was devoted to the history of children's literature. However, it presented very few examples of approaches other than traditional pedagogical-pragmatical. (See *Aspects and Issues in the History of Children's Literature*, ed. Maria Nikolajeva, Greenwood, 1995.) During this conference the German scholar Hans-Heino Ewers proposed the new look at the history of children's literature that I attempt to develop here.
11. See Algulin, 1989, pp. 253-256; Svensson, 1989; Svensson, 1990. Although Algulin's book has only four pages devoted to children's literature, it is symptomatical, since Algulin is not a children's literature expert.
12. See a survey of semiotic reading theories in Toivonen, 1990. Golden, 1990, is a semiotically oriented narrative study, which to my mind is conventional and superficial. I find it significant that Golden uses the designation "childhood literature," apparently to raise the status of her study.
13. See Lundquist, 1985. I use double quotation marks for foreign book titles that have not been translated into English. I use single quotation marks for short story titles.
14. Patricia MacLachlan in an interview with the author, May 28, 1993.
15. See Lotman, 1977.
16. Toijer-Nilsson, 1987; Toijer-Nilsson, 1990.
17. Nikolajeva, 1988; Nikolajeva, 1993.
18. Hunt 1984a; Hunt 1984b; Hunt 1991b. Hunt's theoretical volume on children's literature is wholly based on the premises of "childist criticism" (Hunt, 1991a).

WORLD LITERATURE FOR CHILDREN

The term "world literature" was coined by Goethe. Although we constantly use this notion, it is not always defined. By the "world library" we probably mean a number of texts from different epochs, countries and nations which have endured the test of time and are deeply imprinted in the minds of many generations of readers.

The notion of "world literature for children" is even more complicated. Its history has not yet been written and probably never will be, not only because there are no scholars versed in the literature in different countries, but also because world literature is not merely a sum of literatures from various countries.

The many reference works on children's literature in particular countries or on children's literature in general, need not be enumerated here. Those which treat children's literature in general are always biased by the origin of their authors, who give priority to the literature from their own countries, overestimate the importance of certain writers from that country, and so on.[1] Many American sources do not mention international literature at all, as if it never existed,[2] or they treat it in a separate brief chapter, in parentheses, as it were, as something marginal and secondary.[3] The "touchstones" of children's literature in the United States are not only Anglo-Saxon but very distinctly North American.

On the other hand, in Swedish, Norwegian, Danish or Dutch sources the author's own country will be presented as the capital of world children's literature, while the Anglo-Saxon tradition is somewhat diminished. One of the most central American children's books of the twentieth century, *Charlotte's Web,* is in Sweden mostly known in the form of an animated cartoon and is nowhere mentioned as a touchstone.

In the former Soviet Union, where translations of foreign children's literature were subject to very special and entirely extraliterary regulations, the picture of foreign children's literature was sometimes seriously distorted. Thus in a standard textbook used by schools of education, contemporary (twentieth century) American children's authors are represented by Carl Sandburg, L. Frank Baum, Upton Sinclair, Dr Seuss, John Ciardi, Lincoln Steffens, Erskine Caldwell, John Steinbeck, Marjory Kinnan Rawlings, William Saroyan, Carson McCullers, Harvey Swados, and Robert McCloskey.[4]

Nowhere has there been any effort to view children's literature as a whole, as sharing a common literary evolution. Naturally, this is a very difficult if not impossible task, since it demands not only a huge body of concrete facts but also new instruments which differ radically from those used to describe children's literature in a particular country. The only feasible thing is to attempt to sketch the historical poetics of children's literature rather than a history of children's literature as such, to ignore details, concrete works and authors, and instead look for tendencies, recurrent phenomena, typological similarities and possible paths of evolution.

ARE FOLKTALES CHILDREN'S LITERATURE?

To my mind, the first big mistake that historians of children's literature usually make is to start with folktales. Folktales existed and were told long before childhood was apprehended as a category. Folktales, myths and legends were never created for an audience of children. Indeed, folktales, fables, moral tales, often with religious overtones, were a makeshift solution at a time when there appeared to be no special literature for young readers. The fact that folktales were part of this solution does not mean that they became children's literature. Most oral folktales are not suitable for children because they often contain violence and child abuse. Moreover, they are sometimes obscene and amoral, contradicting the ideals of proper upbringing. Today we know that the Grimms decided to purify their tales after the first edition of their collection was published to make them more suitable for children. We also know that the Grimms did not wander at all among people and collect material, as was earlier believed, but found most of it in the kitchens of respectable bourgeois families, which means that the versions they wrote down had most probably already been purged of the most offensive details.[5]

Folktales also differ from children's literature in terms of communication. They belong to a fundamentally different type of culture—the oral one.[6] When children listen to a narrated folktale, the communication process differs radically from that involved in reading. Reading a collection of folktales is also different from reading a children's book. Instead of a writer—the sender of information in a simple communication model—we have in the case of folktales a mediator (the person who tells the story orally), a collector (the person who makes a transcript of the oral text), and an editor or publisher (the person who is responsible for the published version of the text). As I have just mentioned, in editions for children texts are usually subject to still further transformation, that is, they are adapted to prevailing moral and pedagogical views. The picture of the world that children receive during this communication is completely falsified and has nothing to do with the original world view of folklore. Although ordinary children's books are also subject to purging by the editors, we can nevertheless assume that in modern, non-adapted books for young readers information passes more or less directly from sender to addressee.

By this I do not at all mean that folktales are not suitable as children's *reading*. Many exciting studies show possible ways of using folktales in childhood education. Two widely disparate treatments of folktales are Bruno Bettelheim's psychoanalytical[7] and Jack Zipes's sociological approaches.[8] It is noteworthy that in countries in Africa and Asia today that lack children's literature, there is an effort to use myths and folktales to satisfy their young people's needs for reading material. Although folktales are essentially not children's literature they do have significance for its emergence since so many children's books in some way or other are based on myth and folklore, not only directly, in subject matter or action, but also with respect to narrative, characterization and the use of symbols. This is naturally something that scholars of children's literature must take into account. Indeed, some fascinating archetypal studies of children's literature do take as their point of departure parallels between children's literature and myth or folktale.

ARE THE "CLASSICS" CHILDREN'S LITERATURE?

Another common denominator in children's reading in most countries is the so-called classics. By classics we usually mean a rather heterogeneous group of texts which were not originally written for a young audience. The most remarkable thing is that while these originally adult texts were rewritten, abridged and adapted to children's needs, there were hundreds of other useful, educational, didactic, moralistic texts being produced directly for children. Unlike international classics, such books remained local and were very seldom translated into other languages. Today they are hopelessly obsolete. Usually written by second-rate authors, they scrupulously followed the established and rapidly changing conventions and views on child education. In contrast, the so-called children's classics, which were never meant for children, are eternal and universal.

At least one of these, Daniel Defoe's *Robinson Crusoe* (1719), has been enormously popular and well-known among generation after generation of children in many countries. When in the eighteenth century Rousseau recommended *Robinson Crusoe* as suitable reading for his ideal pupil Emile, he most probably did it for lack of anything better. If he had had access to the children's books available today, he probably would not have chosen *Pippi Longstocking*, since that work is too far from his educational ideas; but in his time there were not many texts to choose from. Depending on the country, children read Aesop's or Lafontaine's fables or carefully selected tales from *Arabian Nights*; British children had King Arthur or Robin Hood. None of these texts was originally created for children and, as I suggested earlier, they provided a makeshift solution. Charles Perrault's fairy tales were thoroughly purged before they were allowed into the nursery.

Robinson Crusoe was regarded as suitable for children partly because of its moral values, partly because it contained useful information about such things as nature and human activities. Its central theme is the eternal striving of the young to break free of the parents, to be grownup and mature, to become independent. These elements reflect the Age of Enlightenment when the book was written, but they are also an important component of children's literature. Although not intended for children, *Robinson Crusoe* contains the most essential narrative pattern of children's literature, namely the structure: Home—Departure—Adventure—Homecoming.[9] In its original version, however, the book was far too long and sometimes too difficult for children, and this paved the way for all manner of adaptations and rewritings.[10] Since the German educator Joachim Heinrich Campe's adaptation of *Robinson* in 1779–1780, numerous versions of adult texts regarded as suitable for young people have been adapted and retold for children. Two selection criteria have usually been taken into consideration here: usefulness and pleasure. Often satisfying the criterion of pleasure were adventure books with elements of suspense, most of them from the periods of Enlightenment and Romanticism. The demand for usefulness could be fulfilled by the practical knowledge that the books contained or by the moral and ethical values originally present or added to them by retellers. These values sometimes seem rather obtrusive to modern reader. Ethical norms grow outdated sooner than practical information, but even facts can become obsolete and confusing.[11]

Another adult text that in some countries enjoys the same popularity among young readers as *Robinson Crusoe* is *Gulliver's Travels* (1726) by Jonathan Swift. While the different retellings of Defoe have more or less retained the central idea of the book, most of Swift's satirical elements, his allusions to contemporary persons and events, and his deep philosophical reflections have been removed from children's editions. What remains is adventure and the humorous play with dimensions: the giant Gulliver among the Lilliputs, tiny Gulliver among the giants. The third and forth parts of *Gulliver's Travels* are often omitted.

Robinson Crusoe and *Gulliver's Travels* are found in most histories of children's literature, that is, in my view, in histories of childhood read-

Tyl Ulenspiegel: *well known to Russian young readers. Illustration from the Russian "World Library for Children"*

ing. But there are other adult texts which are included among children's classics in some countries but are completely unknown in others. I am thinking of books like François Rabelais' *Gargantua* (1535), Miguel Cervantes' *Don Quixote* (1605–1615) or Charles de Coster's *Tyl Ulenspiegel* (1867). They contain the same ingredients which have made *Robinson* and *Gulliver* successful children's reading: the same classical adventure composition with home—wandering—homecoming, suspense, and a chain of more or less independent episodes. They are also humorous; the hyperbolic characters of especially *Gargantua* border on the absurd, while *Tyl Ulenspiegel* is both romantic and funny. Ulenspiegel's faithful friend and squire Lamme Goedzak is a figure appreciated by children in countries where the text is known, while children who are given a chance to get acquainted with the wandering Spanish knight Quixote and Sancho the jester usually come to love them. But in many countries these characters fall entirely outside the range of children's reading.

There are also some curious cases of an adult text from one country becoming known as a children's classic in another. In Russia, one of the most beloved children's classics is a book entitled *The True History of A Little Ragamuffin* by a certain James Greenwood. It is a sentimental story that takes place in the slums of London, somewhat in the style of *Oliver Twist*. However, the book is not mentioned in any British reference source on children's literature,[12] the reason being that the work, published in 1866, was never intended for children, was never reprinted and in Britain was never regarded as a children's book. Not many experts on British nineteenth century literature have even heard of it. But in Russia the book was retold for young readers only a few years after the appearance of the original. In the 1920s the great Russian children's writer and educator Kornei Chukovsky made a new version which secured the book a prominent place in Russian children's reading. It has been reprinted in more than forty editions totalling more than twenty million copies. A third-rate British adult text has thus become a children's classic and a component of Russian childhood reading.

Sometimes I have an uneasy feeling that we overestimate the importance of "classics" in our children's reading today. The criteria for the publication and evaluation of the classics have been inherited from older generations who read *Robinson Crusoe*, Jules Verne, James Fenimore Cooper and Baroness Orczy as children and therefore believe that these texts are the best they can offer modern children. But older generations did not have Winnie-the-Pooh or Moomintroll, they were not acquainted with Maurice Sendak, Roald Dahl or E.B. White. Grandparents of today who go into a bookstore to buy a Christmas present for their grandchildren recognize with a pang of nostalgia the good old stories of their childhood and buy them, believing that they are purchasing literature of quality. Sales figures create the illusion that the books are still in demand, and publishers continue to publish them.

The interesting aspects of, to take one example, Jules Verne's books, are his various scientific and technical ideas—even if some of them, such as the giant cannon in *From Earth to the Moon Direct* (1865), proved to be impossible. Especially *Captain's Grant Children* (1868) and *Twenty Thousand Leagues Under the Sea* (1870) also contain important ethical issues. Among his best known, these books are featured in many textbooks as indispensable childhood reading. Again, what makes them attractive to young readers is their adventurous, dynamic, slightly mysterious plot.

Jules Verne, however, wrote a vast number of books, many of which are little more than travelogues furnished with a superficial plot to resemble novels. Some of them are remembered today thanks to vivid characters such as the witty servant Passepartout in *Around the World in 80 Days* (1872). The central character in the novel, the correct British gentleman Phileas Fogg, travels around the world to win a bet. He is completely uninterested in the journey itself, and whatever description there is of foreign countries is from the naive perspective of Passepartout. Many other books, like *The Giant Raft* (1881), lack even this element. The characters are bleak and schematic, the villains are totally evil and the heroes totally good, magnificent and noble. Of course, this is the way novels were written in Jules Verne's time, but why expose modern children to this?

The foreign countries Jules Verne described for his readers (and they were adults!) were unfamiliar, fascinating and exotic. Although some small part of the geographic and historical facts are still valid, the mass media have made modern children much more familiar with foreign countries than were Jules Verne's contemporary adults. Today's children and young people prefer to get their information from non-fiction. Jules Verne's readers did not have access to a hundredth of the information available to a modern child. The many facts he showers upon his reader (longitudes and latitudes, cubic meters and nautical miles, endless depictions of places and milieus) today seem superfluous in a work of fiction, but if they are deleted, not much will remain. To continue publishing such novels as children's books is like offering children stale bread when there are so many delicious cookies to choose among.

In other words, the simple fact that a book counts as "classic," is written by an established writer, featured in textbooks and constantly reprinted is in itself no guarantee of either quality or suitability as reading for modern young people. At the risk of hearing many indignant voices I submit that we tend to overestimate the significance of classics for today's young readers, although in most countries they still play an important role in publishing (many respected publishing houses have their "Classic Series") and in education. Some of them are by now played out completely and contain little that can provide modern young readers any valuable reading experience.

However, since they have for so many years functioned as substitutes for "real" children's books, they are as literary and social phenomena enormously interesting for anyone dealing with the history of children's literature. They have also contributed to the establishment of children's literature as a system, and have created our concepts of genres and modes.

What Is National Children's Literature?

When we proceed to look for texts written directly for children, the situation immediately becomes more complicated, since the obvious milestones on one horizon are in other countries and cultures eclipsed by more significant texts.

The Wonderful Adventures of Nils (1906-1907) by the Swedish Nobel Prize winner Selma Lagerlöf is a text that many in all countries would acknowledge as one of the absolute peaks of children's literature. Ironically enough, not many Swedish critics would definitely agree. Another common denominator for different literary systems would probably be Hans Christian Andersen's fairy tales; it is significant that the most prestigious international children's book prize is called the Andersen Medal, and that Andersen's birthday, April 2, is celebrated internationally as children's book day.

It is tempting to continue listing writers and works which must be considered absolutely indispensable in world children's literature, but as stated earlier, I do not think that is possible. Besides, paradoxically enough, the closer we come to our time, the more there is a parting of the ways among the children's literature in various countries. Children's literature becomes national and isolated. It also becomes even more difficult to discern common patterns of evolution.

If anything, national literature is still more difficult to define than world literature, and here many factors must be taken into consideration. National children's literature can be defined either prospectively or retrospectively. There are historical and contemporary examples of prospective approach, which is taken when a nation discovers that its lacks a children's literature of its own and sets about creating it. This is possible only when there already exists an established children's literature in other countries.

With the retrospective approach—the most common one—historians of literature judge on the basis of certain criteria that certain texts from the

past can be considered to belong to the children's literature of a given nation. These criteria, however, cannot be themes or subjects, nor are they ideology, moral and ethical values, or styles since these change too rapidly.
Among points of departure we instead find ethnic, linguistic and cultural
criteria. Through language, tradition and cultural values, writers identify
with a certain culture. Readers recognize texts as their "own" through language, national mentality, "credible" descriptions, and so on.

Unfortunately, reality is not quite as simple. The boundaries between
national literatures cannot be defined precisely, for they are constantly changing under the impact of various factors. In the first place, they can only be
defined in opposition to other national literatures and to world literature.
For instance, the scope of Swedish children's literature will be different if it
is defined as (1) all children's books published in Sweden (including translations from other languages); (2) all children's books written in Swedish (including books by the Swedish minority in Finland and books written and
published by Swedish immigrants in the United States); (3) all children's
books written by writers who live in Sweden (including those who write in
minority or immigrant languages). In the process of definition, Swedish
children's literature can be opposed to (1) Norwegian and Danish children's
literature; (2) children's literature in Finland; (3) Scandinavian children's literature; (4) West European children's literature; (5) East European children's
literature; (6) American children's literature; (7) Asian or Latin American
children's literature. The boundaries between literatures will be drawn in a
different way depending on the opposition chosen.

One feature worth contemplating is that the barriers do not correspond to geographical but rather to linguistic boundaries. Seen from the
Scandinavian horizon, English-language children's literature has most suc-
cessfully crossed national frontiers. Although reference sources most often
but by no means always mention the origin of writers, within the English
language domain relatively little attention is paid to whether the writer is
British, Anglo-Scottish, Anglo-Irish, American, Canadian, Australian or New
Zealand. For extraliterary reasons, books from certain countries in Asia and
Africa also occasionally make their way into this community.

However, this last observation is not entirely unproblematic. The
inhabitants of each English-speaking country are often well aware and
proud of their particular authors, although they seldom can pinpoint the
distinctive traits of their national literature. There is evidently a certain dissimilarity between British and American children's literature. John Rowe
Townsend has chapters in his study, *Written for Children*, entitled "Realism, British Style" and "Realism, American Style."[13] Brian Attebery has

noticed the difference with regard to American fantasy,[14] but I think his statement is valid about American children's literature in general. Early American children's writers and educators rejected imaginative literature as escapism, and American children's books are on the whole more down-to-earth, pragmatical and oriented towards material matters than the British. American fantasy authors who do not fit this description, like Lloyd Alexander or Madeleine L'Engle, often find inspiration in the Old World. Today many excellent American children's novels will not sell in Britain, and the other way round.

It happens, too, that English-language writers move within the English-language area of the world. Susan Cooper started writing children's books in Britain but lives today in the United States. As far as I can see this has not affected her themes or her style; she still belongs to British rather than American children's literature.

Australia has been part of the English-language children's literature community until recently, when several writers emerged who develop specifically Australian themes. One example is Patricia Wrightson, whose books make use of the Aboriginal heritage. Some recent Australian studies emphasize the specifically Australian features of children's literature on this continent.

The most prominent Canadian children's writer, L.M. Montgomery, is very much a part of North American literature. Not many of her readers outside Canada are aware of her origin. There is little in the *Anne of Green Gables* series that makes the books specifically Canadian; they could have been American or British. But in Canada as in Australia writers have appeared who dwell on the native culture: for instance, Welwyn Wilton Katz in *False Face* (1987). Both in the United States and Canada there are authentic native American children's writers who write in English, but they are a tiny minority.

Canada is an example of the peculiar literary situation where a boundary cuts across the country, dividing it into two language areas with two separate literatures for children. These seem to exist independently, happily and consistently ignoring each other; mutual translations are rare, all institutions of children's literature are doubled throughout the country. The bilingual journal, *Canadian Children's Literature*, cannot bridge the gap between the two literary systems. Unlike English-language Canadian literature, which is famous for *Anne of Green Gables*, French-speaking Canada has not contributed to world children's literature anything of the same dimension.

A European country with a similar bilingual situation is Belgium, where children's literature is clearly separated into French and Flemish parts. The French-language Belgian literature has produced something familiar to almost everyone, although not many are aware that it comes from Belgium: the world-famous comics "Asterix," "Tintin" and others. Flemish children's literature has yet not been able to boast of anything that could put it on the world map of children's literature. Besides, it has been obliged to compete with children's literature from neighboring Holland, which is likewise not well-known internationally, although it was honored in 1988 by the Andersen Medal awarded to Annie G.M. Schmidt. Flemish children's literature is thus faced with the dilemma of whether to join efforts with the Dutch or to fight for recognition in its own right.[15]

An example from Scandinavia is the bilingual Finland. The minority language, Swedish, has produced Tove Jansson (still another Andersen Medal winner, if we can tentatively apply this as a criterion of quality or at least a token of recognition). Both Tove Jansson and some of her internationally less known but excellent colleagues, like Irmelin Sandman Lilius and Bo Carpelan, are treated in Swedish reference sources as *Swedish* writers.[16] Finnish sources would, however, include these names among Finland's children's authors. The Swedish-language children's literature in Finland is translated into Finnish, but seldom the other way round.

Internationally, there is little awareness of any borders between Sweden, Norway, Denmark and Finland, and everything is treated as "Scandinavian" or "Northern European" children's literature. Those who happen to know that Tove Jansson comes from Finland are mostly ignorant of the fact that she writes in Swedish. Many reference sources present the Norwegian authors Thorbjørn Egner (*The Singing Town*) and Alf Prøysen (*Little Old Mrs Pepperpot*) as Swedish. In creating boundaries between "native" and "foreign," international readers and scholars make no distinctions within the "foreign." In Sweden different English-speaking countries are seldom distinguished in the context of children's literature. Children's literature in Latin America is treated as an entity.

But there are examples when the boundary between literatures goes across the language. One instance is German children's literature, which suddenly found itself on different sides of the Berlin Wall. During the forty years the nation was divided, Western German children's literature was well-known and appreciated in the GDR, while East German children's literature was totally unknown not only in West Germany but also internationally, probably with the exception of the rest of Eastern Europe. After the unification, Eastern German children's literature was ruthlessly cast into the dustbin.[17]

On the other hand, Austrian children's literature is sometimes re-garded together with German, since it is written in the German language. Scholars are aware of Austrian children's literature thanks to Christine Nöstlinger. This is a good example how just one writer, especially one as-sociated with the Andersen Medal, can change our image of a children's literature in a particular country. Swiss children's literature, from another German-speaking area in Europe, is completely unknown. Although some authors such as Erich Kästner, Janosch, Ottfried Preussler or James Krüss might have been known earlier, German literature itself did not arouse any broad curiosity in the Anglo-Saxon world until Michael Ende became in-ternationally acknowledged for *Momo* (1973) and especially *The Neverending Story* (1979).

Sometimes countries with a common language do not share children's literature at all. This is the situation in Latin America, which shows no continuity with Spain or, in the case of Brazil, Portugal. Arab countries also seem to be totally separate in this respect, and children's books from one country never reach any of the others.[18] A possible expla-nation is that children's literature in these countries has emerged (or is emerging, in some cases) at a very late stage, when national identity is more important than linguistic.

Further, there are instances of minority children's literature—for ex-ample, Lapp in Sweden and Norway or Sorbish in Germany—existing within another, larger children's literature community. Sorbs are a very small Slavic minority who live in a limited territory in eastern parts of Germany. They have a children's literature of their own which is written and published in Sorbic and translated into German.

In the former Soviet Union, twenty or more national children's lit-eratures were forcibly brought together under the label of "multi-national Soviet" children's literature. In practice, all forms of national individu-ality were suppressed. Many of these literatures, especially Estonian, Latvian and Lithuanian, are today struggling to restore their national identity.

A children's writer can also for various reasons live outside his own country and lack contact with it. This is the case, for instance, with politi-cal refugees like Salman Rushdie, who is both an adult and children's writer. One of the best known Czech children's writers, Jan Prochazka, wrote his children's books in exile, and these were not mentioned in the official his-tories of Czech children's literature.

The children's literature of Swedish immigrants in the United States, a fascinating and little studied phenomenon, was deliberately created to differ in themes and style from children's literature in Sweden, but it was written exclusively in Swedish and had never any ties with American literature either.

The diaspora phenomenon, which is of general importance in defining national literature, especially in our times of political persecutions throughout the world, is less prominent in children's literature than in that of mainstream. In Sweden a barely visible Estonian children's literature has existed in exile, although at least one Estonian refugee has achieved a significant profile in Swedish children's literature—Astrid Lindgren's illustrator Ilon Wikland.

In Sweden today there are not many exiled children's writers who continue writing in their mother tongue. One of those few, Mahmud Baksi, comes from Turkey, writes in Kurdish, and translates his own books into English, whereupon they are translated into Swedish. To which culture does he belong?

There are many bilingual writers, especially in Asia and Africa, who translate their books between the two languages; there are also writers who sometime in their life begin writing only in the other language. Choosing a language is a conscious act of identifying with a specific culture, but the fact that many African children's writers write in English can be an economical, political, or a cultural choice. Here again the picture of a bilingual/bicultural author proves to be more complicated than it may seem at first glance.

Semiotics tells us that in every system it is the boundary and the periphery that are the active zones. Sweden, which has been in many aspects a peripheral country as far as children's books are concerned, has recently gained international acknowledgement for, among other things, its excellent picturebooks.

Today we are witnessing a rapid expansion of children's literature in cultures such as the Flemish mentioned above which are not normally associated with a strong tradition of children's literature. Under such conditions children's literature seems to undergo a more compressed evolution. Countries which were late in establishing their own children's literature may soon catch up with those where children's literature is well developed as a system and may even eventually produce something more exciting. To take just one example, some of the most interesting fantasy authors today are from countries not usually associated with a strong fantasy tradition: Lygia Bojunga Nuñes (Andersen Medal winner of 1982) and Ana Maria Machado from Brazil, Marja-Leena Mikkola and Lena Krohn from Finland, and Benno Pludra and Krista Koszik from former East Germany. Their books are different from traditional Anglo-Saxon fantasy, and they must therefore be appreciated as innovators within the fantasy genre rather than representatives of en existing tradition.

Inadequate first-hand knowledge does not allow me to digress from the areas of Europe and North America. Because an in-depth discussion of Asian and African literature would oblige me to trust other people's sources, I will confine myself to considerations of a very general nature. Europe alone, however, provides ample material for reflections.

From my Russian background I am familiar with a number of brilliant Italian children's writers such as René Reggiani and Gianni Rodari, the latter of whom also is an educator and theoretician of children's literature. But Italian children's literature after *Pinocchio* is an unknown territory for most international scholars, although the two above-mentioned authors have been translated into English. How much is known internationally about French children's literature after *Babar*, *The Little Prince* and at best *Tistou of the Green Thumbs*? What Spanish children's writers are familiar to us, to say nothing of those from Greece, Poland, Hungary, and Bulgaria?

As I indicated earlier, Scandinavian children's literature is often treated as a single entity in other countries, but even within Scandinavia there is no balanced mutual acknowledgement. Swedish children's literature is much better known in Norway than Norwegian children's literature in Sweden. The situation may have changed slightly when the Norwegian Tormod Haugen was awarded the Andersen Medal in 1990—one cannot overestimate the impact of literary awards and prizes on the acceptance of literary phenomena by other cultures. But the "grande dame" of Norwegian children's literature, Ann-Cath. Vestly, is practically unknown in Sweden, although some of her books have been translated into Swedish (it may seem ridiculous to foreigners that books in closely related Scandinavian languages should have to be translated, but they do). One reason may be that when Ann-Cath. Vestly started writing her books in Norway in the 1950s and 1960s, simple, unsophisticated, everyday stories of hers such as *Hello Aurora* (1966) and its sequels were among the first in Scandinavia that radically questioned gender stereotypes. When her books came to Sweden they had to compete with Astrid Lindgren's childhood stories in *The Children of the Noisy Village* (1947), and later with Maria Gripe, Gunnel Linde and the everyday realism which dominated Swedish children's literature of the 1960s and early 1970s.

This brings us to a most fascinating question: how is literature transferred from one country to another? How is one culture received by another culture? What are the mechanisms that govern this process? I will here ignore the political governing, which accounts for the fact that in the Soviet Union, for instance, translations from other Eastern European countries were given priority, followed by those from the third world, and then by an extremely careful selection from the West, which often was determined by the author's Communist sympathies or other extraliterary factors. Publishing was limited thematically as well. Non-realistic, imaginative literature was unwelcome, which meant that Soviet children got acquainted with *Winnie-the-Pooh* (1926) in 1960, with *Peter Pan* (1911) and *Mary Poppins* (1934) in 1968, with J.R.R. Tolkien and C.S. Lewis in the 1980s, while Edith Nesbit, E.B. White or Lloyd Alexander are still practically unknown. One of the effects of this isolation is that contemporary Russian fantasy seems hopelessly old-fashioned, since writers have not been able to follow the evolution of the genre in the world.

The ideological control of book publishing is an extraliterary factor. I would like instead to take a closer look at some of the factors which influence the transposition of one literature into another literary system and ask some questions about the process by which a particular national children's literature, a writer or an individual book is received into another culture. Since a significant part of national literature is usually affected by foreign texts, especially during the early stages of its history, these questions exert a decisive influence on the formation of the recipient literature.

CULTURAL CONTEXT AND TRANSLATABILITY

The way in which children's books cross boundaries into another cultural region is not merely a question of translation and publication in a new language, although this problem in itself deserves attention.[19] Semiotically, it has to do first of all with the young readers in the new country and their ability to accept and utilize the book. It is, in other words, a problem of reception.

In his preface to the translation of *Alice in Wonderland* the well-known Russian children's writer Boris Zakhoder refers to the following episode. For many years his friends had wondered: "Why don't you translate *Alice?*" whereupon he would answer: "It would be easier to transpose England." However, when Zakhoder eventually started on this impossible task he was probably better equipped for it than most translators, since he was so conscious of the intranslatability of this seemingly simple tale for children.

On the question of translation of children's books, I share the views of colleagues such as Anthea Bell from Britain[20] and Riitta Oittinen from Finland.[21] I agree with them that the best translation of a children's book is not necessarily the one that is most accurate and closest to the original (incidentally, I would argue for this view of translation in general). The idea of accurate translation has been developed, among others, by the famous Swedish scholar Göte Klingberg.[22]

Much more than in the case of adult literature, translations of children's books require not simply the transmission of meaning but the ability to arouse in the reader the same feelings, thoughts and associations experienced by readers of the source text (Riitta Oittinen calls this translation method dialogical, on the analogy of Mikhail Bakhtin's theory). It is not only permitted but highly desirable to deviate from the source text if this is demanded by the reader's response. Boris Zakhoder takes this approach to *Alice* when he offers Russian children parodies on Russian rather than English poetry, that is, texts as recognizable to Russian readers as the originals are to English readers. It is noteworthy that Åke Runnqvist opts for the same solution in his Swedish translation of *Alice*. There is nothing wrong with the translation becoming a retelling or adaptation if the child reader receives an aesthetic and informational message adequate to that apprehended by their counterparts in the source context. The process of translation implies finding not qualitative but significative (semiotic) equivalents to the signs of the source text. The best confirmation of this is the fact that the process is irreversible: a translation back to the source language would result in a totally new text. Besides, the paradox of the process is that in spite of seeming losses, the amount of information in the target text is not reduced, but on the contrary can sometimes increase (provided that the translation is more or less correct). From a semiotic point of view, every interpretation of a sign increases the amount of transmitted information.[23]

My study of this aspect of children's literature in this light will use as a point of departure the concepts of cultural context, semiotic space, and semiosphere as developed by Yuri Lotman.[24] Lotman defines the semiosphere as the semiotic space necessary for languages to exist and function; by languages are of course meant not concrete languages like English, Russian or Swedish, but languages in the broader sense of languages of culture. Beyond the semiosphere there can be neither language, nor communication.

An adaptation of Lotman's semiotic model of communication produces the scheme of interaction of contexts in translation shown in Fig. 1. In this model we ignore the difference between the author's (adult) and reader's (child) semiotic spaces, which would make the whole picture still more complex.

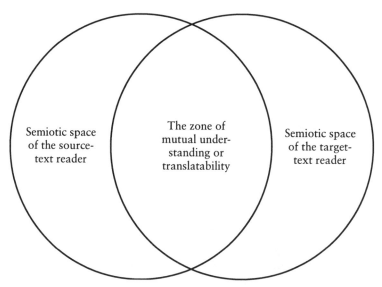

Fig. 1.

Below I propose some examples of real or hypothetical confrontations between the three contexts that I know best: the Swedish, the Russian, and the American. The discussion of three contexts rather than two will show that the "zone of non-translatability" of the source text appears to differ radically depending on the choice of target semiosphere. One might assume that the Swedish and the American ("Western," "democratic") contexts would have a great deal in common and that both would differ from the Russian ("East European," "totalitarian"); but it is not always the case.

In all the examples below, to provide the target-text reader an adequate literary experience, it is necessary to leave the "zone of translatability" and intrude into the territory of the untranslatable and non-understandable. If for some (most often extra-literary, for instance, political or religious) reason this is not possible, the source text is simply rejected by the recipient culture.

For the sake of clarity I will restrict my examples to just a few very elementary levels of the semiotic space, beginning with its structurally simplest part—everyday life. Everyday objects, food, clothes, routines and pastimes in a children's book are semiotic signs or tokens which in the reader's mind create a multilevel system based on previous experience of both life and books. In the terminology from modern reception theory, as developed by, for instance, Wolfgang Iser,[25] these signs help the child to fill the "telling gaps," that is, to relate details to a whole system existing outside the text.

When signs are transposed into another cultural context they are disconnected from the original system and can no longer fill the "telling gaps" in the same manner. Moreover, when the target-text reader places them into a new semiotic space, these signs are interpreted in a new way which, from the point of view of the original context, is most often incorrect.

For example, in "Amanda! Amanda!" (1989) by Annika Holm the characters take along some caviar sandwiches on a picnic. A Russian child reading this book will assume that the characters belong to the privileged class, since the correct interpretation of the sign "caviar" presupposes this connection in a Russian context. The foodstuff in question is, however, not the famous Russian caviar but the cheap cod paste in a tube that has long been a great favorite among Swedish children. In the Swedish context the sign is neutral; in fact, it is not a sign at all, since its connotation is no different from cheese, ham or sausage.

When a Russian child reads a story about a schoolboy taken by his parents to school in a car, the message behind this sign is: the parents are well-off, the boy is spoilt and most probably a negative character in the story. A Swedish reader will simply not notice the detail since in the Swedish context it is not a marked sign. Many Swedish children who cannot walk to school are driven by their parents. American readers might react, but not like their Russian counterparts; they might wonder what was wrong with the school bus that day. There are no school bus systems in Russia or in Sweden.

When, in a translation from Swedish or English, Russian readers encounter signs such as jeans, gym shoes, a walkman and other gadgets which are neutral in the Western context but attractive to the Russian child, the social status of the book character will be seriously misinterpreted. It is normal in both Swedish and American children's books for even very young characters to have a room of their own, often adorned with a poster saying "No trespassing." Russian readers are likely to interpret such details very incorrectly.

I once happened to be present when an American colleague discussed the cultural context of Maurice Sendak's *Where the Wild Things Are* (1963) with his class. With his cultural background, it never occurred to him that the simple fact that the very young boy Max has a room of his own to be sent to is a powerful cultural sign, which is foreign and strange to a Russian child (not to mention Greek, Chinese, or African children).

The social context in one recent translation from Russian into Swedish is so alien for Sweden that the translator feels obliged to write an afterword explaining: "Many things in this book may seem strange compared to what we in Sweden are used to. But in the Soviet Union both children and grownups behave differently. For instance, Soviet children know very little about where babies comes from. This is why it is so strange for us to read that the boy did not guess why his mother went to hospital." Well yes, Swedish children will certainly be perplexed by the total sexual ignorance of Russian children. But they will find the puritan attitudes in many American books no less puzzling. In Patricia MacLachlan's splendid novel *Arthur, For the Very First Time* (1980), the central conflict arises because the parents cannot bring themselves to tell the child they are expecting the arrival of a new baby. In a Swedish book, children might participate in the planning of a new baby, and they will certainly be the first to hear the good news. Pregnant mothers in Sweden are encouraged to take their children along to pregnancy checks in order to give them time to accept the arrival of a sibling. Each in its own way, both Russian and American attitudes to sex and sexuality are shocking and alien to Swedes.

How could a Russian translator deal with Barbro Lindgren's fictitious diary "Top Secret" (1972), in which a major part of the young heroine's pondering focuses on her coming menstruation? Even to mention this word is taboo in Russia among children or adults alike. Or Gunnel Linde's marvelous novel "If Life Is Dear to You" (1977), in which a thirteen-year-old girl plans her sexual debut in detail? Russian educators, publishers, reviewers would consider this outrageous, but in Swedish children's books these signs are as neutral as in the everyday life of Swedish children. The latter book has not been translated in the United States, although the sequel, *Trust in the Unexpected* (1979), has. More than the alien cultural context may be responsible, of course, but very probably American publishers will find the book offensive. In Sweden, where sex education begins in nursery school and where masturbation and homosexuality are frequent topics in the magazine *Kamratposten* read by elementary school children, there is nothing extraordinary or controversial in this or similar books. Lesléa Newman's *Heather Has Two Mommies* (1989), a book which created heated discussions in the United States, is likely to be welcomed or ignored in Sweden for its artistic or social values, but its theme will not be regarded as offensive. There is one cultural sign in it that would prove alien in Sweden, however, since artificial insemination described in the book is not legally available to lesbian couples. Also, the Swedish movement for children's rights might oppose the message of the book on the grounds that the child is denied her right to have a father (which has motivated the above-mentioned legislation). The reasons for rejecting the book will thus be totally different.

In Russia, on the other hand, it was until recently not officially admitted that homosexuality existed at all (although male homosexuality was a punishable offence), and the book would be treated as dirty pornography. With respect to prejudices and hostility towards "otherness," American culture stands closer to that of Russia than of Sweden.

Many American reference sources mention the case of Maurice Sendak's *In the Night Kitchen* (1970), which prompted indignant teachers to paste diapers or underpants over the boy's nakedness. At least one Swedish picturebook has been subjected to a similar censorship in the American translation: in Lennart Hellsing's joyful nonsense poem *The Pirate Book* (1965) a perfectly innocent "striptease dancer" appears properly clothed in the illustration, while in the text she has become "a smashing lady."

I can recall much more harmless signs (or rather absent signs) from Russia which are puzzling when they are transposed into either the Swedish or the American context. For instance, Russian girls are not allowed to wear pants in school. Again, American children who attend private schools and are required to wear uniforms will most likely not pay any more attention to this non-sign than Russian readers, while other American and all Swedish readers will wonder why this is so.

In Irina Grekova's "Anya and Manya" (1978), a nice little book recently translated into Swedish, a little girl boasts in front of her friend that she is allowed to drink unboiled water. A Swedish child will fail to understand what makes this permission so special.

A more sophisticated level of the semiotic space is constructed of human relations, that is, communication and behavior rituals. Everyday signs can be changed in translations without ruining the plot. It does not really matter what the two Swedish children have in their lunchbox, and although the striptease dancer is a funny figure, her disappearance does not destroy the story. Relationship signs, on the other hand, are both more complex and usually more dependent on the narrative. In books as well as in reality, relations between children and parents and between pupils and teachers are based on totally different principles in Sweden, Russia and the United States. Swedish schoolchildren address their teachers by their first names. Russian and American children generally do not. If a translator mechanically uses the form of address of the source text, the teacher-student relationship might acquire the wrong flavor. Many American mothers stay at home with their children. Swedish and Russian mothers do not. An American reader may get the wrong impression of a poor Swedish child sent off to day care after school because his mother works. Russian readers will envy the availability of child care, since Russian children are most likely to return to an empty home.

The severe discipline in Russian schools will seem unnatural to a Swedish child, as well as the race for marks and awards, while American children will recognize their own reality in such details. Spending hours in the principal's office is an experience shared by Russian and American schoolchildren, but it is completely unfamiliar to Swedish children. Often marks are the very cornerstone of a Russian narrative, the source of the conflict, while in Sweden schoolchildren are not given any marks until the eighth grade. It is difficult for a Swedish child to imagine that a bad mark may mean no cinema, or no pudding, or some other parental punishment. Such penalties are usual in Russian and American children's books, but they lie beyond the frame of the Swedish child's semiosphere. In Sweden, corporal punishment, even by parents, is prohibited by law, and this is something children learn already in nursery school.

On the linguistic level of the semiosphere there is the semiotically significant use of colloquial, dialect, babytalk and four-letter words. By tradition slang and obscenities are not used in Russian children's literature. In Swedish, as well as in English and some other languages, obscenities have penetrated into the culture of teenagers and even younger children; Salinger's *The Catcher in the Rye* (1951) may have played a certain part in this process. But when it is a question of a book for young children, American publishers can suddenly become puritanical. In the Swedish original of Barbro Lindgren's charming story *A Worm's Tale* (1985), parents are warned on the title page: "There is a swearword in page 22!" Needless to say, the word is very innocent (something like "Darned!") and, had it not been emphasized like this, it probably would not have been noticed at all. In the American translation it has been deleted.

What shall Russian translators do when they meet regular four-letter words in Swedish poetry for pre-school children? In Russian these language signs will be much more marked than in the source context, and should therefore definitely be softened in translations into Russian. Swedish authors may object to such wilfulness on the part of the translator, but it really is necessary. It is not hypocrisy, but is motivated by the need to achieve a more adequate reflection of the emotional coloring of the source text. Dialect and babytalk will also be more marked in Russian contexts. Russian dialects are much more socially contingent than Swedish.

Finally, here is one example of how changing a title in translation—a very common practice!—can influence the reception and interpretation of a text. *Charlotte's Web* (1952) is in Swedish called *Fantastiska Wilbur*, "Fantastic Wilbur." This shift of focus from one character (female) to another (male) basically imposes a new viewpoint on the reader.

The arguments presented here are, of course, very generalizing, and many of them can be countered with examples pointing to the contrary. However, I am intentionally generalizing here. All the above examples show, in the first place, that a simple rendering of a meaning never provides the target-text readers sufficient cultural-contextual information. Second and related to Riitta Oittinen's reader-response translation, they indicate that the culturally dependent "zone of untranslatability" is determined by the target rather than by the source context.

The single rather gloomy conclusion that emerges from my argument is that children's literature is basically non-translatable, since children's semiotic experience does not allow them to interpret the signs of an alien semiosphere. It is indeed often non-translatable in a literal sense of merely substituting words for words, but the practice of translation shows that superb translations can be achieved when translators use some of the ideas outlined above (although just as many are undoubtedly bad). Lotman's model of cultural interaction is dynamic and provides for an approach to mutual understanding. Also, Lotman believes that the periphery, or boundary zone, is the most dynamic and fruitful, and that it is through confrontation at the boundary that new and exciting phenomena can occur.

How Literature Is Rejected

The process by which children's literature today is becoming more and more national and diverse can impede the painless transposition of one literature into another that was common during the age of *Robinson Crusoe*. As we have seen, self-evident texts of contemporary American children's literature may be totally unknown in Russia, while modern Swedish classics will not be known in the United States, and both will be equally unfamiliar in France. This may seem a paradox, but it is a fact. Another fact is that while American children's literature dominates translations in, for instance, Scandinavian countries, the non-Anglo-Saxon European literatures are virtually terra incognita in the United States. The reason for this cannot primarily be ethnocentrism, since the multicultural United States is hardly likely consciously to reject literatures from other parts of the world.

Simple statistics show that approximately forty Swedish novels for children and young adults and a couple of dozen picturebooks have been translated and published in the United States during the past twenty years. The fact that a book is translated and published, however, does not mean that it has been accepted. As was mentioned earlier, *Anne of Green Gables* belongs to both American and Canadian children's literature (incidentally, to that of Sweden as well). *Pippi Longstocking* or the Moomin novels are not a self-evident part of American children's literature. Thus we must distinguish between a book which is published as one among hundreds, and which very probably never even gets a review and soon disappears from bookstores, and a book which becomes a significant phenomenon in a given culture. Some American reference works feature Astrid Lindgren, and some university courses not specializing in Scandinavian children's literature may occasionally include Pippi. But *Pippi* is still a foreign phenomenon in the United States. I think this is very clear in the American film version of *Pippi*, which is a perfect misinterpretation of this very peculiar character.

The questions I would like to pose here are: why is European children's literature accepted with such reluctance in the United States? What specific traits in the works of Swedish children's authors prevent them from bridging the Atlantic? Is it themes, characters, style, message? And in what way are they specific? The only model that seems capable of providing satisfactory answers to these very complicated questions is once again the semiotic model. My ambition is thus to investigate the *mental* conditions in the United States that ensure that certain literary phenomena from Sweden, Scandinavia or other parts of Europe are received and appreciated while others are rejected.

The publication of authors in American translations involves more than simply transposing texts from one language into another and then printing and distributing them. Beyond that the interaction implies that works of foreign children's literature are assimilated into the American children's culture, meaning that they become a natural part of it and begin to function within a new semiotic space which is largely independent of its further existence in the home country. This is what happens very seldom, or almost never, and it is this phenomenon I would like to examine.

How can we study the interaction of two cultures on the level of mutual understanding, mentality, ideas, values, and beliefs? This is no longer a question of simple facts. What elementary particles of the source culture can be studied one by one and then set in relation to their counterparts in the other culture? How are we to approach the mentality of a nation? As I have shown in the previous section, the natural language of the text represents just one tiny level of meaning. What code or codes enable us to interpret a verbal text from a foreign culture after it is translated into our own language?

Once again, according to Lotman, the foremost condition for a fruitful interaction of cultures is "creative misunderstanding," mutual non-translatability—that is, the existence of an active boundary zone where cultures intersect. In this theory, elements of foreign culture that are either too familiar or too alien are most likely to be rejected, while a well-balanced mixture of "native" and "exotic" is the best recipe for ensuring the success of a literary phenomenon in another culture.

The prerequisite for acceptance and further assimilation of foreign phenomena is that the recipients be able to receive the foreign codes on the basis of their own cultural codes; that is, they must be able to relate "foreign" and "native," accepting or rejecting that which is foreign owing to understanding or non-understanding. The codes can pertain to themes, problems, genre, or style.

My intent, then, is to investigate the cultural translatability of European children's literature into an American cultural context. My point of departure is that the American semiosphere—the set of codes available to American recipients—sometimes interferes with the correct interpretation of European cultural signs. I would like to illustrate this very briefly with several examples of American film adaptations of famous European texts. *The Little Mermaid* by Hans Christian Andersen is a subtle existential text about a non-human being longing for an immortal soul. This heavenly immortality, and not the earthly love of a mortal man, is the little mermaid's goal; to obtain it she is prepared to sacrifice everything and to endure tremendous suffering. In the end, her hopes are dashed when the prince weds another woman. Not much is left of this very complex story in the Disney version.[26] Also, to take an example from England, the tragic figure of Peter Pan, a person who can never mature into adulthood and who is thus doomed to everlasting loneliness, has in the Disney interpretation acquired an adventurous, carefree, light tone. In the same manner, the psychological and existential dimensions of *The Neverending Story* by Michael Ende have been turned into breathtaking and amusing adventures in the film version. Bastian's painful search for identity and the high price he must pay for his fulfilled wishes are absent from the film.

These examples show that there is a tendency to oversimplify the psychological and existential contents of the originals in order to adapt them to what obviously is believed to be the needs and interests of young Americans, also using overtly entertaining media. I have mentioned the American film version of *Pippi Longstocking*, in which Pippi's goodnaturedness is supplanted by a destructive, naughty slapstick à la Donald Duck, which is totally alien to Astrid Lindgren. The original Pippi's asset is not primarily her physical strength but her enormous verbal talent, imagination, and creativity, which give her power over adults and which are completely lost in the film—and partially lost in the American translation of the book. The normal narrative principle of American film and certain modes of literature is action. Thus whatever characters have to say or whatever they feel or think is apparently believed to be less significant to a young American reader or filmgoer than what they do.

While contemporary Scandinavian children's literature often explores the traumatic processes of childhood, American readers are much more oriented towards rationalism, everyday situations, comic events, down-to-earth problems and material things in general. As a young, dynamic and expanding nation raised on the national myth of a strong and active hero (Superman, the invincible cowboy, the brave cop), America favors characters who acquire material wealth rather than spiritual knowledge and maturity. The "spirituality" of European children's literature is alien to Americans. One recent American work of criticism notes this introspective tendency of European children's books as fundamentally different from American literature.[27] American readers will doubtless wonder about many contemporary Swedish children's books, in which nothing really "happens," the development is slow, and there is no happy ending or no ending at all. Not many of my American colleagues have discovered Maria Gripe's excellent psychological studies of a young child, *Elvis and His Secret* (1972) and its sequel, *Elvis and His Friends* (1973). There is no plot in the traditional sense in these novels which lack the logical beginning, conflict and resolution typical of the structure of an epic narrative. We learn about the character's feelings and experience of events, but not about the events themselves. In the American translation of Maria Gripe's *Elvis and His Secret* the present tense of the original is rendered with the past tense. Present tense narrative conveys a very intense, immediate and direct empathy, while the past tense creates distance and alienation. I think the translator's wilful substitution is not accidental but instead represents an adaptation of the emotional intensity of the Swedish original to the American aspiration to spare the reader excessive involvement.

One of the best contemporary Swedish juvenile writers is Peter Pohl, the author of brilliant, ruthless stories of abandoned, maltreated adolescents, in which very sophisticated narrative techniques are used. He has not been translated into American yet (his first novel has appeared in Britain), and if he ever is, he will most probably be perceived as merely a Swedish version of Robert Cormier, which means that he will never be able to disturb and shock readers the way he has done in Sweden. Because of his similarity to Cormier, he will probably be rejected in the United States, since the semiotic space that he represents in Sweden is already occupied by another author.

Some of the most prominent genres and types of Swedish children's literature today, such as the historical and the retrospective novel of the new type, which lack great battles or events and instead explore the sources of national identity, are probably totally irrelevant to American young readers. Stories involving the everyday life of Swedish children will also prove too unfamiliar, for the Swedish child's social network and life-style are entirely different. Themes which are abundant in American school stories, like running for the class presidency, talent show or athletic achievements, are almost never found in Swedish books. The spirit of competition is foreign to a nation whose motto is "Don't think that you are worth anything." The self-pity and self-contempt of the Swedes, which has produced so many abandoned, desperate, unhappy characters in children's literature, does not appeal to the American public, and the absence of solutions in these works will irritate American teachers and librarians.

Here again it may be objected that I am being very general in my judgments, and indeed I am. I am raising questions rather than offering solutions, but I think that the type of issues that I am trying to address are extremely important to an understanding of the situation in world children's literature today.

THE IMPORTANCE OF ASTRID LINDGREN

Astrid Lindgren is the most prominent, most loved and most famous author in Sweden. In Swedish public libraries she has been at the top of the list for many years, far ahead of any other author, children's or adult. She is also one of Sweden's most important export products, her books having been translated into more than sixty languages, including Frisian, Catalonian, Kymrian, Swahili and Zulu.[28] Astrid Lindgren's world fame, however, is not as uncomplicated as it may seem. Indeed, I have in several international contexts discovered that my colleagues from Western countries have a rather vague notion of her. They may courteously recall a few titles, but at the same time they wonder if Astrid Lindgren is something like Enid Blyton, an author loved by children but frowned upon by critics. This is by no means the case: in Sweden, Astrid Lindgren has been the subject of a doctoral dissertation in literature and several volumes of serious criticism.[29]

The fact that Astrid Lindgren is translated and published in so many countries (in the United States alone, over four million copies of *Pippi Longstocking* have been sold) is in itself no criterion of popularity. A published book is not necessarily read and appreciated, nor do the many academic essays about Astrid Lindgren in different parts of the world reflect her importance in their country of origin.

There is one area of the world, however, in which Astrid Lindgren is really a concept, namely Russia and the former Soviet republics, and prob-

Astrid Lindgren in many tongues

ably also the former Soviet satellite states in Eastern Europe. The first work of hers to be translated into Russian was *Karlsson-on-the-Roof*. It appeared in 1957, only two years after the original, which is very unusual for Russia, and has since then sold several million copies. Karlsson, the selfish, greedy, funny fat man with a propeller on his back, has marched triumphantly through the Soviet Union. There is not a single child—or adult—who is not familiar with him. On the other hand, what they know is not the original Astrid Lindgren figure. In the 1970s two animated cartoons were made in Russia based on the Karlsson stories but not on the original illustrations by Ilon Wikland. Cartoons are very popular in Russia, and they have been frequently shown on TV. Later came two picturebooks based on the cartoons. In these anonymous retellings of the plot in the cartoons, nothing remains of Astrid Lindgren's text (her name is not even mentioned on the cover). Numerous Karlsson dolls, badges, postage stamps, mugs, rugs, curtains, chocolate boxes, and other commercial products portray the cartoon Karlsson in much the same fashion as Disney figures in the West. In Moscow a theater performance of *Karlsson-on-the-Roof*, alternating every other Sunday with *Pippi Longstocking*, has been running for full houses for over twenty-five years. It is not Astrid Lindgren's own stage version of *Pippi*, however, but a Russian adaptation of the novels.

What is the secret of Astrid Lindgren's popularity in Russia? What needs do her characters fulfil in the Russian children's reading? If we are not satisfied with simply stating the facts, only semiotics of culture seems capable of providing an answer to this question. To a greater extent than Western recipients, Russian readers have evidently recognized and accepted her books as "their own," as something understandable and welcome. In other words, the Russian readers' interpretation of the cultural codes in her works creates favorable conditions for their appreciation. What are these codes?

In a totalitarian society, to question power is an act of subversion. In Astrid Lindgren's books, the foremost symbol of protest against authorities is of course Pippi Longstocking, but there is also Emil, master detective Bill Bergson and Ronia, the robber's daughter. At the source of Astrid Lindgren's strong impact and popularity in Eastern Europe is the fact that she overtly takes the part of the child—that is, of the weak, the powerless, the oppressed: the lonely younger brother in *Karlsson-on-the-Roof*; the emotionally de-prived orphan in *Mio, My Son* (1954); the mortally sick child in *The Brothers Lionheart* (1973). Moreover, she allows her characters to defy the dictator-ship of norms and conventions, of dull reality, of authority, of structure and order. Bill Bergson challenges the world of adults through his wit and cour-age; Karl Anders Nilsson,[30] also known as prince Mio, challenges it through his creative imagination; Karlsson on the roof challenges it through his bad behavior. Karlsson, the great favourite of Russian children, is together with Pippi Longstocking the most prominent of Astrid Lindgren's characters, those who have definitely stepped out of the societal hierarchy as dissidents and trouble-makers. Pippi gains freedom through her enormous strength, Karlsson through his propeller. Both qualities belong to the world of fan-tasy, which has been more or less closed to Russian children for many years. To read *Pippi Longstocking* or *Karlsson-on-the-Roof* in a Russian context was equal to reading a clandestine, underground protest pamphlet against oppression on the part of society, school, or authoritarian parents. Luckily, the Soviet rulers never noticed the controversial messages of the books, most probably because children's books were not regarded as a threat to the re-gime. They were, of course, because concealed within them was an explo-sive freedom of thought and spirit.

Pippi Longstocking, the rebel, the norm-breaker, the "chaos fac-tor," as one Swedish scholar has labeled her,[31] has been subjected to se-rious critical scrutiny in the English-speaking world. Because of her to-tal lack of respect for adults she has been treated as a bad example for young readers. Her endless supply of gold has won her the label of capi-talist. She has been called a racist because of her adventures on the sav-age island and her supposed contempt of the natives. And she is regarded as strongly anti-feminist and sexist because of her attitude towards her well-behaved playmate Annika.[32]

Needless to say, such critics have completely failed to see the irony of the *Pippi*-stories. But in the first place they have failed to see their anti-power, anti-conventional, anti-totalitarian pathos. It is remarkable that Astrid Lindgren, born and living in a Western democracy, has such a strong and subtle feeling for the oppressed. With her deep insight into the mechanism of tyranny, she is in a way the Orwell of children's literature. Because she writes books for children, however, she cannot be as pessimistic as Orwell but lets the child win over tyranny. Pippi Longstocking violates conventions. She is the feminist in the patriarchal world, the independent individual in the world of collective mediocrity, the rebel against society where children should be seen but not heard, the little Robin Hood who showers golden coins and sweets over the poor and the oppressed. She is also an immensely creative linguist who seemingly violates the norms of language and logic, but who in fact defies the conventional way of thinking and looking at things. The creative use of language to outwit censorship has always been an important typological trait of subversive Russian literature.

Like Peter Pan, Pippi does not want to grow up. Unlike Peter Pan, she does not want to grow up because she does not want to grow into a respectful lady "with a veil and three double chins." She does not want to become what the authorities want her to become: ordinary, obedient and dull. She is what every child dreams of being: strong, independent and free in confrontation with the world of adults. But this is also what all Russian intellectuals dream of being in their confrontation with the regime. In the West, Astrid Lindgren's anti-totalitarian messages have never been grasped as strongly as in Russia. When you have enough water you are not as eager to quench your thirst.

In Denmark Astrid Lindgren has irritated many critics by her supposedly escapist themes. She has been accused of deceiving her readers by offering them daydreams instead of good, solid, realistic problems and solutions. My Danish colleagues are welcome to their firm belief in realism. I would like to reflect further upon the subversive effect of Astrid Lindgren's imaginative writing.

Idyllic books like *Happy Days in Noisy Village* (1952) or *Rasmus and the Vagabond* (1956) were in Eastern Europe a welcome contrast to social realism, this false, artificial style prescribed by the powers for both children's and adult literature. Imaginative books like *Pippi, Karlsson-on-the-Roof* or *Mio, My Son* were able to liberate the imagination of children and extend their horizons beyond the narrow confines of everyday realism. In most Western countries there existed before or parallel to Astrid Lindgren imaginative books such as *Alice in Wonderland, Winnie-the-Pooh*, or *The Wizard of Oz* that performed the same function in children's reading, and her overall revolutionary impact was therefore not as evident there.

In Russia fairy tales, fantasy and all imaginative literature were long banned. It is most probably only Astrid Lindgren's undisputable reputation which made it possible for her fantasy novels to appear in Russian translations. Her books filled a gap, a vacuum, serving as a safety valve for children suffocating in stuffy classrooms dominated by the literature of social realism. In *Mio, My Son* an orphan boy dreams away his colourless existence and makes up a breath-taking adventure in Farawayland. Is it escape? No, for the world of make-believe gives the boy the strength to cope with his anguish, his loneliness and fear. Dreams make him strong in spirit and he matures. This is something that could be adopted by any child, but it was especially attractive to Russian children, chained as they were by harsh discipline in school and at home, chilled by traditionally strict, unemotional relations between parent and child, and often paralyzed by fear of those stronger than themselves. The sick boy's fancies in *The Brothers Lionheart* are similarly a means of reconciliation with death and victory over sorrow and fear. Young readers in Russia, of course, never read *Mio* or *The Brothers Lionheart* in this fashion. Nor do children in Sweden or elsewhere. The subversive message enters the readers' minds on the subconscious level as a spirit of freedom and struggle, a call for creative imagination, for conquering the world by play.

It is illuminating to look at Klaus Doderer's evaluation of *The Brothers Lionheart* as a pessimistic book.[33] Why does Doderer fail to see the liberating idea of freedom in this book? Most probably because he does not himself live in a dictatorship state where every sign of an aspiration for freedom—also freedom of the spirit—is appreciated by a keen reader as a challenge to power. Doderer reads Astrid Lindgren's book in a very narrow Western European context of the 1970s, a period of disappointment after the radical end of the 1960s. A Russian or other Eastern European reader sees in the book a much broader depiction of the struggle against oppression, a struggle that in Eastern Europe of the 1970s, directly after 1968 in Czechoslovakia, could only take place in dreams and the imagination. For the Eastern European reader, Astrid Lindgren's little boy who overcomes fear and anguish through imagination holds a lesson of will, hope and courage. It is also a poetic image of struggle, a brilliant counterweight to hundreds of dull Russian stories about glorious child heroes of revolution and war.

In *Ronia, the Robber's Daughter* (1981) we find once again many of the traits from previous books that made them so attractive in Eastern Europe: the child's unreserved protest against the predestined order of things, freedom of thought and spirit, the eternal wisdom of children contrasted with the petty quarrels of the grownups.

I do not usually approve of reading children's books as a direct reflection of social processes. I dislike very much the undisguised political interpretation of *The Brothers Lionheart* as a description of the Vietnam War.[34] To reduce this multidimensional novel to such a primitive plot would be to question Astrid Lindgren's talent. Still, among many other levels of the text, it is enticing to see in *Ronia, the Robber's Daughter*, written 1981, a vision of the future in which the gorge that divides the robbers' castle is a powerful symbol for the Berlin Wall, the iron curtain between East and West—which young people are called upon to tear down.

SUMMING UP

The notion that there is a "common" children's literature in all countries in the world is a misunderstanding. The idea of touchstones of children's literature, popular in the United States and widespread elsewhere, is ethnocentric. With very few exceptions, children's literature in different countries has little in common. Besides, these universal texts are mostly collections of retold fairy tales (Perrault, Grimms) or adapted adult novels (*Robinson Crusoe*), none of which are children's literature as such, even if for different reasons they have become part of children's reading. Of texts written directly for children it is probably only *Alice in Wonderland* that I would very cautiously name a truly universal children's book, with the reservation that it is most probably unknown in some countries in Asia, Africa and Latin America. The texts that are most often discussed in English-language sources as "touchstones"—*The Tale of Peter Rabbit* and *Charlotte's Web*—are not as unanimously regarded as indispensable in other countries.

Another controversial postulate of this chapter is that, although the general exchange of information in the world is growing, children's literature is becoming more and more national and isolated. Worldwide, the share of children's books occupied by translations is tending to decrease, and foreign books have great difficulties competing with national texts. Inadequate translations contribute to the mutual mistrust. By comparing European and American children's literature and by analysing the reception of Astrid Lindgren in Eastern and Western Europe I try to indicate some sources and consequences of this process.

1.   The Swedish book monthly *Boken* requested 100 writers and critics of children's literature to suggest the ten best children's books of all times and nations. From these, a list of fifty was selected and published in *Boken* 1 (1991). Not unexpectedly, there was an obvious dominance of Swedish books among them. An American scholar would be amazed at the absence of some self-evident English-language texts. Of the 28 texts mentioned in the first volume of *Touchstones* (Nodelman, 1985) eight are included: *Alice in Wonderland, The Wind in the Willows, The Jungle Book*, the Narnia suite, *Winnie-the-Pooh, Anne of Green Gables, Treasure Island* and *Tom Sawyer.*

2.   I can refer to one of the most recent books, Nodelman, 1992.

3.   Lynch-Brown, 1993.

4.   Chernyavskaya, 1982. In another Soviet source, characteristically entitled "One Hundred Books for Your Child," the only contemporary English-language book included is *The Adventures of Chunky* by Leila Berg (Timofeyeva, 1987).

5.   For a detailed discussion on the Grimms see Bottigheimer, 1987; Tatar, 1987; Zipes, 1988.

6.   See Ong, 1982.

7.   Bettelheim, 1975.

8.   Zipes, 1979, 1983. See also Bottigheimer, 1987.

9.   This pattern is discussed in Edström, 1982, as the most essential pattern of children's literature. See also Nodelman, 1992, pp. 77ff.

10.   There are some interesting studies of *Robinson* adaptations in different countries; see, e.g., an annotated bibliography of versions of *Robinson* and robinsonade-theme in Germany: Stach, 1991; on various editions in Sweden: Winquist, 1973.

11.   A comprehensive study of adaptation of children's classics has been made by the Norwegian scholar Kari Skjønsberg; see Skjønsberg, 1979.

12.   James Greenwood is mentioned in Green (1965, pp. 238f) for some of his other books.

13.   Townsend, 1983.

14.   Attebery, 1980, p. 185.

15.   For the insights into Flemish children's literature I am indebted to Myriam Paquet.

16.   One of the recent sources, which includes these writers, is "77 Swedish-language children's writers" (Toijer-Nilsson, 1989). The volume published by the Swedish public library service is clearly subtitled "Modern Swedish Writers" (*De skriver*, 1990).

17.   For information on East German children's literature I am indebted to Rigmor Granlund-Lind.

18.   Information submitted by Mona Henning.

19.   Many international conferences have been devoted to the problem of translations of children's literature, see, e.g., Klingberg, 1978.

20.   E.g., Bell, 1979.

21.   Oittinen, 1993.

22.   Klingberg, 1986.

23.   One of the central figures of modern semiotics, C.S. Peirce, has articulated the sign as something with the help of which we learn about something else. This seems to be such a commonplace in the works of Peirce that I am unable to give a correct reference.

24.   Here and below my arguments are based on Yury Lotman's central work on cultural semiotics, Lotman, 1991.

25.   Iser, 1974a.

26.   Perry Nodelman defends the existence of Disney versions as cultural

works in their own rights (Nodelman, 1992, pp. 54f). I am not questioning this, but here I discuss Disney films as typical American interpretations of European texts.

27. Lynch-Brown, 1993, p. 183.

28. Ørvig, 1977, pp. 184-245; Ørvig, 1987, pp. 116–217.

29. Lundqvist, 1979.

30. In the Swedish original the boy's name is Bo Vilhelm Olsson—another example of mysterious, unmotivated name changes in translations of children's books.

31. Edström, 1990.

32. See, e.g., Reeder, 1979.

33. Doderer, 1978.

34. See, e.g., a newspaper review of the novel, reprinted in Ørvig, 1977, p. 173.

2

CHILDREN'S LITERATURE

A CANONICAL ART FORM

For many years children's literature research in Sweden was governed by the notion of *adaptation*. Briefly, this idea, which has also influenced researchers in Germany and elsewhere, implies that children's texts are adapted, or adjusted, to what writers and educators believe to be the needs, interests, experience or perception of young readers. In Sweden Göte Klingberg has proposed a whole system of different adaptation types according to subject matter, form, style and medium.[1] In his latest works he suggests other terms that probably better describe the various phenomena he previously categorized as adaptation.[2] One of these terms is *purification*, which means that a children's text is purged of whatever does not suit the taste, ideology, morals or religion of an adult mediator.[3] Purification is the most common form of interference in children's books. My favorite example is a passage in the Russian edition of Selma Lagerlöf's *The Wonderful Adventure of Nils* (1906–07), in which the parents go to the market, while in the original they are going to church. In the atheistic Soviet Union, a church could not be mentioned at all in a children's book. Some contemporary Swedish children's books have been subjected to purification because of the strict American attitude to nakedness. The latest such example is Pija Lindenbaum's *Else-Marie and Her Seven Little Daddies* (1990).

There are also some really ridiculous cases. In 1988 the Swedish publisher Rabén & Sjögren brought out a new edition of Astrid Lindgren's bedtime story "I Don't Want to Go to Bed," illustrated by Ilon Wikland. The book was first published in 1947 with illustrations by another artist. Missing in the new edition are two lines describing Mrs Bear's nice little maids who are hanging little Bear's wet socks and shoes. The maids are not portrayed in Ilon Wikland's illustrations. In Sweden of the 1980s children have little experience of maids, and class differences are not so obvious in children's books. But it is remarkable that a book should have to undergo plastic surgery in order to be accepted by educators today.

However, by adaptation in children's literature we usually mean not these cases (which otherwise can also be regarded as censorship), but a conscious endeavour on the part of writers to make their texts accessible for young readers through the use of shorter sentences, easier and shorter words, uncomplicated syntax, abundant dialogue, straight plots, a limited number of characters, and few abstract notions.

A deeper study of children's literature immediately reveals that adaptation theory is totally untenable. The Swedish scholar Vivi Edström was probably the first to challenge it, evidently because her approach to children's literature is not pedagogical but artistic. She shows, among other things, that the conscious simplicity and naivete of children's literature does not mean that it has been adapted, at least not to a greater extent than any work of art is created with a view to its possible recipients. In her pioneer study "Form in Children's Literature" Vivi Edström stresses repeatedly that the statistically shorter sentences and the sparing use of "difficult" words do not imply impoverished or simplified artistic devices. The simplicity of children's literature is an artistic device in itself, something that adult literature sometimes lacks.[4] If the adaptation theory were correct, the whole development of children's literature would have been exclusively in the direction of further simplification and "order," which contradicts the inherent *entropy* of art, that is, a tendency towards irregularity and chaos. Vivi Edström regards the most revolutionary Swedish children's book, *Pippi Longstocking*, as representing precisely chaos.[5]

Edström proposes adopting a much broader view of children's literature, which, among other things, is based upon the notion of the *implied reader*, developed in modern reception theory.[6] In the field of children's literature, Aidan Chambers is one researcher who has made use of this notion.[7]

Another aspect of children's literature we must consider before we can judge it fairly is its apparent secondariness as manifested in a similarity of patterns, limited plot variations, and so on. Perry Nodelman has recently drawn our attention to this "sameness" of children's literature.[8] While I think this question is of overall importance for our understanding of the nature of children's literature, I cannot but regret that Nodelman stops halfway in his argument, more or less supporting the adherents of adaptation theory. He does not directly condemn children's literature, but he states somewhat resignedly that children's literature is *sui generis* and cannot be investigated by conventional instruments. He comes quite close indeed to Peter Hunt's "childist criticism."

I think we get a more positive view of what we are doing if, instead of comparing children's literature with modern Western literature, we attempt to identify other text types similar to children's texts. What does not seem to have been recognized is that the majority of children's texts, at least up to the very recent period, belongs to the category of art which may be called *canonical*.

Nodelman's concept of "sameness" can be viewed as corresponding directly to the traditional notion of *loci communes* (common places) or rhetoric formulas. He shows that children's texts belonging to the same genre—in his case the time shift fantasy—are sometimes so similar that we may wonder whether we have to do with imitation. He argues, however, that it would be wrong to see children's texts as self-repeating and secondary with regards to their predecessors. I would formulate the same idea by saying that children's literature is more imitative than adult literature, if the word "imitation" is not understood in any pejorative meaning. When today's critics analyze contemporary adult novels, they mostly look for original and innovative features which they refer to with terms like "radical issues," "stylistic experiments," or "revolutionary devices." If we attempt to analyze children's literature with the same instruments we would soon discover that almost all children's literature is merely a boring variation of the same text.

The main point of Nodelman's essay is that critics of children's literature must stop making excuses for children's books; as he says with a reference to Harold Bloom, they must reject "the anxiety of influence."[9] What makes each text unique is not superficial similarity but the way writers explore the potential of these superficial narrative devices. From Nodelman's arguments I can draw one conclusion: that traditional children's literature is an essentially different text type than twentieth-century mainstream literature. When we contemplate the differences, we realize that children's literature emerges and develops under very strict canonical, that is, normative rules.

Nodelman does not make use of the notion of canon. I am using it in the sense it is used by Yuri Lotman in his fascinating essay "Canonical art as informational paradox."[10] This essay was written during a period in Lotman's scholarly career when the semiotic studies of the Tartu school began to develop a growing interest in text rather than language, and in text viewed as an important process of confrontation with the recipient rather than a static representation of language. The poetic, or artistic, text in this view not only *contains* but also *generates* information. The recipient figures prominently in the emergence of the text. A text is never a ready message, but rather a generator of the message. To a certain extent this approach is reminiscent of the primary postulate of reception theory: the reader creates the text. This view has been enthusiastically adopted by children's literature researchers.[11]

The feature of the artistic text that makes it generate information is of course present in all text types. The chief accusation leveled at children's literature by its detractors is that children's books are so similar that "children do not learn anything new" from them. It is thus preferable that children read adult literature, the preaching goes. People tend to forget, however, that not all adult literature is informative either. It is meaningless, as the adversaries of children's literature normally do, to compare children's literature *as a whole* with the rather limited top layer of quality adult novels. Comparing Francine Pascal with James Joyce is quite fruitless, although it might prove interesting to compare her with Sidney Sheldon, since both write within a canon.

Thus I would like to go one step further than Perry Nodelman, who states that children's literature is subject to different rules than adult literature. With the help of Lotman's hypothesis I shall attempt to show that these different rules imply not only that children's literature is not artistically inferior but that, on the contrary, it is at least as rich or even richer than certain adult novels.

TRADITIONAL AND MODERN ART

Canon, a central notion in Russian literary and art criticism, shares certain features with ideas developed by Ernst Robert Curtius in his classical study *Europäische Literatur und lateinische Mittelalter*,[12] and there are also similarities with Northrop Frye's studies of literary modes.[13] I do not intend to present any detailed analysis of the notion of canon, but will simply state that Lotman discusses canonical art forms from the viewpoint of his very broad attitude to art and culture as text characteristic of the Moscow/Tartu semiotic school in general. When he says "canonical text," he may mean a folktale or myth, a medieval icon, a church or temple, a rite, and so on. According to Lotman, there are two principal types of art. The first is based on the canonic system and can be called "ritual," "canonical" or "traditional" art. The other is based on violations of the canon, that is, the prevailing norms. This type is called "modern" art. Aesthetic values in modern art emerge not out of adherence to norms but out of deviation from them. While in ritual art breaking of the norms is comprehended as wrong, and in extreme instances as criminal (for example, blasphemy), in modern art it is seen as innovation and creativity. In my earlier example Francine Pascal—and most children's literature—as well as Sidney Sheldon, belong to the category of canonical art, while Joyce—and much so called "quality" contemporary literature—represents the non-canonical, or modern, art.

The breaking of the canon in children's literature has been prevented by the dominating norms in subject matter (themes considered unsuitable for children are dismissed), behavior (descriptions of sexual intercourse are improper) and language (writers are not supposed to use slang and abusive language; language should be grammatically correct).

Some researchers have questioned whether art can even exist outside a canon. One argument is that unique, non-recurrent objects cannot communicate, and that every "individual," "outstanding" work of art is created by a combination of a limited number of standard elements. Undoubtedly, if a work of art is so innovating and unique that it does not contain one single element which recipients can recognize, this work of art is "closed" for the recipient; in other words, it is meaningless. To take an extreme and hypothetical case: a book written in a language which no one beside the author understands, which depicts totally incomprehensible settings, creatures and events and is based on natural laws alien to those of our universe is, to put it mildly, very unlikely to be read and appreciated. The innovations which Western culture has advocated during recent centuries as a prerequisite for successful art have mostly been very tiny deviations from the norms. As many examples show, when these deviations became too obvious, works of art have often encountered disgust and condemnation. It is this experience which has led certain art theoreticians to pose their almost metaphysical question about the possibility of art outside a canon. No one, however, has questioned the existence of the canonical art, that is, art which adhered to norms and rules. It is quite remarkable, therefore, that scholars, scholars of children's literature in particular, should so often ignore the basic principles of canonical art.

COMMUNICATION IN CANONICAL TEXTS

Lotman argues that a system which has a purpose to communicate, a limited vocabulary and a rigid grammar can reasonably be expected to resemble a natural language and that it is therefore possible to study it in the same manner. In the beginning semioticians were tempted to study canonical texts as analogues to natural languages and investigated their morphology (classifying parts of speech, establishing rules for conjugation, etc.) and syntax (studying sentence patterns, establishing rules for word combinations, etc).

Throughout several historical epochs artistic activity consisted in following rules, not breaking them. This can be observed in oral narrative and during the Middle Ages and the period of Classicism. There are also certain countries and cultures—for example, Japan or among the Australian Aborigines—in which most art is created within predetermined rules. Studies of texts from these epochs and countries produce the most fruitful results when they utilize structural methods. Vladimir Propp's well-known *Morphology of the Folktale* (1928) is an example of this approach; the title itself reflects its methodology.[14]

The seemingly self-evident parallel with natural languages, however, immediately creates problems. When a text is created in a natural language, the *signifier* appears automatically. In other words, when I speak or write, I do not think about parts of speech or sentence patterns; these are irrelevant for successful communication. The mechanism which governs the use of grammatical forms or sentence structures is invisible. If I make grammatical mistakes when I speak a foreign language, my interlocutor will understand me anyway, provided that the topic of the conversation is interesting for us both. Both in correct and in grammatically or syntactically deficient language I can produce an unlimited number of messages on any subject. The *signified* of the message in a natural language is endlessly free.

Canonical texts are built up according to a reverse principle. The informative side of the text is regulated, while the "language" of the system is a non-automatic mechanism of which we are constantly aware during communication. In other words, the important part is not *what* is told, but *how* it is told. Fixed contents are the most prominent feature of ritual art. In a natural language like English, or Russian, or French, you can speak about anything. In the folktale language you can only speak about certain things. The relationship between the signifier and the signified is different. In art the process of "codifying," that is, creating a text with the help of codes, cannot occur automatically, as when we speak or write in a natural language, or it is not art. Once again, the essential part is *how* the message is formed.

We are thus confronted by a paradox. On one hand we have a system, a "language" which produces a vast number of texts and, since it uses a recurrent type of codification, is very similar to a natural language. For instance, when we tell the story of Little Red Riding Hood, we must use a certain amount of elements and this specific number of characters and specific number of events must also occur in a certain order—more or less like words and grammar rules in a language. The same would be true about ritual texts such as the whodunit, the Western or the romance.

On the other hand, the system behaves in a strange way—it does not produce language automatically and it does not have a free content. That is, although we can decorate the story of Little Red Riding Hood in many ways without changing its essence, we cannot insert Snow White into it or it will cease to be the story of Little Red Riding Hood. There must be something beyond a superficial similarity between general linguistic communication and the communicative process of, for instance, a folktale or a children's book.

THE SAME TEXT OVER AND OVER AGAIN?
I have allowed myself to dwell on the general communicative issues of canonical texts in order to approach the following question: how can a sys-

tem consisting of a limited number of recurrent elements and rigid rules for their usage retain its informative value? In other words—something that many children's literature experts have wondered—why are children not bored by their endless Biggles and Nancy Drew? What joy can they get out of fantasy novels, in which the final victory of the good is predictable from the beginning? What information do they gather from girls' books, in which the heroine will inevitably marry her prince?

Lotman's answer is categorical and shows the doubts of adults to be groundless. If in folktales or medieval art or any other ritual texts we perceive only the maintenance of certain rules, then we have dealt with just one layer in the complicated structure of the text. Lotman exemplifies this by comparing two messages: a written note and a handkerchief with a knot. Both can be "read." In the first case, the text itself contains the message which can in its whole be extracted from the text. In the other case, the "text" (knot) has a mnemotechnical function. It reminds the recipient about something that the recipient already knows. Here it is not possible to extract the message from the text. The handkerchief of this example can represent many different text types, not only the "string writing" of North American Indians but all cases where a fixed written text serves merely to jog the memory. Medieval monks were often illiterate. When reading from the Holy Scripture, they read by heart, but they still needed the sight of pages. In the same manner a very young child can "read" the verbal text in a picturebook from memory with the help of the pictures which the child immediately associates with the story.

Lotman shows that there are many more similar text types. "Reminding" is merely one case among a vast category of messages in which the information is neither contained in the text itself nor extracted from the text, but is found outside the text and needs the presence of the text in order to be received and decoded.

This can be seen more clearly if we imagine the simple communicative process. There are basically two ways in which individuals or human groups can receive information. First, we can get information from outside. Information is produced outside the individual or group and is transferred *in toto* to the addressee along the simple communicative chain: source→sender→code→recipient. Because it is commonly believed that this is *the only* possible way to receive information, it is often advertised in children's books, especially by pedagogically oriented mediators; children's books should have "issues," they must "teach" children something useful.

But there is another type of communication in which the information received from outside is only a part of the whole and stimulates an increase of information in the mind of the recipient. This self-increase structures and organizes unstructured information in the recipient's brain. The recipient plays a much more active role in this process than in a simple transference of a stable body of facts. The most primitive examples, proposed by Lotman, include the beat of a railway car or rhythmical music stimulating meditation, the human predilection for regular patterns or geometrical figures, and the fascination of word repetition in, for instance, poetry. In all these cases, inner information increases under the influence of organized outer information. The same phenomenon in a more complicated form apparently underlies canonical art, and this makes it easier to explain the paradox we observed above.

If we compare folklore, medieval art or children's literature with the mainstream aesthetics of the nineteenth and especially twentieth century, it is obvious that fixed texts are related in a different way to the amount of information that the text contains. A "modern" or "unique" text contains *all* the information in this particular work of art, and the information is, or at least is supposed to be, "new." A folktale, a medieval picture or a children's book contains merely a portion of the information which its creator intends to mediate and which its recipients—provided they have the will and the capacity—can "read." Because the signifier is extremely rigid, the form, the relation between signifier and signified, between form and content, are no longer as unequivocal as in natural languages. Instead, they function in the same manner as the handkerchief and the memories that the knot is supposed to evoke.

A children's book, which is a work of art, contains more information than is printed on its pages. There is also a reminiscence of other books the child has read. There is a reminiscence of the child's personal experience. There is an emotional charge which works in various ways depending on the child's temperament, upbringing, previous knowledge, mood, and atmosphere under this particular encounter with the text.

Provided that they have read similar texts earlier, when young readers open a book of adventure stories they do not in the first place expect to learn anything new. The fascination of traditional children's books is based on their predictability, the "joy of recognition." It is also here that fairy tales and classics play their decisive role in children's reading.

Recipients of a "modern" text, for instance, an adult "quality" novel, are in the first place listeners who are prepared to extract information from the text. Information is in this case equal to something new. This novelty can pertain to the plot, the setting, the characters or the style, language, or artistic devices. This is precisely what literary critics pay attention to when they evaluate works of literature. Recipients of a canonical text are merely favorably situated to listen to themselves. They are not only listeners, but co-creators as well. This is why canonical art does not lack an ability to mediate information. Listening to a folktale—or a children's book—is more like listening to a musical piece than reading a modern novel. It is normal to listen to musical pieces more than once, under different circumstances, and performed by different musicians. In contrast, most adult readers are certain they have gotten everything from a novel which they have read just once. Aren't children cleverer when they demand to hear the same fairy tale or book over and over again? In the one case, the "work" is equal to the graphically fixed text; it has limited boundaries and a stable body of information. In the other case, the fixed text is just a part—albeit the most tangible part, but still merely a part, probably not the most essential part of the work. The text demands more interpretation, which among other things means putting the work into its context.

The relation between art and the interpreted reality is radically different in the two text types. In a "realistic" novel you can easily identify the text and the real life, while it is the creative process or emergence of the text which demands most effort. If text and reality can be identified at all in canonical art, this process itself is creativity. In semiotics, this process is called *semiosis*, which very primitively means discovering the structure of signs in the world, identifying signs with their signified. The process in realistic novels has been named *mimesis*, or reflecting reality.[15]

In canonical art, which is dependent on rules and norms, most signs are *conventional*, that is, the relation between the sign and the signified is based on some form of agreement between the sender and the addressee. In modern art, most signs are *iconic* or *indexical*, that is, based either on a similarity between the sign and the reality behind it (icon) or a direct indication from the sign to reality (index).[16] Conventional signs can only be interpreted when the recipient is familiar with the code.

A non-canonical text is the source of information, while a canonic text is the evoking force. In non-canonical texts, formal structures are a link or information channel between sender and receiver. In canonical texts structure is the very essence of information. The structure is transmitted to the receivers and helps to organize information that already exists in their minds. Once again we may recall the example of children reading an adventure story: they relate the text they are reading to all earlier adventure stories they have read, they compare and confront—subconsciously, of course. This is the child's creative work during reading, the process we ignore when we wonder why children keep choosing the same book type.

From Lotman's argument we can thus see that in order to generate information readers must necessarily confront the text with their earlier experience (master the code) and compare with previously known texts (that is, set texts in their intertextual relations). Children's literature, therefore, places high demands on the readers' previous knowledge in order, for instance, to relate a book to a "genre": Is this a Western? a horse story? a criminal novel? a fairy tale? Canonical texts have markers to guide recipients.

All this means that when we examine the inner structures of canonical texts ("plots" or "motifs" in children's books), we may get a good idea of an important layer of the text, but this is not its only layer. When we have stated that all adventure stories have the same narrative pattern, or that all books for girls pursue the same basic plot ("the Cinderella story"), or that all fantasy novels present the same structure with a passage between two worlds—shall we then feel satisfied, like Perry Nodelman, and say that we need not be anxious about the inferiority of children's literature? Nodelman goes so far as to claim that children's literature is "a sort of women's literature."[17]

Lotman, who primarily deals with canonical texts created long ago, encourages us to investigate the deeper meanings of texts. What did the text—a folktale, a myth, a rite, a picture—mean for the group of humans who created it? How did it function in a community? This question can be very difficult to approach, since it can most often not be answered on the premises of the text itself. "Modern" texts often have reference to social functions. A novel is a novel and can hardly function as a religious service (at least, not primarily). Canonical texts of the type Lotman discusses—myths, folktales, rites, icons—generally give us no clues about their functions in human community. The pragmatic and social meaning of these texts must be reconstructed from outer sources (at best, from representatives of the culture). Ethnologists try to do so with folktales and myths, archeologists interpret cave paintings and megalithic monuments, art historians examine icons and murals. But we cannot be sure whether their explanations are correct, for the mentality behind canonical texts may be totally alien to us members of Western civilisation. An Aboriginal corroborree is not, as it is often mistakenly thought to be, a representation of an event of long ago but the event itself, and its participants are not portraying characters in the same meaning as modern Western actors in their roles.

Unlike the folktale, children's literature has a clear social and pedagogical function, and we have little doubt about its meaning. But children's literature presents yet another problem not confronted by Lotman. It is one of a few types of texts in which senders and recipients always belong to two different human communities, each with its own experience, previous knowledge and expectations. With very few exceptions, children's literature is never created by the same group of humans to whom it is addressed, that is, to children. This means that children's literature as a form of art is in one respect more complex than adult literature; it has always two systems of codes, one addressed to the child, another addressed, often unconsciously, to the adult beside or behind the child. This feature of children's literature has encouraged scholars to suggest the notion of *ambivalent texts*, that is, texts participating in two different literary systems. The concept of ambivalent texts has been elaborated by the Israeli semiotician Zohar Shavit,[18] while a similar notion of *duplex fiction* has been independently proposed in Sweden by Danuta Zadworna-Fjellestad.[19] The weakness in both scholars' arguments, as shown, for instance, by Vivi Edström, is that they underestimate child codes in ambivalent texts and, rather than accept the inherent value

Alice in Wonderland—*an ambivalent text. Illustration by Grigory Kalinovsky from a Russian edition. Note the adult pictorial code.*

of these texts, they try to raise the status of certain children's books (*Alice in Wonderland* in particular) to the level of adult fiction.[20]

The ambivalent addressee in children's literature is examined at length by Barbara Wall, whose study is subtitled "The dilemma of children's fiction."[21] Wall makes a distinction between *double address* in the negative meaning (cf "double morals") typical for Victorian children's literature, and *dual address* on equal terms in contemporary children's books. Whatever terms we prefer, the distinction is indeed significant. This circumstance, the double system of codes in children's books, demands that all our communications models take into consideration the interaction of communicative processes on the two levels.

Lotman concludes his essay on canonical art with the following statement: canonical art has played an enormous part in the history of art and culture. It is in no way fruitful to treat it as a lower or obsolete stage. It is, on the contrary, necessary to investigate not only the structure of canonical texts but also the hidden information sources which make a seemingly simple and well-known text a powerful mechanism of human culture.

SUMMING UP

Accepting children's literature as a canonical art form will have several consequences for us as scholars. We can once and for all abandon the defensive attitude towards "serious" literary criticism. No one accuses ethnologists or medievalists of studying something of less value than modern art or literature. We can also stop arguing against the supposed artistic inferiority of children's literature. As Perry Nodelman points out, it is ridiculous to analyse Proust and Edith Nesbit with the same instruments, but not because Edith Nesbit is a worse writer than Proust. She is "worse than Proust" only in the same sense that the Japanese artist Hokusai, who painted 36 landscapes of Mount Fuji, is "worse" than, for instance, van Gogh. They are phenomena from different categories. They cannot be compared.

Applying the notion of canonical art to children's literature allows us to view it in a new light. Studying children's books as canonical texts leads to new and unexpected conclusions as compared to traditional methods. To take one example, we can explain why children like to read many similar books—both *paraliterature*[22] and "quality" literature with similar motifs—in a row. Children are not stupid and unable to extract information from the text during the first reading. Children's books may convey less information, but they generate more information. Texts create a flow of information in the mind of readers; the more the recipients are familiar with the canon, the richer this flow. I think Perry Nodelman reduces the significance of this aspect when he simply says that "young readers of formula books may be learning the basic patterns that less formulaic books diverge from" and "perhaps we cannot appreciate the divergences of more unusual books until we first learn these underlying patterns."[23] Canonical texts are not only a training exercise for more sophisticated literature but have a value in their own right.

Finally, we must realize that canonical features of children's books and their young readers' devotion to these works are as indispensable to the history of children's literature as to all other forms of art.

NOTES

1. Klingberg, 1972, pp. 95–102.
2. See, e.g., Klingberg, 1981.
3. Klingberg, 1986, pp. 12f, 58–62.
4. Edström, 1982, pp. 177–198.
5. Edström, 1990.
6. Iser, 1974a.
7. Chambers, 1985. See also Tabbert, 1980; Golden, 1990; Skjønsberg, 1990; Johansson, 1992.
8. Nodelman, 1985.
9. Bloom, 1973.
10. Lotman, 1973.
11. Cf. Tabbert, 1980.
12. Curtius, 1954.
13. Frye, 1957.
14. Propp, 1968.
15. The classical study of mimetic structures in world literature is entitled *Mimesis* (Auerbach, 1974). See also Hume, 1984.
16. The division of signs into icons, indices and conventional signs, or symbols, appears in the branch of semiotics associated with C.S. Peirce. I prefer to use the term "conventional signs" to avoid confusion, since in non-semiotical criticism "symbols" have a different connotation.
17. Nodelman, 1992, p. 96.
18. Shavit, 1980; Shavit, 1986, pp. 63–92.
19. Zadworna-Fjellestad, 1986.
20. Edström, 1992b, pp. 18ff.
21. Wall, 1991.
22. I prefer the term *paraliterature* ("side-literature") since it does not contain any qualitative evaluation. Some more conventional terms are: mass literature, trivial literature, popular literature. I have also come across the pertinent term "instant literature." Less biased scholars use the notion of "formula fiction." Common examples of paraliterary texts are Enid Blyton, Carolyn Keene (pseud) and, in our days, *Sweet Valley High* or *The Baby-Sitters' Club*.
23. Nodelman, 1992, p. 89.

3

THE HISTORY OF CHILDREN'S LITERATURE FROM A SEMIOTIC PERSPECTIVE

In the previous chapter I suggested that children's literature can be viewed as a fixed, canonical art form. If this is the case, how can any evolution take place? How do new forms emerge and old ones disappear? For evidently even the canon changes throughout history.

The historical method in literature inevitably tends to be descriptive. Because research on children's literature on the whole lags behind general literary criticism, the descriptive tendency is all the more evident there. There are no established models addressing the development of children's literature, whether a national literature, a general outline, or studies of certain periods.

If we want to do more than simply state certain facts and proceed to questions of causes and interrelations, we will be obliged to search for adequate methods and models in other fields of research. One such field of special interest here is the semiotics of culture as it is understood by the Russian semiotic school and presented in the works of Yuri Lotman.[1] On the basis of this approach, children's literature will be viewed as a particular *semiosphere*, and its history will be regarded as a succession of changing cultural codes. The whole body of children's texts is thus a complicated, stratified system of signs, a special semiosphere, that is, a continuum of semiotic signs. The codes which govern this system or continuum differ in some respects from those of mainstream literature. As I showed in the previous chapter, what sets children's texts apart from mainstream literature is the presence of a *double* code system consisting of a "children's code" and an "adult code."

Many notions borrowed from the semiotics of culture can contribute to an efficient model for describing the history of children's literature. The most important aspect of semiosphere is its dynamic character, which means that the "children's code" and the "adult code" change throughout history, converging, diverging and overlapping at various points. The best example of this process is the way in which so many books comprehended as "adult" become part of children's literature. Attitudes towards children's literature as opposed to mainstream literature also vary.

The code shift within children's literature implies that central phenomena are eventually supplanted by borderline phenomena. When J.D. Salinger's *The Catcher in the Rye* appeared in 1951 it was unique, but today is has become the central archetypal text for a whole tradition sometimes called "jeans prose." The term was introduced by the Jugoslav scholar Aleksander Flaker in his study *Modelle der Jeans Prosa* (1975).[2] It is widely used in German and Swedish scholarship to designate novels emphasizing special tokens of teenage culture—clothes, food, music, language. Thus Salinger's book has generated what may be named "jeans code."

Many taboos that existed in children's literature during its early periods are today being withdrawn. This does not, however, happen suddenly. Texts that take up some earlier forbidden theme such as violence or sex first appear on the borderline. Since in any semiosphere it is the borderline that is active, while its centre is passive, the borderline texts move successively towards the centre. Today we can discover candid descriptions of sexual relations in children's books on a scale unheard of twenty years ago. We can also see a further breakthrough in the periphery; for instance, *Dance On My Grave* (1982) by Aidan Chambers was among the first young adult novels to take up homosexuality, but it was soon followed by more. Today, homosexuality has also entered literature for very young children, one example being Lesléa Newman's *Heather Has Two Mommies* (1989).

Discoveries of new peripheral codes constitute a semiotic process known as the "semiotization" of codes (see Fig. 2). As the central code is

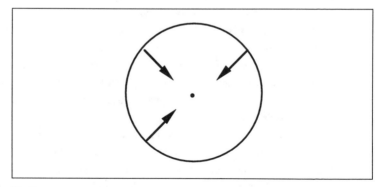

Fig. 2

forced aside, it becomes less and less effective and is "desemiotized." Through centripetal movement the peripheral code acquires the central position.

There are several criteria which determine the central code and several conditions for its existence. Among the criteria may be mentioned a wide distribution (most writers use this code), great frequency (the code is used statistically more often than others) and high status, which means that during a certain period this particular code is appreciated as the most important. It is very easy to give examples, and we intuitively associate every historical period with a certain dominant type of children's literature.

Paradoxically, the conditions of the existence of a central code are also the reasons it is inevitably superseded by new codes. In the first stage, the central code becomes a model for all new texts. For instance, *Robinson Crusoe* became the model for later robinsonades as different as Scott O'Dell's *Island of the Blue Dolphins* (1960), Jean Craighead George's *Julie of the Wolves* (1973) or Michel Tournier's *Friday and Robinson* (1971).

In the second stage, the code becomes more and more elaborate and detailed. Now it is standardized and transformed into a system of instructions, rules and prescriptions ("This is the way a good children's book should be"). This means that the code becomes an obstacle to evolution, it becomes automatized, a stereotype which is no longer appreciated by the receivers as new and exciting. A good example is the Kunstmärchen in Sweden, which after a short period of bloom at the turn of the century very soon became a stale and conservative genre.[3] The longer a code has been central, the greater the risk that it will become petrified and lose its appeal to readers. At this point, peripheral and therefore more flexible codes come and take its place.

As stated earlier, the semiotic system of children's literature consists of several levels. A complete description of changes in a code system must therefore take these into consideration. We can start with the linguistic level: the first appearance of dialect in a Swedish children's novel (*The Children of the Moor* by Louisa Fitinghoff, 1907); the abolition of plural verbal forms in *The Wonderful Adventures of Nils* (1906-07) by Selma Lagerlöf; the first appearance of teenage slang in *The Catcher in the Rye*.

There is then material culture, the system of concrete objects, or *artifacts*, significant for children's books. The printing press was apparently the essential prerequisite for the emergence of children's literature, since handmade books were too expensive to be put into children's hands. In our time the appearance of computers cannot be neglected.

Further we can investigate social culture: the changes in societal processes, institutions, behavioral patterns and other *sociofacts*, or social signs of the texts.

The most difficult to capture is the mental level, mentality or mental culture: the reflection of the changing history of ideas and values, or *mentifacts*.[4] Changing gender stereotypes in children's literature are a very good example of the code shift on the mental level. Different manifestations of "political correctness" in children's books may also be included among phenomena from this area.

Changes do not occur simultaneously on all levels. In "The Black Spot" (1949) by Harry Kullman, which is usually mentioned as the very first Swedish young adult novel, there is a discrepancy between the jeans code on the level of setting or relationships and the conventional, correct language of the work.

Consequently, the movement between center and periphery is not a mechanical oscillation back and forth. The only area where such a swing of pendulum can be observed is the abrupt turns of educators demanding utility versus pleasure in reading—between the notion that children's books should be educational, didactic or ideologically correct and an opposite emphasis on entertainment and imagination. This fluctuation has been going on at varying rates since the emergence of children's literature, and it is not until now that the division itself has been called into question.

In any other respect, a simple pendulum movement would mean that in the long run no innovations would be possible. Sometimes we may indeed wonder whether they are possible, considering the traces of old genres such as adventure, suspense, historical novel and so on, that can be discovered in the children's literature of today. The movement between center and periphery, however, is more complicated. In the first place there is an intensive interaction between the different levels of the semiosphere. New themes (social signs) demand new forms (linguistic or stylistic signs). New mentalities stimulate new themes. New artifacts arouse interest for stylistic experiments, for instance, imitations of a computer printout.

Further, the semiosphere is permanently bombarded by outside phenomena, from the areas which in the semiotics of culture are called non-culture and extra-culture. *Non-culture*, or anti-culture, is everything that members of a culture do not recognize as culture but regard as "the other"—barbarianism, paganism, heresy, exoticism, alienness, the subconscious, the pathological, as opposed to what we under certain circumstances believe to be culture. Dialect and slang are initially non-cultural phenomena which eventually penetrate into children's literature, as is the homosexual "sub-culture." Motifs from Australian Aboriginal beliefs in Patricia

Wrightson's Wirrun trilogy are examples of earlier non-cultural elements which are accepted into the semiosphere of children's literature.[5] In our time, impulses from film, TV, video, teenage fashion, rock texts, the toy industry, advertisements, cartoons and entertainment are important in the evolution of children's literature. These phenomena can be called *paraculture* ("side culture," "parallel culture") existing outside the boundaries of culture as such.

Adult literature as well is non-culture vis-à-vis children's literature (and the other way round, of course). When adult books become part of children's literature, this must be seen as a crossing of boundaries from adult non-culture into the peripheral areas of children's culture. As we have seen, works such as *Robinson Crusoe*, which from the perspective of children's culture are non-cultural phenomena, can acquire an absolute central position within children's literature.

Extra-culture is everything that lies beyond the awareness of members of a culture, meaning especially foreign cultures. Extra-cultural phenomena enter culture through crossing of the boundaries between native and foreign. Translations of children's books, and information and research on foreign children's literature, are examples of interaction between culture and extra-culture. As I have shown earlier, in today's world most foreign children's literature is unknown in any given country. That is, for any particular children's semiosphere (American, Swedish or Indonesian), the bulk of children's literature elsewhere is indeed extra-culture. If and when members of a culture become aware of the existence of extra-cultural phenomena, these appear in opposition with their own culture. They can then either be eliminated (destroyed) by the native culture or integrated into its marginal areas—and later start slowly moving towards the center. I have demonstrated this mechanism in an earlier chapter.

Children's literature, which for so many years has not been accepted into the general literary system but treated as non-culture (similar to the criminal novel, the romance and other "paraliterature"), has now very tentatively started to be integrated both into the history of literature and into teaching. Since children's literature also exists in an interaction with adult literature, the crossing of boundaries becomes still more complex. Children's literature can take over new codes from adult literature directly, but children's codes can also come from other semiospheres than adult literature (for instance, film, comic strips or computer games). Therefore children's literature can possess codes that are totally absent from adult literature.

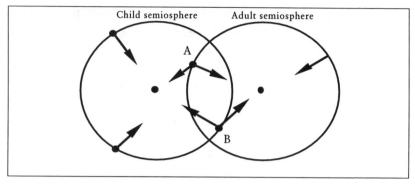

Child semiosphere   Adult semiosphere

A

B

Fig. 3

The centripetal movement of peripheral phenomena in the semiosphere of children's literature is disturbed by duplicated semiospheric centers, as in phenomena A and B in Fig. 3.

All this explains how evolution of the children's literature system takes place. The model may, however, appear too deterministic and insensitive to the random factors which have become a great concern for modern research, especially in various chaos theories. Recent contributions from Tartu semiotics include Lotman's model for the unpredictability of culture. Lotman shows that the evolution of cultural semiotic systems is predictable only to a very limited extent. This idea, like so much in Lotman's theories, comes from the natural sciences, more specifically from the Russian-born Belgian chemist and physicist, the Nobel prize winner Ilya Prigogine.[6] In Lotman's model, which is constructed after Prigogine's description of chemical, physical and biological processes, cultural evolution is only predictable to a certain point, a critical moment when something crucial happens. Prigogine calls these moments *bifurcation points*. After these, evolution may take an indefinite number of possible, unpredictable paths. In reality, however, only one of these is followed and thus becomes predictable—up to the next bifurcation point[7] (see Fig. 4).

Going back to *The Catcher in the Rye*, we may say that the appearance of this "non-cultural" text was the crucial moment in the history of children's and youth literature. After that, children's literature changes in ways that nobody could possibly have predicted before. On the other hand, it is easy to predict the appearance and further evolution of jeans prose up to a certain point which most probably has not taken place yet. Astrid Lindgren's *Pippi Longstocking* is doubtless a bifurcation point in Sweden. The year of its publication, 1945, is often considered as year zero in the history of the modern Swedish children's book.

Thus it is the task of the semiotically minded historian of children's literature to discover these bifurcation points, that is, literary or sometimes extra-literary phenomena (extra-cultural, non-cultural, paracultural) which dramatically change historical evolution. At the same time it is essential to investigate predictable evolutionary lines, that is, the slow movement of new, innovative literary phenomena from the periphery of the semiosphere, where they first occur, towards the center. Although this model naturally makes higher demands on the researcher, it can help us view the history of children's literature in an essentially new light.

In the mechanism of culture the code functions as *collective memory*, another important concept of cultural semiotics. Collective memory is stored during the evolution of culture in language, in individual texts, text types, and genres. Mikhail Bakhtin speaks of "the memory of genre."[8]

The semiotic model for historical literary research can be applied to various types of investigations, for instance: to examine the development of poetics of children's literature at various periods; to interpret more accurately the history of any particular genre or kind of children's literature; to explain the evolution of some patterns generally believed to be essential to children's books (such as the journey, the homecoming, the happy ending); or to account for the appearance of earlier taboos (such as death, sex or violence) in modern books for young people.

I will now give a few examples to illustrate how the model works. It is not my ambition to produce a comprehensive historical analysis. My examples may seem to have nothing to do with each other, but they are purposefully chosen from different genres and text types to show that the model is indeed universal and applicable for historical studies on a larger scale.

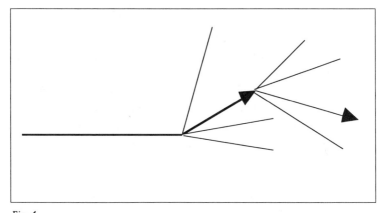

Fig. 4

The 1960s and 1970s in Sweden were a period of social commitment in children's literature. Authors addressed a vast variety of problems affecting children in society: parents' divorce, alcohol addiction or criminal behavior; the nightmares of starting school and the failure of teachers to understand the child's psychology; the trauma of moving from a countryside community to a large city, and subsequent mobbing by cruel classmates; sibling jealousy, unmarried teenage mothers, etc. Sometimes it feels as though writers were competing to see who could put the most misery into children's books. All the dark sides of reality penetrate children's literature. Gone are idyllic and sentimental solutions to conflicts, and books are filled to the brim with lonely, unhappy children with cruel comrades, indifferent parents and uncomprehending teachers. The most common feelings are fear and despair. Everything that had been taboo in children's literature suddenly makes itself manifest.

Often the social problem is proclaimed already in the titles. For instance, the child's longing for a real father is reflected in titles like Maria Gripe's *Pappa Pellerin's Daughter* (1963) and *The Night Daddy* (1968) or Kerstin Thorvall's *And Leffe Was Instead of a Dad* (1971). Almost everything in a child's life is presented as a problem: to get a new sibling, to start school, to move into a big city. At the same time there is a treatment of more serious questions such as the child's response to death. In Sweden of the 1960s and later, where most old people die in hospitals and the majority of the children never see a dead person, death becomes something alien and dreadful. More and more commonly, therefore, death and the child's contemplation of death appear as a secondary motif in some children's books and the central theme in others. Young adult novels went still further in this direction, depicting young people's suicide attempts or, in extreme cases, even accomplished suicides.

This was a necessary and understandable reaction to earlier idyllic children's literature, which wished to spare young readers the less attractive sides of the society. But as the socially committed code dominated children's literature, all other codes were banished to the periphery, among them the imaginative code of the fairy tale and fantasy. Fairy tales were considered outdated and simply harmful to young readers because they were believed to distract the child from real problems, from everyday life with its misery, loneliness, anguish—the key words of the Swedish children's book of the 1960s.

In 1973, Astrid Lindgren's *The Brothers Lionheart* burst all the boundaries in the tight ghetto of children's literature. The book is imaginative, romantic and full of adventure; it describes an alternative world and deals with death as something positive or at least nothing to be anxious about. All these aspects and many others aroused a storm of criticism. Today one reads with amazement the immediate reviews which accused Astrid Lindgren of escapism, of misguiding her young readers in existential problems, and of using the fantasy form. But the book had its subversive effect and initiated a total shift of the main trend in Swedish juvenile prose.

Thus I think we can regard *The Brothers Lionheart* as a bifurcation point. Before it the evolution of children's literature in Sweden was more or less predictable and consistent with the dominant code. After it children's literature returns to imaginative writing. Today Swedish children's literature is following the path paved by Astrid Lindgren's novel. We cannot predict when the next bifurcation will occur. True, the novel remained for quite some time in the borderline zone, and during the whole of the 1970s social-realistic juvenile novels continued to appear. But as early as in 1980–81 two basic studies were published in Sweden on fantasy for the young,[9] and the genre was generally accepted as appropriate and even welcome. In the early 1980s a wave of mostly translated fantasy swept over Sweden, filling in previous gaps and bringing literature abreast with the development of the genre around the world.

It is noteworthy that the code shift has not directly affected Swedish children's literature. Despite a few vivid exceptions Swedish fantasy as a tradition is still practically non-existent. Some attempts in the early 1990s are mostly derivative. The indirect impact of the shift, however, is all the more remarkable. The socially committed juvenile novel has not vanished completely. It still exists in the periphery where it attracts very little attention from critics or readers. What has happened instead is an often romanticized historical and retrospective literature exemplified by Maria Gripe's *Agnes Cecilia* (1981) or her so-called "Shadow" books, which at first glance have all the traits of the Gothic novel. Mystery, adventure and the supernatural are keywords in today's Swedish literature for the young, but this new code is by no means identical with the traditional adventure code familiar from R.L. Stevenson or Walter Scott. The focus is not on adventure or mystery or the supernatural for their own sake, but on their effect on the young personality.

In this way this new kind of literature—I will not venture to call it a genre since it involves many different genres and also to a great extent a convergence of genres—often manages to discuss the same problems and convey the same ideas as the purely realistic literature of the 1960s and 1970s without the frequent didacticism of the latter. Historical and retrospective novels play today the same role as fantasy in some other countries; as Susan Cooper has put it: "Fantasy is the metaphor through which we discover ourselves."[10]

Moreover, when we today reread some of the best Swedish children's books from the 1960s and 1970s, for instance, Maria Gripe's *Elvis and His Secret* (1972) and sequel *Elvis and His Friends* (1973), we discover that they, too, are not realistic throughout, but also contain tiny elements of the supernatural and the fantastic. The *Elvis* books and the *Hugo and Josephine* trilogy (1961–66) include features of mysticism and fantasy which are connected to her early books such as *The Glassblower's Children* (1964), *In the Time of the Bells* (1965), or *The Land Beyond* (1967), and to later ones such as *Agnes Cecilia*. The child's immediate contact with the supernatural, with the world beyond life, and the mystical idea that "everything that is alive belongs together" are themes which are unbroken through Maria Gripe's works from the early 1960s to the present. The reason why this continuity was completely ignored by the critics of the 1960s and 1970s is that their attention was focused exclusively on the social, mimetic codes of the texts.

It is tempting to extrapolate the Swedish model onto other countries, but this is risky unless we take into account the specific features of other semiospheres. In the 1970s and 1980s in the United States there was a similar trend in children's literature towards problem-oriented books in the works of such writers as Katherine Paterson, Cynthia Voigt or Betsy Byars, which superseded earlier, more idyllic or slightly humorous alternatives of Vera and Bill Cleaver, Elaine Konigsburg or Beverly Cleary. Unlike Sweden, however, this realistic wave has in the United States developed parallel to a well-established fantasy tradition represented not only by world-renowned authors like Lloyd Alexander, Madeleine L'Engle and Susan Cooper, but a whole constellation of equally exciting writers: Natalie Babbitt, John Bellairs, Jane Yolen, Anne McCauffrey, Robin McKinley, Meredith Ann Pierce and many more. It is therefore much more difficult to foresee any unexpected turn from social realism towards imaginative writing in American literature. Rather, as it progresses from the periphery towards the center, the psychological-realistic code merges with the psychological-fantastic code, producing, as in Sweden, genres such as the more imaginative historical novels. Here an examination of this slow movement will prove more fruitful than a search for sudden bifurcations.

FROM CERTAINTY TO HESITATION

In his famous study of fantastic literature the French scholar Tzvetan Todorov makes a clear distinction between the fantastic, the marvelous and the uncanny. His material is eighteenth and nineteenth century literature, and he is not concerned at all with fantasy for children. If he were, however, he would most probably put traditional children's fantasy, represented best by Edith Nesbit or by C.S. Lewis's Narnia books, into the category of the marvelous and have them stand as models for central codes. For Todorov, the foremost criterion on the fantastic is the hesitation of the protagonist (and the reader) when confronted with the supernatural.[11]

In early fantasy for children the matter of belief is often taken care of in some way, most commonly by explaining the wonderful adventure as a dream, as in Lewis Carroll's *Alice in Wonderland* (1865). Another device is the introduction of a visible instrument of the supernatural events such as a magician or a magic object. This pattern is well known from fantasy novels by Edith Nesbit and many of her followers around the turn of the century. Nesbit's magical agents (the Psammead or the Mouldiwarp) and her magical objects (amulets, rings or flying carpets) create a tension between the marvelous and the everyday. But there is no room for wonder or hesitation. Magic is accepted both by the protagonists and the readers as part of the game.

In adult fantasy from the same period, which has strong links to Romanticism, there is a tangible tendency towards mysticism, the unuttered, and many possible interpretations. It is almost certain that clear boundaries and rational explanations in early fantasy for children were conscious or unconscious compromises with prevailing educational views. To leave a child reader in uncertainty was pedagogically wrong.

As early as in the 1950s, however, the fantasy code begins to change. In books by the British authors Lucy M. Boston and Philippa Pearce, for example, the mechanism of the marvelous events is not revealed, and both readers and characters are confronted with mystery and hesitation as to reality of the magic—that is, exactly what Todorov's definition of the fantastic prescribes. Astrid Lindgren's *Mio, My Son* (1954) is also open to conflicting interpretations.

On contemplating the reasons for this change we must note that modern fantasy is created within a different cultural context. The evolution of science and technology has radically changed our attitude towards a rich variety of phenomena dealt with in fantasy novels. These include parallel worlds, non-linear time, extra-sensory perception and other supernatural events that modern science cannot explain but accepts as possible. This wider attitude is manifest throughout world literature, especially in so-called postmodern literature. Naturally, children's literature could not but be affected by the shift, and modern fantasy for children must therefore be viewed against this general cultural background. Since modern science tolerates alternative explanations, writers can also allow for ambivalence, encouraging young readers to draw their own conclusions and accept the existence of more than one truth. Today's readers, who are aware of scientific progress, possess different and more sophisticated codes than their grandparents, which means that writers can use more complex codes without fear of being misunderstood. The bifurcation itself may thus be said to have extra-literary sources, but it is quite easy to discover texts which mark the bifurcation point: *The Children of Green Knowe* (1954) by Lucy M. Boston and *Tom's Midnight Garden* (1958) by Philippa Pearce. Alan Garner's *Elidor* (1965) confirms the code shift. The later in the evolution of the genre, the more hesitation we discover in fantasy texts. The boundaries between reality and the magic world are dissolved and become evasive and ambivalent. The passage between reality and the magic world or between two different times becomes less pronounced and often invisible.

Thus the marvelous code—the "children's code"—gives way to the fantastic code in Todorov's meaning—the "adult code," which during the earlier periods was present in the periphery, on the frontier between children's and adult literature.

Another very important aspect in the development of the fantasy genre is that adventure as such becomes subordinate to the psychological dimension of the text. The fantasy form is merely a literary device used to convey whatever the writer wants to get across. In the early stages of the evolution of the genre, for instance in Edith Nesbit's fantasy novels at the turn of the century, magic adventures were self-sufficient, combined with some practical knowledge, a bit of history, a bit of didacticism. The further we follow the development of the genre, the better we see that innovation involves not variation of subjects and motifs, but above all the problems, ideas and values behind the adventure in the psychological dimension. This means that fantasy can treat the same questions as the best realistic stories.

Alan Garner's novels are perhaps the best illustrations of this. Of all British fantasy writers Garner is the most equivocal. Not even in his earliest books can we find ready interpretations or distinct boundaries between good and evil. In his later works this ambiguity is reinforced. This is a conscious effort on Garner's part; he states that a writer must not offer readers solutions or happy endings, but instead make use of something he calls "the method of an open hand"[12] where readers must discover for themselves what the writer has to show. It was the publishers who requested that *The Moon of Gomrath* (1963) be given a "happy" ending instead of an open and therefore disturbing one.[13]

Garner is not interested in alternative worlds as such or time shifts as such, but only in the way his own contemporary society is affected by the past and possible alternative worlds. He is not alone in this attitude; many fantasy writers today are above all concerned about the way encounters with the supernatural—in whatever form it may take—change the protagonist. Magic is for these writers a mirror which reflects reality with special clarity and sharpness.

One text type in which this becomes particularly obvious is fantasy with a time shift motif. Whenever time travel was involved in earlier fantasy, the authors applied Edith Nesbit's principle that the time traveller could not affect history. Both in Nesbit's books and in fantasy from the 1950s and 1960s the characters traveling in time could witness horrible events in history, but they could do nothing to prevent them. Writers assumed that the faith of young readers in the stability of the universe should not be shattered. To use an image from Ray Bradbury's short story 'A Sound of Thunder,' this phenomenon may also be described as the "butterfly syndrome."

Today we read that the whole purpose of time travel is to change history, either the private history of the character, as in *Playing Beatie Bow* (1980) by the Australian author Ruth Park, or *The Root Cellar* (1981) by Canadian Janet Lunn, or the history of the world, like *A Swiftly Tilting Planet* (1978) by Madeleine L'Engle. In this book the character changes the past so that the third world war does not break out in his own time. Time travelers are no longer passive observers, but must take upon themselves responsibility for their actions in the past.

Even the terminology in studies of fantasy has changed recently; scholars no longer speak about time travel, which implies the characters' active and conscious participation, but about time displacement, which often occurs without the character's knowledge and creates the atmosphere of hesitation emphasized in Todorov's definition.

In fantasy from the 1980s and 1990s innovations are not primarily variations of themes and motifs, but concern problems, messages and values (*mentifacts*) that can be discerned behind magical adventures. They also concern psychology, which enables fantasy to treat the same issues we find in the best non-fantastical novels for children. Magical adventures in recent fantasy become a quest for identity, and protagonists are no longer obedient pawns in games played by higher powers but are developed into active and engaged participants who are often central to the plot.

Diana Wynne Jones is an indisputable innovator, and in her books the hesitation principle is most tangible. Unlike the writers of traditional fantasy, she often describes alternative worlds from within, while the real world, our own reality, becomes "the other world" for protagonists. This pattern is naturally much more difficult to elaborate upon; generally it is a daring idea which harks back to the question in Lewis Carroll's *Through the Looking-Glass* (1871): "Which Dreamt It?" or the similar argument in *Mary Poppins in the Park* (1952) by Pamela Travers.[14] The play with alternative worlds in Jones's books becomes a discussion of existential questions: what is reality? Is there more than one definite truth? The idea itself is not alien to modern natural sciences, but we do not yet have any answers.

The strongest side of Diana Wynne Jones's novels is her characterization. In early fantasy, including C.S. Lewis's books, the protagonists are schematic because they are totally subordinated to the plot. In the usual narrative pattern in fantasy, a young person (or a group) encounters supernatural creatures, events or objects. In Jones's *Archer's Goon* (1984) the protagonist himself is a supernatural creature—but we do not realize this until we are four-fifths of the way through the text, although we may begin wondering and guessing much earlier. It is not a first-person story, but it is still told solely from the protagonist's viewpoint. Howard is faced with a hard dilemma. He is trying to find a great villain—the wizard who is threatening his family. As it turns out, he is himself this evil wizard who, together with his six powerful siblings, rules the town and plans to rule the world. The total shift of perspective makes an already serious and frightening story even more solemn.

In *The Lives of Christopher Chant* (1988) Jones again attempts to convey the feelings of an omnipotent wizard. It takes some time before the very young protagonist Christopher realizes what unlimited powers he possesses. Using magic, however, involves more than a simple wave of the hand and is hard and painful labour. To be a wizard is an enormous responsibility.

Diana Wynne Jones's power lies in the unconventional solutions, sharp observations and deep examinations of human nature in her works. Magic adventures are not there for their own sake, and the struggle between good and evil is merely a background for the protagonists' struggle with themselves, a struggle that is somewhat more common in real life. Incidentally, good and evil are no longer absolute categories for Diana Wynne Jones or other sophisticated fantasy writers. In this very delicate question as well, writers take the risk of allowing young readers to hesitate and choose sides for themselves.

Thus the changing fantasy code has many different manifestations. The movement towards the fantastic in Todorov's meaning implies more subtle and refined narrative techniques, more elusive boundaries between magical and real worlds, more relative categories of good and evil. The interaction of real and magical worlds has more serious consequences. All this naturally makes higher demands on readers. Due to at least two factors, however, today's young readers are better prepared to accept complicated fantasy codes. First, there is an overwhelming science fiction culture in both literature and film. Especially because science fiction is so widely distributed through movies, television and video, young readers acquire the necessary training to follow easily and unquestioningly intricate time paradoxes and other advanced narrative techniques. Children who easily cope with *Back to the Future* will not have problems with fantasy novels either. Computer and role-playing games ("Dungeons and Dragons") which are often based on (mostly rather primitive) fantasy stories also create favourable conditions for young readers to cope with fantasy novels. Here they doubtlessly have advantages over adults who are stuck in old conventional narrative patterns. Paraliterary elements have entered children's literature, bypassing adult literature. Incidentally, the structures of many of Diana Wynne Jones's novels have parallels to computer games.

At the same time, many fantasy writers continue to produce books using old primitive codes, like the very schematic and derivative *The Castle in the Attic* (1985) by Elizabeth Winthrop, where the adventure flows smoothly, the conflict is solved neatly and the protagonist is not affected at all by his experience. Sometimes the old codes can be camouflaged in supposed complexity. The intricate plot of Geraldine Harris's four-volume story *The Seven Citadels* (1982–83) displays upon closer examination a total lack of depth, and the abuse of letters X and Z in personal and geographic names creates a false exoticism which conceals flat and uninteresting characters.

The Incredible Mungwort Quest (1990) by the Canadian writer Moe Price is predictable from the very first page, and is merely an unexciting outline for speculative fantasy. A good witch and a bad witch competing for power over the world, two children (a boy and a girl, to insure an identification object for the reader) and an odd companion on a quest that only humans can accomplish, playing against time just before Halloween—the plot is painfully familiar. The children are just instruments in a superficial quest, they go obligingly wherever they are sent, move neatly from station to station, pursued by enemies and assisted by friends, until they reach the final destination, fight a quiet final struggle and are brought back safely by a magic ring. Not even the scientifically minded Danny becomes any wiser, while Louise just thinks: "This was better than any romantic fantasy" (!). All memory of the experience is wiped from the children's minds, and they emerge from the quest as innocent or ignorant as they were before. Moe Price has evidently failed to observe the evolution of the modern fantasy genre, and although the book is not without humour, it is nothing but speculative.

These primitive fantasy codes still linger in the periphery, but they have little chance of moving back into the center.

From Female to Male Monsters

Among many interesting examples of code shifts in fantasy we can also note the depiction of evil. This evolution is investigated thoroughly in an essay by Nancy Veglahn.[15] I do not wholly share her approach, but below I draw on some of her arguments and complement them with my own examples.

Veglahn chooses for her analysis four male writers who portray evil as female, and four female writers who portray evil as male. According to Veglahn, these are two recurrent patterns. She also means that there is a clear chronological development from the first pattern (male writer—female monster) to the second (female writer—male monster). Although Mary Shelley's *Frankenstein* appeared in 1818, it is correct that early fantasy, for children as well as for adults, was dominated by men.

The struggle between good and evil is the most common motif in fantasy. In early texts, often written by men, evil is depicted as a female figure. Nancy Veglahn uses the word "monster" about any deviation from normal human form, including the possession of magical powers. Veglahn's viewpoint is primarily psychoanalytical, and she interprets these female monsters as sexual symbols, basing her approach on Ursula Le Guin's collection of essays *Language of the Night*[16] and on the Jungian Marie-Louise von Franz's book *Shadow and Evil in Fairy Tales*.[17] Both emphasize that personified evil in folktales and fantasy represents the subconscious and suppressed parts of the psyche, which create anxiety and pain and are therefore perceived as evil. We can expect writers who personify evil in figures of the opposite sex to create these figures out of hidden impulses of their own selves, as reflections of their own fears. At the source is a concept of the opposite sex as not fully human.

I am not questioning this very exciting interpretation, but I still believe that we can equally well trace evil female images back to traditional witches in folktales or the ambivalent good/evil progenitor in myths. Fantasy undoubtedly has its roots in folktale and myth. Some might prefer to use the term "archetype" about the female monster, whereas a scholar with Jungian training will suggest the notion of "Anima." Whatever theory to which one chooses to adhere, the pattern "male writer—female monster" is found in practically all early fantasy novels. The victory over the monster of the opposite sex becomes the natural solution of the plot and creates its emotional charge. Among Nancy Veglahn's examples are the Queen of Hearts in *Alice in Wonderland* (1865) and her twin the Red Queen in the sequel *Through the Looking-Glass* (1871). Both are absurdly and unreasonably evil through and through, and both books have all the features of nightmares, which suggests a psychoanalytical interpretation.[18] Carroll's contemporary George MacDonald had a number of evil female characters in *The Princess and the Goblin* (1871) and *The Princess and Curdie* (1882). The wicked witch in Frank Baum's *The Wizard of Oz* (1900) is well known. Finally, evil in C.S. Lewis's Narnia stories of the 1950s is personified in the central figure of the series, the White Witch.

To these examples proposed by Nancy Veglahn we can easily add several more. It has been pointed out that the witch in C.S. Lewis's books has much in common with the Snow Queen in Hans Christian Andersen's tale,[19] yet another hateful female portrait by a male writer. Both images may have a source in the writers' biographies. We know about Andersen's problems with women, and C.S. Lewis also had some traumatic experience. There is splendid material for the psychoanalytically minded literary critic.

The White Witch comes to Narnia as an intruder, an unwanted companion to the two protagonists in *The Magician's Nephew* (1955). She comes from yet another alternative world that she has destroyed through her endless evil. Narnia is created as a happy and carefree country, a paradise, but in the White Witch the country acquires a permanent threat. Humans must therefore be summoned when the threat comes too near. Strangely enough, however, the Witch does not play any part in the final destruction of Narnia.

Another common feature in the above-mentioned male texts is that in all of them the protagonist is an active and independent girl who alone or almost alone triumphs over the evil. Veglahn's interpretation of these positive female figures in male fantasy is that no healthy person sees the opposite sex as totally evil; negative emotions are counterweighed by attraction and love, which is expressed through the good female images: the reasonable Alice, MacDonald's emancipated princesses, Dorothy who perceives herself as helpless and passive but who is both courageous and resolute if need be. Finally, in C.S. Lewis's books Lucy is his favorite among the four siblings. Still, Lewis's view of women is revealed in *The Lion, the Witch and the Wardrobe* when it is explicitly said that women will not participate in the combat because it is unbecoming.

As a contrast to the four male writers Veglahn chooses four later female writers of fantasy: Madeleine L'Engle, Ursula Le Guin, Susan Cooper and Natalie Babbitt. Evil in their novels is incarnated in male figures. Besides, with the exception of Natalie Babbitt's *Tuck Everlasting* (1975), the central figures of the texts are boys who vanquish evil. To these examples I can once again add Astrid Lindgren's *Mio, My Son* and *The Brothers Lionheart*, where evil is represented by male figures—Sir Kato in the former, Tengil in the latter. There are also male protagonists in both books who are sent on quests to struggle against evil.

The pattern shift from "male writer—female monster" towards "female writer—male monster" must be seen as a code change in fantasy, although it is very difficult to discover a bifurcation point. The earliest female text, *Mio, My Son*, appears at the same time as the Narnia suite.

Nancy Veglahn generalizes too much and grounds her argument on an arbitrary choice of texts which suit her patterns. Her examples are representative enough, but she neglects texts that do not fit in her model, for instance J.R.R. Tolkien's *The Hobbit* (1937) and *Lord of the Rings* (1954–56) which have almost no female figures at all, good or bad. This in itself is significant. Veglahn safeguards herself against criticism by pointing out one exception to her pattern—Lloyd Alexander, who in his Prydain suite (1964–68) has a male figure as the leader of evil forces. But she disregards the obvious fact that Alexander also has a female monster who is indeed more threatening than the male, since the witch is much more involved in the action and is therefore a more immediate incarnation of the evil. The witch changes throughout the suite, and in the final battle she is on the side of good, against her earlier ally. Thus there is an essential line of evolution in recent fantasy which Veglahn, in keeping with her point of departure, ignores. Her model is not adequate to describe modern multidimensional texts. The duality in the representation of evil must be seen as a movement towards a new code shift, a new bifurcation.

In Alan Garner's first novel, *The Weirdstone of Brisingamen* (1960), there is, as one might expect, an evil female creature—the Morrigan, a traditional figure in Celtic mythology which also appears in other fantasy novels. In Garner's book, however, the figure is slightly more complicated. The Morrigan is just one side of the triple Celtic goddess. Her evil is not as unambiguous as in other, more "common" witches. One of the two protagonists, Susan, has a bracelet that appears to be part of a powerful triple amulet serving the Morrigan. The amulet is also ambivalent, for it can both protect the bearer and help evil forces to trace her. Therefore we cannot describe Garner's female supernatural figure in terms of only good or only evil, and this naturally gives the text a new dimension. As to the protagonists, Susan and her brother Colin are equal in their roles as vanquishers of evil, although Susan has to pay a higher price. In another novel by Garner, *The Owl Service* (1967) there is one more female creature with a double nature. The young girl made of flowers is through evil charms transformed into an owl, and good turns into evil. This duality is much more typical for recent fantasy than it was for MacDonald or even C.S. Lewis.

There have also appeared several interesting female figures created by female writers, active heroines who often represent a new attitude towards woman's independence and freedom of action. These include characters in Meredith Ann Pierce's *The Darkangel* (1982) or Diana Wynne Jones's *Howl's Moving Castle* (1986). In both books there is a male villain who eventually appears to be a victim of other—female—evil powers. The ambivalence of the male monster demonstrates once again the code change towards hesitation in the portrayal of the supernatural which I discussed in the previous section. Both Pierce and Jones describe the female protagonist's sexual attraction to the male monster. Such intricate play with male and female patterns is typical of modern fantasy novels, in which writers—mostly women—are trying to free themselves from sex stereotyping and create new patterns.

Once again, there are many examples of writers who continue to use old, conventional codes. Regretfully, there are both male and female writers among them.

FROM CIRCULAR TO LINEAR JOURNEY

The basic pattern in children's literature is the circular journey. That is, the plot follows the trajectory home—departure from home—adventure—return home. This pattern, which has its origin in European Romantic philosophy, can be traced in practically any children's text, not necessarily belonging to what is commonly labeled as adventure genre. It can be found on different levels and in different shapes anywhere from picturebooks (*Where the Wild Things Are*, 1963) to psychological novels (*Back Home* by Michelle Magorian, 1984). The purpose of the journey is the maturing of the child (protagonist as well as the reader), but the return home is a matter of security; whatever hardships and trials, the safe home is the final goal.

A splendid example of this pattern is Edith Nesbit's short tale 'The Town in the Library,' written in 1898. The two children get into the toy town they have built, and, escaping from hostile toy soldiers, find their own house there. In that house there is one more town which they in turn enter—and Nesbit plays with the idea that this could go on forever, as the children penetrate "deeper and deeper into a nest of towns in libraries in houses in towns in libraries in houses in towns in. . . and so on for always—something like Chinese boxes multiplied by millions and millions for ever and ever." But this way, Nesbit continues, they would be getting further and further from home every time, and she hurries to take the characters back to their own world and bring the story to a safe and happy ending.

The circular journey code has dominated children's literature since its very beginning, but very early we can discover seeds of the opposite code far away in the periphery. One of the first authors to break the circular pattern, ɪf only tentatively, was George MacDonald in *At the Back of the North Wind* (1871). The ending of the story can be perceived as both happy and unhappy. We know that Diamond dies. But we also learn that he is in the beautiful country at the back of the North Wind that he previously was only allowed to watch. The duality reflects the attitude to death that was common in MacDonald's time. Death was nothing alien to child readers, but was the natural way into the happy life after this one. The ambivalent, good/evil female supernatural force, the North Wind, is one of the most universal images in world literature. It is never mentioned in MacDonald's book that she is Death herself, but an adult and even a keen young reader has no difficulty identifying the image. However, what is interesting for us here is that MacDonald leaves his hero in the secondary world, after recurrent returns from journeys which apparently have only approached the threshold. This text must be among the very first in children's literature to depict a linear journey.

Another example is to be found much later in the last book of the Narnia suite by C.S. Lewis. In the previous volumes the children are brought into Narnia to perform a task, whereupon they are transported safely back into their own world. But in *The Last Battle* (1956) they die in a railway accident and are thus allowed to proceed into a world beyond this, beyond the point of no return. I will not discuss the possible interpretations of this passage here; I am interested in the pattern—the subversive linear code within the dominant circular code of traditional children's literature. Here, as in many other respects, Astrid Lindgren was far ahead of her time, describing a linear journey in *Mio, My Son* and repeating the

Mio, My Son—*a linear journey (left to right). Illustration by Ilon Wikland*

pattern twenty years later in *The Brothers Lionheart*. Even today critics are uncertain how to interpret the endings of these two novels. This uncertainty makes them deep and exciting.

The linear code is, of course, much more daring and presupposes total confidence in the reader on the part of the author. It demands a good deal of courage for a child to accept the absence of the return home that offers the protagonist security. The reader's own belief in the security of the world is shattered. But at least some modern authors accept the challenge. The so called "open ending" that is gradually gaining more and more acceptance—first in young adult novels and then also in books for younger children—should be viewed as a modification of the linear code.

Children's books with ready solutions bind the child's imagination and free thought. It is treachery towards the modern sophisticated child reader to offer a "rational" explanation at the end: "And then he woke up, and it has only been a dream." We should not think that this ending is a thing of the past, for we remember it from *Alice in Wonderland*. It is repeated in much later texts, and one discovers it somewhat reluctantly in Mordecai Richler's prize-winning book *Jacob Two-Two Meets the Hooded Fang* (1975) and in a many even more recent texts. Critical and creative authors find such resolutions very unsatisfactory, and regard the open ending as the only possible way of appealing to modern young readers. I see the open ending as the utmost transformation of the "telling gap" discussed in reception theory. The presence of telling gaps in the narrative can be viewed as a criterion of literary quality; the more contemplative questions the reader confronts, the better the writer has performed his task. The German scholar Reinbert Tabbert suggests a distinction between didactic and creative texts depending on the number of telling gaps.[20]

The open ending is a means to stimulate questions. Even the traditional formula of the folktale "And they lived happily ever after" leaves room for questions for an inquisitive writer; what does it mean to live happily ever after? Thus the Norwegian writer Tormod Haugen's "The White Castle" (1980) starts where the folktale ends.

I see the code shift towards the dominant open ending as one of the most interesting features of modern children's literature. Peter Pohl, one of the best Swedish juvenile novelists of today, has definitely given up the old code. His characters are never brought back into the safety of home and family; they leave security and move towards whatever fate awaits them. To summarize the experience of the 1980s, Peter Pohl's greatly appreciated debut novel *Johnny My Friend* (1985) is undoubtedly one of the central events in Swedish juvenile literature of the past decade—the bifurcation point which will set up a new code for the coming authors.

FROM VISUAL TO VERBAL CODE

Before 1917 children's literature in Russia was dominated by sentimental and moralistic stories and verses, often written by not very talented women authors. The views on children and education of that time, which can be compared to Victorian attitudes in Britain, dictated the norms of writing for children; the world of children's literature was restricted to the nursery, and the characters were sugary, well-behaved children in starched clothes.

It was not until the 1920s that children's literature in Russia stood on the threshold of renewal. The reason, naturally, had to do with the general change in artistic norms brought about by societal development—the process of building up the new "socialist" culture in the new Soviet state. The primary principle for this new culture was to repudiate every old, "bourgeois" form in art. For instance, the central thesis of the so called Proletkult movement (from *prolet*arian *cult*ure) was the following: art is the "forming" of the collective experience of the people into "living images"; since the experience of the working class has nothing to do with the experiences of the former social classes, the art and culture of the working class must be totally different from art and culture of the past. The Russian working class was to create its own "socially pure" culture. This is probably one of the most obvious cases in the history of human culture where artistic norms were directly guided by social and political circumstances.

There were no available models for the new forms in art. Thus the 1920s in Russia became a period of ardent experiments in all kinds of art. This was also the only period in Soviet history when different trends, movements and styles in art and literature were allowed to coexist, before the slogan of socialist realism became the only guideline for all culture (I would add in passing that today it is commonly acknowledged in the former Soviet Union that the so-called socialist realism was a bluff). In the 1920s education and propaganda were the two extremely important missions of art. Large segments of the Russian population were illiterate or half-literate; it was essential that art should be comprehensible for the masses, and for that reason it was primarily visual. This is most obvious in political posters of the period, the so called "ROSTA-windows" (ROSTA was the Russian news agency, later called TASS), which became for the masses both the first ABC-book and the propagandistic newspaper. In accordance with the new role of art in society, the new artistic norms rejected everything that could be apprehended as "elitistic," or "decadent" as it was commonly labeled, in art and literature. This meant that many styles and genres in poetry or figurative art were condemned as being too complicated. "Art for art's sake" had no right to exist in the new society; it had to be pragmatic, purposeful and ideologically correct.

The central idea of the new aesthetic in popular art such as the poster was to make both text and illustration simple, concise, and loud—easy to memorize, easy to recognize. The typical propaganda posters from that period use vivid colors and simple, concrete contours, with an accompanying catchily rhymed short verse of usually two lines. The principle for the first picturebooks for children was exactly the same. To see the striking

"Red Army and Navy Defending Russia" by Vladimir Lebedev

similarity, it is sufficient to compare Vladimir Lebedev's poster "The Red Army and Navy Defending Russia" (1920) with his picturebook *The Ice Cream Man* (1925, verse by Samuil Marshak). Such resemblances arose not only from the fact that many ROSTA artists also produced picturebooks for children, but especially because post-revolutionary art was generally oriented towards the concrete and visual.

Everything old and "bourgeois" was discarded within children's literature as well, and there was a great demand for new books for young people. The number of young readers multiplied rapidly, and children's literature became more democratic. The "bourgeois," pre-revolutionary children's book was primarily addressed to children from well-off families.

Отличное,
Земляничное,

Прекрасное
Ананасное

Именинное
Апельсинное

Морожено!

The Ice Cream Man *by Vladimir Lebedev*

They were the only children who could read. Books were also often intended for family reading, where the adults could support and guide, explain and educate. The new children's book was meant to be available for young readers from all social groups, especially children with working class backgrounds. The new book necessarily spoke down to these children, who could hardly read and often had illiterate parents. The layout of the first Soviet picturebooks had a great deal in common with that of the propagandistic posters, containing colorful illustrations and very short texts, preferably in verse to aid memorization.

It was only during the 1920s that true picturebooks—that is, books in which the verbal and visual aspects are an inseparable whole—were ever produced in Russia. Among these first attempts the books with texts by Vladimir Mayakovsky are quite remarkable. This is no coincidence, for Mayakovsky was also a well-known name from the ROSTA windows. His picturebook "The Tale of Fat Peter and Thin Simon" (1925) has exactly the same structure as the posters, with a large-scale, very schematic, colorful picture on every page. The colors are bright, undiluted, free of shades and nuances. The figures of the two children—one rich and fat, the other poor and thin—resemble the opposition between the capitalist and the worker, which is easy to recognize from the popular posters of the time. Mayakovsky tries in this manner to make use of the well-tried political cartoon style on something totally different—a children's book. Other picturebooks with Mayakovsky's versified texts have the same poster structure, with a large diagrammatic picture on every page and two or four short rhymes, for instance his verse about a Zoo called "On Every Page You See an Animal in a Cage" (1926) and illustrated by Vladimir Lebedev. In this book Mayakovsky also tries to conduct political propaganda; the lion is no longer the king of the animals, but the president!

Less didactic, but still working with the unity of visual and verbal images, was Samuil Marshak. Together with Vladimir Lebedev he produced several picturebooks during the 1920s, for instance, *The Ice Cream Man* (1925). The text consists of very short humorous verses which take up very little space on every page compared with the bright and concrete pictures much in keeping with the dominant tendencies in art. Characteristic now but unusual both earlier and later is the fact that the writer's and the artist's names were printed in equally large type on the cover, for it acknowledges that the picturebook was created in equal measure by both. Later, when picturebooks from the 1920s were reprinted, it was customary to take the text and two or three pictures to "illustrate" it. Sometimes this was taken even further, and another artist would illustrate a text from the original picturebook. There is, of course, nothing wrong with these illustrations as such, but not much is left of the picturebook as a specific art form. What remained was a story in verse illustrated with a few pictures. Fortunately, at least some of Marshak's texts are brilliant in themselves, although they naturally lose a lot without the original illustrations. Others are much more dependent on the visual aspect. One example is "The Circus" (1925), where the verses are more like short commentaries while the humor and the dynamic of the story are conveyed through the pictures. Without them, the verses become primitive and even incoherent.

The greatest innovator and pathfinder in Soviet children's literature was Kornei Chukovsky, whose first children's story in verse, *The*

The Crocodile. *Illustration by Re-Mi*

Crocodile (1917), was illustrated by Re-Mi (pen-name for Nikolai Remizov, a well-known prerevolutionary cartoonist). Chukovsky was very particular about the illustration of his verses, most of which have a structure that has become known as the "Kornei-stanza": two, three or more rhymed couplets and one non-rhyming line, which is the most effective and significant. Each of the similarly constructed stanzas is a unity in itself, a complete verbal picture. Among the "thirteen commandments" that Chukovsky created for good poetry for children in his famous volume *From Two to Five*[21] is the demand that verses be graphic, rich in visual images, and that these images shift quickly, that is, the verse must be dynamic. The structure of the stanza called for a special way of illustration: each stanza is a complete verbal scene which corresponds to its own picture or a concrete visual image.

The first edition of Chukovsky's probably most famous verse story *Wash'em Clean* (1923) had a very characteristic subtitle "A Cinema for Children." It was illustrated by the "World of Art" artist, Yuri Annenkov. The verse is full of swift action, from the whirlwind of various household objects in the beginning (the blanket, the sheet, the pillowcase, etc.), followed by a wild race in the streets, through the dramatic encounter with the crocodile—the beast from the previous book appears again in a new role—to the triumphal march at the end. The dynamic character of the illustrations supports the dashing development of the events in the text. The illustrations, as in *The Crocodile*, are black and white, like contemporary film. Short explanatory texts were usual in silent film. The concept of montage introduced by Sergei Eisenstein can thus also be traced in the art of picturebooks.

Chukovsky himself stated in one of his theoretical essays that *Wash'em Clean* should be illustrated by exactly fifty-three pictures corresponding to the fifty-three episodes or "film sequences" in the text. When Chukovsky's books were republished in the 1950s after having been banned by the Soviet censorship for nearly thirty years, the author's wish was completely ignored. The standard version of *Wash'em Clean* published since the 1950s and to the present day carries only ten pictures. There is nothing wrong with them; they are the product of their time and reflect, among other things, better printing technology, but the very idea of a picturebook is neglected. Annenkov's illustrations are in perfect correspondence with Chukovsky's texts: concise, simple and lucid. There are no details, no backgrounds. Modern illustrations make use of better graphic technology; they are rich in detail, which brings them into conflict with the laconic texts. The function of both text and illustration differs from the original.

This is even more evident in "The Cockroach" (1923). Like so many of Chukovsky's verses, it seems to be written down from a children's game upon which the writer has eavesdropped. Various animals are riding on every possible means of transport: bears on bicycles, followed by a cat pedaling backwards; mosquitoes on a balloon, crayfish on a lame dog, wolves on horseback, lions by car, rabbits by tram and a toad on a broom, like a witch. This may seem nonsensical, but it is easy to imagine a child playing with his toys and taking no notice of the fact that they are of different sizes.

In the first edition, illustrated by Sergei Chekhonin, yet another member of "The World of Art," each verbal image corresponds exactly to the visual sequence. Here, too, Chukovsky had himself expressed the wish that the story be illustrated with exactly twenty-eight pictures. In modern editions, beginning in the 1950s, all animals are depicted on the same page or only a few of them are pictured at all; in both cases the composition destroys the dynamic movement which Chukovsky saw as the cornerstone of the picturebook, in which each text-picture unity was consciously built up as a film still. A lack of respect for the picturebook concept is apparent in practically all modern editions of Chukovsky's verses for children. Often they are published as a collection in which—possibly due to lack of space—each verse is illustrated by five to eight pictures or less.

One verbal picture—one visual picture. Illustration by Sergei Chekhonin,
The Cockroach *(1923)*

The first Soviet picturebook experiments ended in the 1930s. Whenever a picturebook text from the 1920s is pulled out from oblivion it is most often illustrated with new pictures, which, whatever their artistic merit, can function only as a decoration. It seems as though the very idea of a picturebook as an organic whole has been essentially alien to Soviet publishers from the 1930s onwards. This seemingly incomprehensible phenomenon can only be accounted for by societal circumstances. There may be various explanations for this evolution, but the core of the reasons is obviously extra-literary. By the early 1930s, illiteracy in the Soviet Union had been defeated. The new visual forms of art became outdated. The educational and propaganda role of painting, sculpture and architecture, as well as of cinema and political posters, was suddenly superfluous. The function of children's literature also changed: from now on the verbal aspect started to dominate literature

for the young. It focused on the contents, the plot and—most important—
the message and ideological values. From the point of view of societal expectations of children's books, the integrated unity of text and illustration
in, for instance, Marshak-Lebedev's picturebooks became redundant.

Children's literature of the 1930s and later was in itself abundant
(and this was in turn the consequence of social circumstances). There appeared stories, fairy tales, juvenile novels—often richly illustrated, but always with emphasis on the text. By the middle of the 1930s, these predomi-
nantly verbal children's books take the place of earlier picturebooks and
occupy firmly the central position in children's literature which they still
enjoy today. The illustrations have become something purely decorative and
subordinate to the text.

The first attempts with modern picturebooks in the 1980s have completely different prerequisites, and their origins should be sought in the
Western picturebook, comic strip, and animated cartoon—that is, in the
context of totally different cultural codes.

FROM SIMPLICITY TO ABUNDANCE

Picturebooks allow many interesting semiotic approaches. The one aspect
I will discuss here is the changing codes in the semiotic space in contemporary picturebooks. My general attitude towards the specific features of
picturebooks is based on the notion of *iconotext*, coined by the Swedish
scholar Kristin Hallberg.[22] It presupposes a unity of the verbal and visual
text which must be "read" simultaneously in an interaction of the two
semiotic systems. Since every system also consists of different levels, the
interaction can become extraordinarily complicated.

The Swedish illustrated children's book has a long tradition; its
golden age occurred around the turn of the century and was clearly inspired
by the British tradition of Walter Crane and Kate Greenaway. The most
prominent author and illustrator of that period was Elsa Beskow, famous
for her rich colors, abundant details and realism in portrayal of plants and
animals. What can be called a modern picturebook tradition began in the
1950s with Inger and Lasse Sandberg, whose very first productions dis-
played their most typical features: an absence of backgrounds, that is, a
reduced pictorial space, undiluted colors, schematic figures, and few details. The Sandbergs' early books—*What Anne Saw* (1964), *Little Anna's
Mama Has a Birthday* (1966), *Daniel and the Coconut Cakes* (1968)—
marked a definite break with the picturesque romanticism of the Elsa
Beskow tradition and represented a transition to a clear everyday tone in
both themes and style. On both the verbal and the visual levels, the sto-

ries are simple and naive. The backgrounds are empty, and details are kept to a minimum. Pictures convey the plot as much as the words, so that only details essential to the plot appear in the picture. This tendency, which is also manifest in Gunilla Wolde's *Thomas Goes Out* (1969), *Betsy's First Day at Nursery School* (1976) and other Thomas and Betsy books, corresponds in a way to the trend in the Swedish children's novel of the 1960s towards everyday realism and a sober narrative which focuses attention on the issue of the book.

You Are a Sly One, Alfie Atkins (1973) and other Alfie Atkins books by Gunilla Bergström can be viewed as the first step back towards a fully expanded pictorial space. But this does not mean a return to the picturesque Beskowian universe. Gunilla Bergström's space, much more rich in detail than the early Sandberg or the Gunilla Wolde products, creates a modern, chaotic, mosaic pictorial space which is stressed by the collage technique in Alfie Atkins books. The space is still reduced, but a variety of everyday objects not mentioned in the verbal text appear in the picture, stimulating young readers to fill the emptiness from their own experiences.

The movement back to the fully expanded and dense pictorial universe may have to do with the general condensation of visual signs in Western culture that can be observed in TV, video, visual advertisements, and visual signs instead of inscriptions. The culmination of this tendency in Sweden must be seen in picturebooks by Sven Nordqvist. Their richness of details has even irritated some critics, who have called them "obtrusive."[23] Nordqvist's books seem to be a bifurcation point in Swedish picturebooks, which once again excel in detail, color and nuances, though in a way quite unlike that of Elsa Beskow. The many dimensions of contemporary picturebooks also mean double, or ambivalent, codes, and this results in picture allusions ("intervisuality") entirely intended for adults. Examples are the Brancusi sculpture from the Stockholm Museum of Modern Art in "The Egg" (1978) by Lennart Hellsing and Fibben Hald, or variations on the "Guernica" theme in *Come into My Night, Come into My Dream* (1978) by Stefan Mälhqvist and Tord Nygren. Many picturebook authors in Sweden today play with postmodern ideas in their creation of pictorial space, uniting the incompatible and including sharp contrasts and unexpected turns. This pictorial space reflects the world around today's children and its multitude of visual impressions. Inger and Lasse Sandberg's evolution also tends toward a fully depicted universe and joyful self-quotations, for instance in "ABCD" (1986).

The new pictorial space is able to include a psychological depth which the simplified, sober picturebooks from the 1950s and 1960s lacked. We can, however, expect that Sven Nordqvist's rich pictorial code has by now become standardized and will soon generate a reaction. Its beginning can already be discerned in the grotesque, caricature-like picturebooks of Gunna Grähs or Anna Höglund.

Summing Up

The semiotic model I am proposing for the description of the history of

Adult code—Brancusi. Children's code—fried egg. "The Egg"; illustration by Fibben Hald

A jungle of allusions. Come into My Night, Come into My Dream; *illustration by Tord Nygren*

children's literature differs radically from most other approaches, because it is not related to any concrete historical periods but rather attempts to discern more universal evolutionary patterns. The most important pattern is the dynamism of central and peripheral literary codes, which basically accounts for the possibility of evolution. The other pattern is the bifurcation point, which causes sudden and unpredictable changes in evolution. Combining these patterns we can describe various processes in the history of children's literature.

I have chosen examples from several periods, literary modes and countries to test the model. In Sweden of the 1960s and 1970s social commitment gives way to more imaginative literature, with *The Brothers Lionheart* as a possible bifurcation. In fantasy literature of the twentieth century hesitation and ambivalence become dominant, and there is a certain pattern shift in the treatment of evil. Earlier circular journey patterns typical of children's literature are gradually supplanted by linear narratives. Visual codes in Russian children's literature of the 1920s are in the following decade firmly replaced by verbal codes. Reduced pictorial space in Swedish picturebooks from the 1960s and 1970s becomes a fully painted and detailed universe in the 1980s. This wide range of examples should prove the universal character of the model.

My analysis of a number of concrete examples does not purport to be a history of children's literature, but merely illustrates how the model can be applied. Its most essential feature is the balance between the slow movement of codes within the system and the abrupt intrusion of bifurcations.

1. The theory of cultural semiotics has been developed by Lotman and his school in a number of studies; to refer to every statement would make my own text unreadable. I can suggest Lotman, 1991, as the most comprehensive volume. A choice of cultural-semiotic essays from Tartu/Moscow are in Baran, 1976; Lucid, 1977; Matejka, 1977; Fawcett, 1984; Halle, 1984.

2. Flaker, 1975.

3. See Nordlinder, 1991.

4. The notion of *mentifact* is not yet universally established. It is introduced by the German semiotician Roland Posner. Mentifacts are products of mental culture in the same manner as artifacts are products of material culture (Posner, 1989).

5. The treatment of these and similar "non-cultural" elements by children's writers has been rightfully criticized. Perry Nodelman takes up the moral implications of reading sacred texts from other cultures as entertainment (Nodelman, 1992, p. 173).

6. See Prigogine, 1984.

7. Lotman, 1991, pp. 230ff.

8. Bakhtin, 1984.

9. Klingberg, 1981; Toijer-Nilsson, 1981.

10. Cooper, 1984, p. 282.

11. Todorov, 1973, p. 25.

12. On Garner's writing method see, e.g., Garner, 1970; Garner, 1978.

13. Information submitted to the author by Alan Garner in an interview, February 2, 1991.

14. See Bergsten, 1978, pp. 68ff.

15. Veglahn, 1987.

16. Le Guin, 1979.

17. Von Franz, 1974.

18. *Alice in Wonderland* (1865) is one of the favourite objects of psychoanalytically oriented critics; see, e.g., Bloomingdale, 1971.

19. See, e.g., Fisher, 1975, p. 374.

20. Tabbert, 1980.

21. Chukovsky, 1963. The Russian original was published 1925.

22. Hallberg, 1982.

23. Schaffer, 1991, p. 148. Obviously the critic is not at all aware of or interested in the evolution that I have outlined here.

By the time children's literature emerged, adult literature had already existed as an established literary system for many centuries. The evolution that took mainstream literature several millennia has been accomplished by children's literature in three to four hundred years, and in some countries considerably less. The traditional division since antiquity of literature into epic, lyric and drama was from the beginning irrelevant to children's literature, and with rare exceptions, even today poetry and drama for children are marginal phenomena within its system. When we speak about children's literature, we most often mean prose, stories, that is, epic. Thus the history of children's literature consists mainly of the evolution of epic structures.

On the basis of my suggested view of the history of children's literature we can try to outline a periodization, which will imply not specific indications of time but general stages of development. These are in turn also quite relative; as we shall see, they can overlap, and many phenomena from earlier stages can remain within later ones. But it seems that children's literature in all countries and language areas has gone through more or less the following four stages:

1. Adaptations of existing adult literature and of folklore (folktales, myths, fables) to what are believed to be the needs and interests of children, according to accepted and dominant views on child upbringing.

A fascinating question concerning this period is why there have never appeared any adaptations of women's literature. Why is there no *Jane Eyre* adapted and abridged to the standards of a girl's book? It is possible that this and similar novels had too open erotic undertones and were too much directed towards marriage, which was considered less suitable for younger female readers. Another possible explanation is that early children's literature was addressed primarily to boys, who were taught to read. When girls became an audience of readers, the practice of writing directly for children was already in existence.

Adaptation of folklore is a visible process today in many countries in Asia and Africa, and should probably often be regarded as children's literature at this stage. In most cases it is established writers in these countries who *also* write for children. Children's literature has not yet been formed as a separate literary system. It is possible—as we have seen, cultural development is unpredictable—that children's literature in these countries will be formed in a radically different manner than in Europe or North America.

2. During the second period there appear didactic, educational stories written directly for children. Most often these two periods overlap. The children's literature system starts to detach itself from the adult system, and sometimes even isolates itself in a kind of ghetto. The most characteristic feature of this period is that it seldom produces anything really worth saving for the coming generations of readers. Since such books are closely related to educational ideas which soon become obsolete, the texts seem outdated and often merely boring. Most of these books are today of interest only to a tiny circle of experts as merely representative of a period. However, there are some recent studies of this stage which show that some of its writers have been unjustly forgotten, and some of them are being rediscovered by critics and publishers. Some have been re-evaluated from a feminist viewpoint, for example, and may once again find readers.

This period probably corresponds to medieval literature of the mainstream, which similarly enjoys no wide general readership today. Countries in which children's literature emerges late simply jump over this period, since they can draw on experiences from other countries.

3. During the third period children's literature is established as a literary system with its different genres and modes. It is during this period that the *canon* of children's literature is created. There are clear divisions between books for boys and books for girls, as well as between different genres. The rigid system allows no deviations or innovations. This period corresponds to Classicism, the Baroque and to some extent Romanticism in mainstream literature. In most reference guides on children's literature with no special historical emphasis we find a synchronic and static description of this particular period.

The most characteristic feature of texts from this period is that they are distinctly epic, that is, have typical epic narrative structure.[1] They tell a story with a clear beginning and end, they present a classical plot with an initial situation, conflict, climax and solution, they have a stable and genre-determined place of action, they render the events in chronological order, their characters have definite and ultimately defined roles, and there is always a clear-cut message and a didactic purpose. All such books display a similarity to classical mainstream novels such as *Tom Jones, Oliver Twist* or *Jane Eyre*. Their structure is also similar to that of folklore, which allows some exciting new interpretations based on the use of instruments from folktale analysis.

It is against this established system that contemporary writers for children revolt with new daring themes and new narrative devices. In Sweden the year 1945, when several major writers published their first books for children, usually is described as "year zero" of modern children's literature. Everything that we see afterwards brings children's literature closer to the modern, or rather, the modernistic, novel, which suggests that children's literature is entering its fourth stage.

4. Polyphonic, or multi-voiced, children's literature.

The notion of *polyphony*, or multi-voicedness (originally a term from musicology), was introduced into literary criticism by the Russian scholar Mikhail Bakhtin.[2] The opposition "epic"—"polyphonic" is the cornerstone of Bakhtin's treatment of the novel genre and the evolution of literature in general. In his evaluation of Russian literature Bakhtin sees in Turgenev or Goncharov representatives for the classical *epic* novel, which also stands closest to the classical European novel. To Bakhtin, a breaking point comes with Dostoyevsky, who takes a definite step away from the epic narrative.

One can argue whether the polyphonic novel is indeed a superior novel form, which is the opinion propagated by Bakhtin's faithful disciple, Julia Kristeva.[3] It is obvious, however, that many recent children's books contain features which Bakhtin relates to the polyphonic novel. Modern writers very promptly abandon the epic narrative in this novel—at least in the sense Bakhtin puts into the term "epic."

When Bakhtin states that Dostoyevsky's novels are not epic he means that they are not life stories.

> What unfolds in his works is not a multitude of characters and fates in a single objective world, illuminated by a single authorial consciousness; rather a *plurality of consciousnesses, with equal rights and each with its own world*, combine but are not merged in the unity of the event. (Bakhtin's italics)[4]

This quotation is from Bakhtin's *The Problems of Dostoyevsky's Poetics*; one of the implications is that the characters in a polyphonic novel are ideological rather than psychological objects whose utterances are not exclusively about themselves and their closest surroundings, but about the whole world. This statement may seem to have very little to do with children's literature until we attempt to understand the essence of the notion of multi-voicedness.

Bakhtin views Dostoyevsky's writings—and to some extent Gogol's—not as realistic narratives but as descriptions of a rite, or, as he prefers to call it, a carnivalized reality.[5] The world of Dostoyevsky's novels is an upside-down world. The characters' behavior is not "normal" but ritual. The episode at Nastassia Filippovna's birthday party in *The Idiot* is for Bakhtin a typical example of a life situation depicted as carnival. This episode and several other similar scenes were criticized by Dostoyevsky's contemporaries for their lack of verisimilitude.

This is something extremely important for modern children's books which so often have been criticized by less sensitive scholars for being "not true to life," or "unrealistic." But modern children's literature, like modern literature and art in general, is not a mirror which reflects reality precisely as it is (or is supposed to be); it is rather a crooked mirror which distorts reality, divides it into hundreds of puzzle pieces which readers are challenged to put together.

In the context of children's literature, "realistic" often means "devoid of magical or supernatural elements,"[6] but it would be essentially wrong to equate "realistic" and "verisimilar." The question "Can this really have happened?" is irrelevant for many contemporary children's writers, who describe not real events, but artistically constructed ones—ritual, in Bakhtin's terminology. This must be borne in mind in order once and for all to dismiss the demand that a children's book should be true to life.

The notion of the carnival does not imply that books become theatrical or unlikely; carnivalization is merely a means to achieve a distance from cruel aspects of reality. It is especially important when we have to do with children's and adolescent literature with elements of violence, like Robert Cormier in the United States or Peter Pohl in Sweden. In Peter Pohl's "Always That Anette" (1988), a ruthless criticism of the Swedish educational system, all teachers at school have names beginning with "Ing": Inge, Inger, Ingemar, Ingegjerd, Inga-Gulla, etc. The immediate association in Swedish is to *inget*, meaning "nothing." This obvious carnivalizing device has irritated many Swedish critics expecting credibility in a text set in realistic surrounding. In the sequel, "Can No One Help Anette?" (1990), the hospital staff have names beginning with B: Björn, Bella, Bengt, Berit, etc. There may be yet another secret code hidden in the letters I and B (Peter Pohl is a mathematician); otherwise they might indicate Institution and Bureaucracy. The names of schools mentioned in the story—Silver Lining School and Dispairy (sic!) School—are typical "telling" names in the style of Gogol or Evelyn Waugh. Both the school and the hospital in "Anette" books are satires with no aspiration to verisimilitude. The persecution of Anette by the teachers in Silver Lining School is driven to the absurd, and the fact that neither Anette nor her father can do anything about it emphasizes the carnival character of the story. A similar device in an adult novel, going back to Jonathan Swift and perfected by Franz Kafka, is naturally accepted, while in a children's book it causes misunderstanding and protests.

The peculiar thing about Peter Pohl is that he seems to be trying to write "issue" books, about child abuse in *Johnny My Friend* (1985), mobbing in "Let's Call Him Anna," incest in "The Rainbow Only Has Eight Colors." But his talent compels him, seemingly involuntarily, to go beyond issues, resulting in some splendid novels. The mirror that he holds up to reality is doubtless crooked, and the universe of his books becomes a carnival. The mental hospital, the setting of the second "Anette" book, is of course a recurrent metaphor in world literature.

Another recent Swedish novel, Ulf Stark's "The Nuts and the No-Goods" (1984), has premises that have troubled critics who tried to see it as "realistic." The protagonist, the twelve-year-old girl Simone, goes to a new school and is mistaken for a boy, Simon. She gladly accepts this to create a new identity for herself. It is not very plausible that nobody discovers the truth, but this is again a carnivalizing device. To change identity by changing clothes is the essence of carnival. The party which the dying grandfather throws for his friends at the end of the book can be viewed as an echo of the many carnival processions in Ingmar Bergman's or Federico Fellini's films.

MULTIPLE VOICES

The central notion of polyphony is naturally that manifold voices present their own different ideas and viewpoints. In Dostoyevsky's novels, as Bakhtin points out, the writer's own voice disappears completely, and the novel becomes an endless discussion of various issues, a battlefield of ideas and existential questions. Can this also be relevant in a children's book?

New themes in children's literature beginning in the 1960s, which I have discussed earlier, also demand new forms—the code shift on one level initiates a change on all other levels. It is no longer possible to write about the innermost thoughts and feelings of a child in the old traditional manner with an omniscient narrator, to say nothing of a narrator whose own voice, with his own ideology, views on education, morals, etc, comments on the behaviour of his figures and monitors the reader's response. One can assume that the first-person narrator is more subjective and insightful and therefore more suitable for conveying the deeper feelings of a child. However, traditional first-person narrators, for obvious reasons in adult literature (Tom Jones, Moll Flanders) and for didactic purposes in early children's literature (Jim Hawkins), most often relate their stories long after the event from the viewpoint of a clever adult, and this allows them to comment on their own shortcomings and provide educational conclusions for the reader.[7]

In the new type of narrative we find a fundamentally different authorial attitude towards the character. The author takes a step back and allows the character to come forward. The described events are filtered through the mind of the character before they are presented to the reader. We as readers thus learn more about the characters' feelings towards the events than about the events as such. We can call this subjective realism, or if you will, carnivalized realism, in the sense that we perceive reality *after* it has been reflected in the crooked mirror of the character's mind. In this sort of narrative we never approach reality in the same way as in an epic story.

Let me illustrate this statement on the basis of the novel *Elvis and His Secret* (1972) by Maria Gripe. There is a constant dialogue going on within the main character, the six-year-old Elvis Karlson, a painful and fruitless discussion in which he himself and his innocently childist (not childish!) view of the world is challenged by the outlook of others: his mother, his father, his grandparents, his older friend Peter, his teacher, his classmate and friend Anna-Rosa. There is a variety of voices and opinions, none of which is distinguished by the author as the only right one. Elvis, and the reader with him, is forced to draw his own conclusions. Within Elvis's mind there is a hopeless battle between the well-behaved, obedient Elvis, which his mother favors, the blindly religious Elvis that his grandmother tries to foster, Elvis the soccer player who is his father's ideal—and the free, independent, intellectually superior Elvis who he deep down really knows himself to be. This "real" Elvis does not always win the battle, for much too often he is obliged to compromise. There can never be a happy ending to this story.

This is one example of how to apply the notion of multi-voicedness to a children's book. With the author totally dissolved within the character, *Elvis and His Secret* and sequels almost feel like first-person narratives. In my experience, students of children's literature often are absolutely sure as they reflect upon the text that Elvis is the first-person narrator. Contributing to this effect of direct experience is the fact that Maria Gripe—and other authors writing in the same period—use the present narrative tense.

Between the narrative technique in *Elvis and His Secret* and the first-person narrator of, for instance, Astrid Lindgren's *Noisy Village* books, however, there is a profound difference. When the seven-year-old Lisa is telling the story, Astrid Lindgren cannot possibly exceed her verbal or intellectual capacity. This creates an air of trust on the reader's part, but the narrative loses in depth. In the *Elvis* books, Maria Gripe translates the thoughts of a six-year-old boy into

Elvis and His Secret—*a book with many voices; illustration by Harald Gripe*

a more grownup language, dresses them in words and sentences which he normally would not master, and allows him to think and reflect at a level far above what would be expected in a child his age. But it does not make Elvis improbable. Verbalizing and articulating the thoughts and feelings of a child character is merely an artistic device. This is not the traditional *Erlebte Rede* (free indirect discourse), but a much more introspective narrative.

The most typical feature in the polyphonic novel is that the writer's voice disappears behind the voices of the characters. There is no self-evident mouthpiece for the writer's views, so that a great deal remains implicit and unuttered—and this is the most prominent trait of polyphony. In modern children's books we very seldom find adult narrators expressing their own opinions, comments, or judgments of the characters' behavior. The didactic narrator constantly intent on conveying the correct message to the reader belongs to the earlier stages in children's literature. That sort of narrator can best be observed in the frame-stories of Joachim Heinrich Campe's retelling of *Robinson Crusoe* or in Madame Leprince de Beaumont's fairy-tale collection. The adult narrator of the frame-story is there to guide the reader, provide explanations and draw conclusions.

The shift from epic to polyphonic narrative patterns implies, in the first place, a disintegration of the basic structure, or generic plot, of children's literature: home—away—home. Epic children's books have a clear-cut plot, that is, a sequence of events within a book or portions of a book ("chapter" composition). In a polyphonic book, nothing really "happens." There is no beginning or end in the usual sense, no logical development towards a climax and denouement; the story may seem to be arbitrarily cut from the character's life, or is even more often a mosaic of bits arbitrarily glued together.

When an earlier approved narrative norm is broken like this, something must appear in its stead, and in fact quite a few narrative techniques can be discovered in recent children's literature.

THE HIDDEN TEXT

Fictitious diaries are a fascinating form of children's book, and although the genre has a long tradition in mainstream literature, it has only recently become a popular narrative device in children's and adolescent books. Sue Townsend's *The Secret Diary of Adrian Mole, Ages 13 1/4* (1982) and Beverly Cleary's *Dear Mr Henshaw* (1983) are two rather well-known examples.

The didactic narrator. From J.H. Campe's The Young Robinson; *illustration by Ludwig Richter (1896)*

HASSE

204 dagar i Hans Henrik
Olssons liv

Siv Widerberg   Rabén&Sjögren

Hasse keeping a diary. Cover by Jan Gustavsson

Most scholars agree that using the diary form is a good way to imitate children's manner of writing, and that this is why young readers appreciate reading novels in diary form. I believe it is the other way round—that in writing diaries or journals children intuitively or consciously use the unwritten rules they have learned from children's books in diary form: for instance, the formula "Dear diary." One of the early models was probably the authentic but purified *Diary of a Young Girl* by Anne Frank. Children's journals not intended to be read by other people may deviate stylistically.

In Sweden several series of children's books using the diary form have appeared recently, and they are equally popular among young readers. They include Barbro Lindgren's "Top Secret" and sequels (1971–73); Viveca Sundvall's "The Diary of a First-Grader" and sequels (1979–86); Siv Widerberg's "Hasse" and sequels (1983–85); and "Bert's Diary" (1987) by Anders Jacobsson and Sören Olsson. These four series provide good material for contemplating the diary form, for they contain a diversity of themes and exemplify a number of purposes for which the device is used. In the first two series the narrators are girls, in the latter two they are boys. "Top Secret" is among the most candid children's books of the 1970s; its very title reflects the author's aspiration to mediate the innermost thoughts of a teenager. "Hasse" is more of an "issue" novel, dealing with problems of a foster child. The narrator/protagonist is much younger than Barbro in "Top Secret," and the limited vocabulary and poor style of an eight-year-old are imitated. Also, presumably for the sake of authenticity, many entries are merely "Nothing happened today." In "The Diary of a First-Grader" the seven-year-old Mimmi is a well-balanced, happy child in a secure home. Finally, "Bert's Diary," the only text written by male authors, is openly entertaining, full of half-frivolous hints reflecting the teenage boy's sexual anxiety; it definitely lacks the depth of many contemporary children's books.

Among both critics and readers there is an opinion that Barbro Lindgren used her own authentic journals while writing "Top Secret" and its two sequels. She may have used them, but this does not mean she copied them directly into her novels. While she may have had recourse to the journals to reinforce her memories, the books are fiction. She is using a naive, or naivistic, viewpoint, which involves descending to the level of a child without losing the mentality or the vocabulary of an adult. That is, Barbro Lindgren uses the same device in her fictitious diaries as Maria Gripe in the *Elvis* books, pretending that the child is the narrator but telling the story herself through the eyes and the mind of a child.

The crucial difference between an authentic autobiographical text (autobiography, diary, journal) and a fictitious one is determined by the dissimilarity between the mimetic and the semiotic process of writing. An authentic autobiography is mimetic, a more or less direct reflection of reality. Modern (or postmodern, if you wish) fictitious autobiography or diary is semiotic. The reader is encouraged to participate in the process of deciphering the text. While an authentic autobiography reveals something (cf the classical genre of "confessions," from Augustine to Rousseau), modern texts hide reality behind an opaque curtain of semiotic signs.[8]

When the diary form is used in children's literature merely as an unmotivated, superficial narrative device—which I believe is the case in "Hasse" and "Bert's Diary," as well as in the *Adrian Mole* books—the texts lack dimension and are not convincing. The form feels artificial and forced. In the "Mimmi" books, on the other hand, there is an inner structure which implies that the books could not have been written in another way. Like Barbro Lindgren's series, the books about Mimmi tell us something other than what they pretend. "Hasse" and "Bert's Diary" do not. Here, precisely, are examples of the difference between the epic and the polyphonic manners of writing.

In the "Mimmi" books there is another dimension besides the epic one consisting of a mere sequence of events depicting a school year through a child's witty, often precocious comments. In analyzing this other dimension, it seems appropriate to make use of the notion of *palimpsest*. A palimpsest is a bit of papyrus or parchment on which the original inscription has been washed or scratched away and a new text has been written on top of it. The term is used in feminist criticism in the method of text analysis which aspires to discover the original, hidden meaning behind the superficial plot and to suggest possible reasons for hiding this meaning. This concept of palimpsest is introduced in Sandra Gilbert and Susan Gubar's study *The Madwoman in the Attic*[9] and has subsequently been used by various scholars, among them some who have also applied it in a "re-vision" (a feminist term, not to be confused with revision) of children's books, mainly books by and for women.[10] I feel, however, that the notion is far too useful to be restricted exclusively to feminist texts.

One very brief example of a palimpsest structure is the treatment of the relationship between Moomintroll and the Snork Maiden in *Comet in Moominland* (1946) by Tove Jansson. We do not know how old Moomintroll is in the stories; he may be about ten, the age of pre-puberty. In *Comet in Moominland* we see his curiosity about the opposite sex developing into love long before he himself can articulate his feelings. The visible, superimposed text consists of Moomintroll's adventures together with his friends, in their efforts to find out about the dangers of the coming comet. The hidden text is about his maturation process, in which breaking free from his mother and developing an attachment to another female is essential.

The remnants of the erased text are scattered throughout the book. The Snorks are first introduced into the story by Snufkin, who tells Moomintroll how beautiful Snork Maiden was. Moomintroll's reaction is: "Pah! Women! . . . Didn't anything exciting happen?" (p. 82) At this point, Moomintroll does not yet know that Snork Maiden is the most exciting thing that is going to happen to him. Four pages later they find a bracelet that had evidently belonged to Snork Maiden, and they assume that she had fallen over a preci-

A palimpsestic narrative: Moomintroll meets Snork Maiden; illustration by Tove Jansson from Comet in Moominland

pice. "Moomintroll was too overcome to speak" (p. 86). Three pages further Moomintroll inquires at the observatory about "a little pale green Snork Maiden. . . all fluffy. . . perhaps with a flower behind her ear. . . " (p. 89). She has already become an image in his mind and his heart. He is so interested in her that he forgets to ask about the comet, which is why the friends have come to the observatory in the first place. Snork Maiden has already eclipsed everything else in his thoughts. "I wonder where the Snorks spent the night. . . . I must give that wretched girl her ankle-ring back" (p. 93). From now on, all his thoughts are about her, and he betrays himself repeatedly by talking about her: "We might easily have rolled one of those stones on to the little Snork Maiden" (p. 97). Eventually they meet, and Moomintroll saves her life, declaring his role once and for all: "I am here to protect you." The relationship develops more or less predictably, but Moomintroll continues to make slips of the tongue. When Snork Maiden asks whether ankle-rings can be made of pearl, he answers: "Ankle-rings and nose-rings and ear-rings and engagement rings—" (p. 106). Finally, Sniff comments: "He's been quite dotty since he met that girl" (p. 118). The emotion is given a verbal expression.

Moomintroll is still very much dependent on his mother, and he hurries home because he believes that his mother can cope with anything, including comets. At the end of the story, it is to her, and not the Snork Maiden, that he gives the biggest pearl.

Thus by allowing us to discover the erased text behind the real one, the palimpsest method enables us to perceive even more interesting levels in the Moomin stories. Hidden emotions are a very important part of Tove Jansson's books.[11]

To return to the diary form, we may ask what the hidden text may be in "The Diary of a First Grader" and why it is hidden. What is Viveca Sundvall trying to convey? To answer this question we must try to see what or who is the center of the text, the point around which the story rotates. It seems that the janitor is such a point in the book. The author is telling us a story about a seven-year-old girl's infatuation with a middle-aged, not very attractive janitor in her school. There may be many reasons why Viveca Sundvall wants to hide this line in the story. It is a slightly controversial theme, even though children's literature has become much more open in depicting young children's emotions. Most probably Viveca Sundvall feels challenged by the very idea of telling the story of a mind behind the superficial plot. This realistic, true-to-life sequence of events is not very exciting. Everything that Mimmi writes in her diary is a superimposed text which hides the real, the innermost, the intimate and secret text. It is so secret that Mimmi cannot even verbalize her feelings for herself.

The hidden text comes through in short, careful phrases, scattered among large segments of text: "I turned around and saw. . . ." "He is dangerous, hideous and evil and strong and stern." "I am allergic to janitors. Not all janitors. Just these ugly types who stroll around in some schools." The further we go in the story, the more obvious the hidden text becomes: "He is so terrible that he is almost sweet. . . . The janitor is a king. If you kiss him maybe new, curly hair will grow on his head. . . . I must think a little more about the janitor before I went to sleep. I wonder if he has a Christmas tree in his little red cottage by the school building."

The portrayal of the janitor becomes longer and more and more intense. Everything else Mimmi is writing about is merely camouflage. She wants to speak about her feelings, but doesn't dare—not even for herself or the yellow notebook she is writing in. She hides her feelings behind lots of everyday details. But the hidden text glimmers all the time. Whatever Mimmi writes about she somehow manages to mention the janitor. Every person, setting or event is worth describing in the diary if only there is a tiny connection to the hidden text. Mimmi's older friend Rebecca is important since she provides information (sometimes totally incredible) about the janitor. School is important because there Mimmi can see the object of her love.

Mimmi does not admit that it is love, but there is a dialogue going on between the Mimmi who is in love and the reasonable, cunning Mimmi who tries to hide her love and therefore calls it hate or fear.

The final encounter between Mimmi and the janitor is anticipated in a subtle way throughout the story. There is one letter missing from Mimmi's typewriter, the letter Z. Therefore she mentions in the beginning of the story that if she ever has to write about a certain striped animal it will prove pretty difficult. It is hard to imagine why Mimmi will have to write about zebras, but it happens to be the janitor's favorite motif when he is painting. If we simply view this as a funny episode we will certainly miss an important aspect in the psychological charge of the text. Mimmi lacks a letter to describe the janitor's secret hobby. It is the missing jigsaw-puzzle bit needed to call the feeling by its proper name.

There is another evidence that Mimmi's love for the janitor is the core of the story. It ends with the final encounter, which takes place on April 30. If the plot had been concerned with school, family, classmates, and so on, it would have been more natural to end the diary year with the end of school.

As in every analysis of hidden texts, one can ask whether it is a conscious device on the writer's part or merely speculation on the part of the scholar. In this case I would suggest that if Viveca Sundvall is unconsciously hiding Mimmi's feelings behind lots of trivialities, this only makes the text more interesting. Palimpsest is the only frame that holds together the story, which otherwise would fall into small, disconnected narrative pieces resembling sketches. In *Elvis and His Secret* the palimpsest is the tension between the mother and the son.

The same kind of hidden text can be found in *Johnny My Friend* by Peter Pohl. The very obvious and erotically charged feelings that Chris, the first-person narrator, has for Johnny are hiding in his account of superficial events. They are toned down, for it is the writer's intention not to let Chris acknowledge his infatuation with Johnny, not to let him accept the truth about Johnny which he keeps pushing away from him and which the people around him (and the keen reader) have already guessed—that Johnny is in fact a girl disguised as a boy, and that therefore Chris's love for her is perfectly normal. One Swedish critic has noted the masterly verbal treatment of Chris's feelings when he and Johnny spend a night in a tent in the forest: if we simply substitute "she" for "he," we will get a marvelously sensual description of the awakening of a young lover in a bridal bed.[12]

JIGSAW-PUZZLE METHOD

We can call Peter Pohl's narrative technique the jigsaw-puzzle method. In *Johnny My Friend* it is the reader's task to put the pieces together and learn about Johnny's secret. This sort of thing is self-evident in a mystery novel, but somewhat daring and innovative in what is supposed to be a "quality" book for children. Again as in most mysteries, the readers also have a chance to get one step ahead of the protagonist and first-person narrator Chris in their guessing process. On re-reading the text, we discover that very early in the text are hidden clues about Johnny's true identity—tiny but relevant details, one-second flashes that eventually make it possible to assemble the whole picture.

Chris's attempt to assemble loose pieces of life is at the same time an inner dialogue with many vices. His secure world comes tumbling down when he meets Johnny, whose life conditions do not fit into Chris's usual concepts. Having lived with a circus her whole life, Johnny is a kind of "child of nature" who doesn't know about school, or religion, or table manners, or gender stereotypes, or what is considered normal behavior. Instead she knows a lot about things that Chris has never thought about, like colors. Johnny's free, unspoiled view of the world stands in sharp contrast to the conventions which Chris has acquired from school, family, his gang and from the mass media—conventions and knowledge which he believed important and which he has meticulously recorded in his filing boxes. These different voices struggle in Chris's mind throughout the book, which spans the short time when he is being interrogated by a police officer and the horrible truth is slowly unfolded before him. The voices merge together in an anguished scream at the end of the book.

In the two books about Anette the discussions take a more conventional form, and the various authorities are given a voice each. Is it never said explicitly whether any opinion is right or wrong, and all views are represented equally. One can argue that young readers may become confused, but I believe that their own notions of right and wrong, just and unjust, and good and evil are strong enough to enable them to take sides. This must also be Peter Pohl's belief, since he never steps forward with his own comments.

The jigsaw-puzzle technique is found not only in Peter Pohl's novels regarded individually, but encompasses his *oeuvre* taken as a whole. The adult novel (that is, it was published and marketed as such in Sweden) "The Rainbow Only Has Eight Colors" (1986) and adolescent novel "Let's Call Him Anna" (1987) seem to have nothing in common. In "While the Rainbow Fades" (1989), however, we find the missing piece of the puzzle: the youth camp leader Micke appears to be the same person as the war child Henrik, and thus the three novels form a suite. The middle novel explores the way the oppressed Henrik becomes Micke the oppressor. Typically, Peter Pohl lets him change his name and identity.

The second Anette book is a companion volume to the first, where the same story is told from a different point of view. There too a mystery technique is used, when the protagonist and narrator, child psychologist Björn, is trying to solve the mystery of Anette's case like a real criminal inspector. If you have read the first book you already know the answer, and the suspense is in following Björn's intense guessing work. There is also a secondary line in the story in which the reader has no advantage. Not having read the first book does not detract from the suspense, although the focus of your attention naturally shifts from Björn to Anette, who is the subjects of investigation.

EXPERIMENTAL FORMS

Pure formal experiments are still rare in children's literature. The reason, apparently, is that writers are afraid they will not be properly "understood"—not by children, but by publishers, teachers, and reviewers, that is, the adult literary establishment. Downright experiments probably never can become dominant in literature; we know of some in adult fiction, but they come and go. They arouse curiosity, but as a consistent narrative technique they are too "non-understandable" to be received creatively. I use the term "non-understandable" in the semiotic sense of Yuri Lotman, who defines it as the creative aspect of our appreciation of art. Only through non-understanding is the recipient able to take in the work of art. At the same time, there must be a balance between understanding and non-understanding—a work of art that is completely non-understandable, "closed," cannot reach the addressee.

Peter Pohl in Sweden and among English-language writers Aidan Chambers and Robert Cormier are prominent examples of formal experiments in adolescent novels. Chambers is perhaps most conscious of what he is doing, since his novels are in a way products of his activity as scholar and educator. His ambition is to renew adolescent literature, and he is not afraid of the most daring devices, which he also tries to explain theoretically in his essays and lectures.[13] *Breaktime* (1978) is the novel which best illustrates Chambers's intellectual play with the possibilities of a modern narrative. It has been characterized as "a collage" by critics. In the novel, first and third person narrative alternate, different typefaces are mixed with handwriting, quotations from guidebooks and handbooks appear in the midst of a story. A totally black page indicates the blackout that the protagonist goes through. In his capacity of scholar Chambers maintains that in a contemporary book for young readers *how* the story is told is more important than *what* is being told. Chambers has done in adolescent literature what Umberto

Eco has done in *The Name of the Rose* (1981); that is, he has created a work of fiction based on the knowledge and instinct of a literary critic.

I think it noteworthy that at the same time the British Aidan Chambers wrote his experimental novel, a similar experiment appeared in the United States: *I Am the Cheese* (1977) by Robert Cormier. Cormier also uses the collage technique in a mixture of simulated tape-recorded dialogue and first-person narrative that, we realize by the end, also may be hallucinations. For Cormier's shocking theme, this technique must have seemed the most effective.

There are many similarities between Cormier, Chambers and Peter Pohl. They do not appear to have influenced each other, although such a possibility cannot be completely dismissed. Both Pohl and Chambers use the simultaneous form of a film script—two events described parallel to each other by means of graphic layout in order to stress a dramatic situation: Pohl at the end of *Johnny My Friend*, Chambers in *Dance on My Grave* (1982), where there appears something he calls "replay in slow motion." Incidentally, the subtitle of *Dance on My Grave* is "A Life and a Death in Four Parts, One Hundred and Seventeen Bits, Six Reports (Consecutive), Two Newspapers Clippings as well as various jokes, some mysteries, several footnotes and a failure now and then to help the story on." Here is a description of merchandise which honestly reveals Chambers's writing principle.

In *Now I Know* (1987) Chambers imitates a tape-recorded speech and a word-processed text, alternates between first person and third person, and inserts fictitious documentary portions. A mixed technique is also used in *The Tollbridge* (1992). These devices are obviously modernistic and are comparable, for instance, to conceptualism in visual art. In Chambers's texts they most probably are meant to reflect the chaos of life, the confusion of an adolescent, and the loose structures of our modern existence. But above all, the various voices in the text become discernible.

Peter Pohl uses the unusual and advanced second-person narrative in his book "Let's Call Him Anna" (1987). There is also a first-person narrator in the text, but the protagonist is a "you." The book becomes indeed a dialogue in which the "I" tries to analyze reactions of the "you."

In the second Anette book, the same technique is developed into something as rare in children's literature as an adult first-person narrator. As I mentioned earlier, the sequel tells the same story from another perspective. This is a common device in modern adult literature, one of its best-known examples being *Rashomon* (1915) by the Japanese writer Ryunosuke Akutagawa (made into film by Akira Kurosawa). Peter Pohl allows a story first rendered through a child with the same empathy as in Maria Gripe's

Elvis books to be told again by an adult in a meticulous jigsaw-puzzle work. The whole book is a series of conversations between the narrator and the various people involved in Anette's case. However, we as readers don't get to know much about Anette. Anette in this book is secondary, just as Johnny is secondary in my interpretation of *Johnny My Friend*. The protagonist of the sequel is a young, lonely and insecure child psychologist Björn, whose work with Anette causes him to take a new look at his own life. But the narrator doesn't reveal this to the reader, just as Mimmi doesn't reveal her true feelings. The palimpsest method in Peter Pohl's book demands of readers that they interpret Björn's own problems through his reactions to the many voices he is forced to confront. This interpretation is confirmed by the very last paragraphs of the book, when Björn starts contemplating what has happened to him. The adult level of the sequel is much more tangible than in the first book. However, Peter Pohl has never stated that he writes for a young audience.

The Swedish writer Mats Wahl uses a multiple first-person narrative in his book "The Lacquered Ape" (1986). Three of those first-person narrators are young people, while the other two are adults: the mother of the main character and his landlady. The young person's dilemma is thus highlighted literally from different viewpoints. It is difficult to imagine a better example of multi-voicedness. I think, however, that in this book the device is too superficial and makes the whole book slightly schematic.

COMPUTER GAMES, CHOOSE-YOUR-OWN-ADVENTURE AND CHILDREN'S BOOKS
Modern children's and adolescent culture ("non-culture" with respect to children's literature) has doubtless influenced the ways contemporary authors write for children. Computers and computer games have also contributed to this process. The thinking in binary opposites typical of the computer age has among other things resulted in the so called "Choose-Your-Own-Adventure" books, which, given their limited scope of action, meagre language and restricted possibilities of variations even compared to computer games can hardly be seen as valuable contributions to children's literature.

The phenomenon of computer games deserves a special study, since they have become such an important part of children's culture and supposedly influence children's reading skills by, among other things, reducing their attention span and affecting use of grammar. From the ethical point of view as well, it is certainly harmful for children to get the idea inherent in the computer game that having once failed, you can "play again." In defence of these games, however, it should be said that they stimulate in children other skills such as the "reading" of pictures or grasping several lines of action simultaneously.

I will not dwell any longer on computer games as such, but I would like to give some examples of binarity as a narrative principle. The exciting idea of allowing the reader to choose the order of events in the story has been used in children's literature long before computer games came into being. In 1967 the Swedish writer Gunnel Linde published a rather peculiar story entitled "The Island of Eva-Sham." It has three final chapters, and the readers are invited to choose the one they prefer:

> Do you want only Nalle to stay on Eva-Sham's island? Then turn to page 110. Do you want only Lua to stay on Eva-Sham's island? Then turn to page 120. Do you want everybody to stay on Eva-Sham's island? Then turn to page 131. (p. 109)

The three final chapters eliminate each other, as do the two sequels, "Eva-Sham and Nalle" and "Eva-Sham and Lua," which both appeared the year after the first book. The third and happiest ending has no sequel, since it is indeed happy and reconciling. Incidentally, the situation immediately preceding the final chapters in "The Island of Eva-Sham" illustrates Prigogine-Lotman's bifurcation model: from this point the story can go in different directions. The fact that Gunnel Linde lets her readers choose the direction is evidence of her great confidence in children.

Unlike Gunnel Linde, Peter Dickinson cannot but be aware of the binary principles of computer games when he in *AK* (1990) has two concluding chapters entitled: "Twenty years on, perhaps: A" and "Twenty years on, perhaps: B." They present two different endings of the story: one promises peace and happiness, while in the other war continues, the hero Paul is murdered, and another little boy picks up his AK, just as he did in the beginning of the book.

THE MERGING OF GENRES

It is in the merging of genres that we find the most radical examples of the interplay of different voices in children's literature. In my introductory chapter I enumerated the different genres that coexist in *Ronia, the Robber's Daughter* and *Johnny My Friend*, two recent books in which this merging is extreme. Among these genres we see those most often associated with paraliterature: the criminal novel, the thriller, the mystery and the romance.

The use of paraliterary forms in so-called "quality literature" must be regarded as a typical feature of the contemporary children's book. The mystery story *The Westing Game* (1978) by Ellen Ruskin, which was awarded the "quality" Newbery medal, is one example. Of course, the same trait is also present in postmodern mainstream literature, which often deliberately operates with building blocks from paraliterary genres. The purpose in adult fiction is aesthetic; to a great degree, postmodern literary values lie in irony, parody, displacement,[14] deconstruction,[15] etc. In children's literature there are additional pedagogical aspects: in order to entice children to read, books pretend to be something other than they really are. Two Swedish adolescent books, Mats Wahl's "The Master" (1982) and Stig Ericson's "Jenny from Bluewater" (1982) can serve as illustration. The first book is seemingly a pirate story, while the second appears to be a frontier story, set in the United States in the 1860s. Both have the necessary components of the adventure story: a clear distinction between good and evil, suspense, dynamic plots. The covers of both books suggest violence and action, with guns aimed at the reader in the good old James Bond or Modesty Blaise fashion to catch readers' attention. What is important in these books, however, is not the plot or action but the individual, the evolution of personality. Unlike the earlier, "canonical" adventure stories, the lives of pirates and settlers are not presented as exciting or romantic. The truth behind the romanticized historical depictions is shown to be cruel and ruthless, consisting of hard work and poor living conditions. "The Master" shows the protagonist confronted by a moral dilemma. "Jenny from Bluewater" can be read as a subversive feminist text about a young girl's way to freedom and independence through, among other things, the mastery of language. The very thought of placing a girl in the center of an action-dominated frontier story is a displacement of the genre principle.

We can find examples of similar connections to adventure in contemporary American books for children as well, including historical novels such as Ann Turner's *Grasshopper Summer* (1989), where the romantic idea of conquering new lands is blurred by hardships, failures and despair. Both the text and the cover illustration, however, contain the features necessary for the reader to recognize the book as adventure. Most of Gary Paulsen's books have the marks of adventure, for instance, robinsonade in *Hatchet* (1987), while at the same time they are psychological, even existential novels depicting the young protagonist's inner quest for maturity.

Writers are not necessarily aware of this pedagogical aspect in modern children's literature. We can once again view it in a semiotic perspective. A "book of quality" containing elements of paraliterary genres has a better chance of being "understood" by readers (who may also be familiar with the genre from other media like TV). But in this case, the "zone of understanding" is merely a tiny layer of the text, while what the writer really intends to tell lies beyond. It will be recalled that non-understanding is the creative factor in art reception, the factor that stimulates imagination and reflection. Really "difficult" books lack this zone of understanding; paraliterary forms, which are easily recognizable, are a suitable means to send signals to the reader saying that the text is indeed "understandable." Covers and flap texts also offer elements of "understanding" in order not to scare the reader.

Among many fascinating examples of authors who work with seemingly popular forms and yet create texts of high literary quality is Cecil Bødker, the most outstanding children's writer in Denmark and winner of the Andersen medal. She is famous for her series about the young boy Silas, beginning with *Silas and the Black Mare* (1967), which today includes twelve volumes. Serialization is in itself a typical trait of paraliterature, and indeed, the first books in the series have a strong air of formula fiction, folktale and fantasy.

Although he has no magical powers, Silas can be described in terms of an "alien child." There is probably something magical in his flute that allures both humans and animals. The flute arouses associations with the figure of Pan, a child of nature; the motif of a hero taming animals and/or punishing evil people with the help of a magic flute is well known from folktales. It is also used in Zacharias Topelius's tale 'Knut the Musician,' which Bødker is of course familiar with. The horse, Silas's recurrent attribute, is an indispensable folktale element as well. Like the folktale hero, Silas takes sides with the weak and the oppressed, against the thieves and villains. As in folktales, he acquires a faithful squire in Ben-Godik. The folktale structure reappears in a later book, "Silas and the Blue Horses" (1985), where Silas goes away on a journey, helps the weak and poor, feeds the hungry with "two loaves of bread and five fish," not unlike a Savior figure, and once again makes use of his magic flute.

Silas is also the hero of the trickster tale, the adventurer, the picaro—a modern Don Quixote who defends the oppressed. But the books are not really adventure stories. Not even the earliest books depict any great adventures. There are, however, many features of the naughty-boy story, which contains a strong protest against the world of adults, and they have much in common with Astrid Lindgren's *Pippi Longstocking* (1945) or *Emil and His Pranks* (1963). Like Pippi, Silas makes witty remarks and has a horse as his best friend. There is a parallel episode to *Emil* where Silas wins a horse on a bet, and both cases exploit a motif from trickster tales.

The horse, on the other hand, also offers a connection with the paraliterary genre of horse stories. We are told a lot about horses and taking care of horses; pictures of horses are on every cover, and this may be regarded as a typical element of "understanding" probably intended to entice readers. In American public libraries, in fact, I have discovered *Silas* books on shelves labeled "Horse Stories." The protagonist is a boy, however, and this violates the canon of horse stories, which are a typical girls' genre.

We can also consider the books within the historical genre. They are not truly historical fiction, for we never learn what country the stories take place in; the landscape and climate suggest Central Europe. Cecil Bødker avoids place names, names of coins, weight measures and anything that can indicate place and time and that usually creates the feeling of a particular historical epoch in fiction. Yet these are not operetta duchies either. The form of government is never mentioned, but there are gendarmes, a town guard and tax collectors; there are also churches and priests. Personal names sound slightly exotic or neutral, like Maria. The societal order and the few historical details suggest perhaps early 1800s: people travel by horse and in carriages, they are afraid of robbers, children are sold to circuses or to forced labor. These signs are related to the early social realism of such writers as Dickens, Victor Hugo, or Hector Malot. Almost all the people Silas encounters are pariahs, outcasts, strange or even handicapped: Maria is blind, Ben-Godik lame, Tyste has a harelip, while others are foundlings and orphans, poor, old and sick. These are elements of "misery" literature which the reader is supposed to recognize.

Beginning with the fifth book, "Silas at Sebastian Mountain" (1977), we find more than merely adventure. Silas and his oppressed friends settle in a deserted village and try to survive as Robinson Crusoe did on his island, which introduces yet another popular genre. The epic style of the earlier books disappears and there is no action whatsoever; the most dramatic events consist in someone getting lost, quarrels or fights with a neighbor or the town guard searching for runaways. The eternal villain Goat is less dangerous and becomes almost a comic figure. Everyday chores, hard work and the struggle for life are described in a slow and detailed narrative. Some chapters are reminiscent of handbooks in survival: how to tend to animals and cultivate the soil, which herbs can be used for medical purposes, how to make cheese, how to hunt and fish, cook, make baskets, do carpentry, sew furs, and so on. Meals are described in detail as an important part of existence. We are allowed to see how a community functions and grows. A picture of societal rather than individual development, it reflects a typical attitude of the 1970s.

It may seem remarkable that romantic and adventurous books like the early *Silas* books could appear at a time when the slogan was social commitment and everyday realism, in Denmark even more than in Sweden. In later books, however, we discover some harsh social criticism, especially in

Silas and the Runaway Coach (1972), where there is a palpable contrast between Silas's way of living and thinking and that of a bourgeois family. In a straightforward and didactic way Silas preaches to Japetus, the merchant's son, about social justice. It is not clear, however, whether it is really Cecil Bødker we hear talking through her character.

Silas's village can serve as a model for collective housing, a popular radical idea in Scandinavia in the 1970s, based on equality and collective efforts for the common good. It is easy to believe that Bødker wants to offer an ideal picture of society, yet what she really shows is a cross-section, a little model of society as it is. Sebastian Mountain is an inevitable compromise between "nature" and "culture" (here is the dialogue again!), anarchy and order, between Silas's earlier life outside society and the organized, bourgeois life represented by the merchant Planke. In this case Sebastian Mountain becomes a utopia, a dream about justice and equality, but like any utopia in literature or in reality, it soon develops into its opposite. The idyll on the mountain can never be totally independent from society. Interaction grows larger and larger in scale, and the villagers are forced to adjust to the conventions of the surrounding world.

School becomes the first step towards civilization. We also notice the first division between physical and intellectual labor when Japetus is fed for being a schoolteacher. Japetus introduces a spiritual dimension into the village which was entirely absent before. He represents the spiritual in contrast to Silas, who is the incarnation of the material. The subtle dialogue between the two becomes the axis of the later books. It is also suggested that the evolution continues towards the establishment of a village council, an armed guard, and a court, and that this development will be marked by a struggle for power and even bloodshed in conflicts with the outer world. These are voices of a society in a violent dialogue.

The mountain accepts "refugees" from the outside world, the sons of merchant Planke, Japetus and Jorim. They express adolescent revolt against parents, a necessary process of liberation and maturation. But they also escape from civilization and the strict regulations of their society. They are the rich man's children who want to live close to nature, while the young villagers long for freedom outside the village and they want to get rich and live under bourgeois conventions. They indicate that the experiment has failed. The ghost of a respectable life torments them and gives them no peace.

A dialogue between male and female, a "gender role debate," also suddenly breaks with the genre conventions. In the early *Silas* books there are no women, for women do not belong in the adventure story. It is peculiar that the writer should choose an ambivalent, male-female figure for the main villain. Goat is indeed the most oppressed of all the miserable figures around Silas. Goat is a hermaphodite, and has therefore been hated, despised and humiliated during her entire life. Abandoned by her own parents, she has become evil and revengeful, but the reader is given a chance to reflect together with Silas whether it is her own fault or whether we instead should pity her. Maria, who is handicapped herself, feels an affinity with Goat, and the abominable woman is eventually accepted as an equal citizen in the tiny mountain realm.

Reformed villains are not unusual in adventure stories, but very seldom does the transformation involve the psychological level, as in Bødker's books. Besides, Goat plays a significant role in the evolution of Melissa, the most fascinating character in the village. We first encounter her early in the suite as a beggar girl in poor harbor quarters. It is Melissa who definitely violates the conventions of society. She does not want to get stuck in a traditional role: "she had no wish to become like her mother—or any other woman she knew." In Goat she sees an alternative: freedom, but at a price of a repulsive lifestyle. Melissa starts contemplating a middle way which she finds in education. Her great dream is to become a merchant, which in the normal order of things is inconceivable for a girl. At first merchant Planke refuses to deal with her, but she perseveres and succeeds.

She also breaks free from Silas, who by this time has become a wise patriarch, and forces him to accept their relationship on her terms, as equals, which is not allowed by the traditional canon of either boys' books or girls' books. Melissa must leave the Mountain because within this very confined society there is no way for her to be free. Before she leaves she plants seeds of doubt about gender stereotypes. Strangely enough, it is the men who question the stereotyping: both Aron the hunter and Silas are willing to do women's chores, while the old Christophine represents the conservative view of women.

It is not without significance that Melissa is red-haired, a true heiress to the strong, independent girls in children's literature, like Anne of Green Gables and Pippi Longstocking.

The most important aspect of this feminist dimension of the Silas stories is that in the end it is women who appear to be reasonable and practical. They decide the fate of merchant Planke's sons, they succeed in concluding a peace treaty, providing for a peaceful coexistence between the utopia and the rest of the world.

What all this demonstrates, at any rate, is how something which started as adventure with a clear epic structure can eventually evolve into a huge cross-section of society containing a complicated network of relationships, deep insights into different characters, and a variety of issues addressed and presented through a variety of voices and opinions. Still, the adventure is there, and has been integrated into stories in a way that holds the reader in suspense.

As I mentioned above, there are now twelve books in the suite, but it is not a series like Nancy Drew. You cannot start reading *Silas* books in the middle, jump back to the beginning, read a chapter here and there. Each book continues its immediate predecessor in a clear evolution, so that references to people and events are impossible to understand without knowledge of the earlier books. Again, a feature of paraliterature is used to entice readers by involving them in something else.

Summing Up

The central idea of my whole study is the general tendency in contemporary children's literature towards the disintegration of traditional epic narrative. Children's literature today is catching up with mainstream literature in its so-called postmodern phase, which has as its most prominent slogan the violation of generally accepted literary norms.

In my analysis of the process I make use of Mikhail Bakhtin's distinction between the epic and the polyphonic novel. In the latter, one of the essential features of traditional children's literature, the didactic narrator, disappears. Conventions of epic narrative such as the relatively chronological order of events, the logical development of the plot towards a solution, the verisimilar depiction of events and characters, and so on, have become secondary and are supplanted by a variety of experimental narrative forms such as the palimpsestic narrative, unreliable first-person narrator, collage, and multiple ending.

One consequence of polyphony is a tendency for genres to merge. When children's books contain elements of many genres it is naturally difficult to relate them to a particular genre. This, of course, is something children's literature experts often wish to do for practical reasons: Where is the book to be shelved in the library? How should the shelf be labeled? In which chapter in the reference source shall we discuss the book? Is it about the family, adventure, siblings, disabled or old people? Since working with children's books is related to education, it is difficult to avoid these problems, which somehow never arise when we speak about mainstream literature (Is *The Sound and the Fury* about the family or about the handicapped?). It is time to acknowledge that genre books constitute a decreasing share of children's literature, which instead includes more and more novels for which genre distinctions are not only difficult but meaningless.

NOTES

1.   Most of the features singled out by Perry Nodelman as typical for children's fiction are epic: "action-oriented rather than character-oriented," "with happy endings," "repetitious," etc. (Nodelman 1992, p. 190).

2.   Bakhtin, 1984.

3.   In an essay on the adolescent novel Kristeva emphasizes the significance of ambivalence versus epic in the novel (Kristeva, 1990, p. 14); ambivalence is for her an indispensable feature of polyphony; see Kristeva, 1986.

4.   Bakhtin, 1984, p. 6.

5.   More about carnival is found in Bakhtin's study of Rabelais (Bakhtin, 1968). The notion of carnival has also been applied by children's books scholars, see, e.g., Harker, 1991; Stephens, 1992, chapter 4.

6.   See, e.g., relevant chapters in some recent reference guides: "Realism" (Lukens, 1990, pp. 14–18), "Contemporary Realistic Fiction" (Norton, 1991, pp. 408–471), "Realistic fiction" (Lynch-Brown, pp. 120–136). Most courses in children's literature throughout the world seem to have a similar section.

7.   Cf the discussion of Jim Hawkins in Nodelman, 1992, pp. 82–84.

8.   For a more general discussion of modern autobiography see, e.g., Kondrup, 1982; Taylor, 1983.

9.   Gilbert and Gubar, 1977.

10.   See, e.g., Åhmansson, 1991.

11.   See Jones, 1984; Westin, 1988.

12.   Lundqvist, 1994, p. 207.

13.   See in the first place Chambers, 1985, 1993.

14.   The term "displacement" comes from Northrop Frye (1957) and has been used in children's literature research by, for instance, Virginia L. Wolf (1985) and in Sweden by Eva M. Löfgren (1992, 1993). See also Nodelman, 1992, pp. 101ff.

15.   The term "deconstruction" comes from Jacques Derrida (1976). See Nodelman, 1992, pp. 106f.

5 CHRONOTOPE IN CHILDREN'S LITERATURE

The notion of the *chronotope*, which I use in my study of fantasy, *The Magic Code*, was introduced into literary criticism by the Russian scholar Mikhail Bakhtin. Bakhtin defines the chronotope as "the intrinsic connectedness of temporal and spatial relationships that are artistically expressed in literature."[1] In other words, and in what is probably a more correct translation from the Russian, it means: "a unity of time and space" presented in a literary work. Bakhtin notes that he has borrowed the term from the natural sciences, where it is widely used nowadays (the word itself comes from Greek "chronos"—time and "topos"—place). In Bakhtin's literary theory the term acquires a specific meaning, denoting the unity of fictional time and place, or, in his own words, "a formal category,"[2] an abstract literary notion.

We are justified in asking whether there is any reason at all to resort to the notion of the chronotope, or whether this is simply another fancy term introduced instead of the old, well-approved literary terms "place of action" (or "setting") and "time of action." On the rare occasions these concepts are treated in handbooks on children's literature, they are regarded as separate entities, and herein is the principal difference.[3] The chronotope denotes the *indivisible* unity of time and space, which according to Bakhtin are mutually dependent.

The most important aspect of Bakhtin's concept of the chronotope and what makes it so useful in children's literature research is that in Bakhtin's view it is a genre category,[4] that is, specific forms of chronotope are unique for particular genres. Bakhtin goes on to discuss the chronotope in both the broad (the medieval chronotope) and narrow meaning of the word (Dante chronotope); different text types as well as particular writers can represent a specific form of chronotope.

The study of chronotopes thus seems to be an appropriate approach to genres, and this is what I attempt to do in *The Magic Code*. Although I have encountered the misunderstanding among both colleagues and students, it would be wrong to assume that chronotopes are only present in fantasy. As Bakhtin shows, every literary mode, epoch, genre and even writer can be defined on the basis of the way in which they organize time and space. The reason why we see the fantasy chronotope so clearly is simply because it is so obvious. Because time and space relations are such significant aspects of fantasy narratives, they deviate from other genres and are therefore easy to single out. However, every genre and every type of children's text has its own, unique forms of chronotope. I am not proposing to make a complete inventory of these, but will merely discuss some interesting cases of chronotopes in children's books. I also intend to show that chronotopes become more complicated as we approach our own time.

THE FANTASY CHRONOTOPE

In my study of fantasy *The Magic Code* I have investigated contemporary fantasy for children in the light of the notion of chronotope as a genre category, that is, the interrelation between space and time inherent to fantasy as a genre. Analyzing the fantasy chronotope seemed to me an adequate means for achieving a better understanding of the fantasy genre as such. I will not recount or summarize my arguments here, but I do want to make some general remarks based on my findings.

First, the notion of chronotope provides us with a very good distinction between fairy tale and fantasy, which quite frequently presents a problem in studies of children's literature. As often as not both genres are treated under a common heading in the same chapter. Fairy tales, both traditional and literary ("Kunstmärchen"), take place in a magical world, which in Russian is described as situated "beyond the three oceans, beyond the three mountains" and in Swedish as "west of the sun, east of the moon" (English does not seem to have a common formula). The time of action is "Once upon a time" ("Il etait un fois," etc). Both time and space in fairy tales are beyond our experience. In the fairy-tale world, magic is taken for granted and does not cause amazement; fairies, witches, wizards, dragons are natural inhabitants of this universe, while magical transformations are the most common events. Both the characters of the fairy tale and the listener/reader are placed *inside* this magical world. The position of the listener has to do with the close connection of fairy tales to folk beliefs and to rites, but I will not dwell on this aspect here.[5] Incidentally, Bakhtin has a section on the fairy-tale chronotope in his study.[6]

Fantasy, on the other hand, has a link with reality and our own time and place, and its characters are most often ordinary children. The magical passage into another world and subsequent magical adventures in this other world create a contrast to reality. The other world has a time of its own, independent of the "real," or primary time. In other words, we can distinguish fantasy from the fairy tale depending on whether there is a one- or two-world structure in the chronotope.

With this definition we can clearly see, for example, that many of Edith Nesbit's short texts, commonly described as "fairy tales" (e.g. 'Billy the King' or 'The Deliverers of Their Country') belong generically to fantasy. The same is true of many of Astrid Lindgren's short texts. In both cases we can see how fantasy novels, especially *Mio, My Son* (1954) and *The Brothers Lionheart* (1973) by Astrid Lindgren, have grown out of shorter texts within the same genre.

Second, the notion of the chronotope enables us to avoid the problem encountered by most researchers of being forced to divide texts into categories such as "secondary-world fantasy" (a typical example is *The Lion, the Witch and the Wardrobe*, 1950, by C.S. Lewis) and "time-shift fantasy" (typical examples are Edith Nesbit's *The Story of the Amulet*, 1906, and *The House of Arden*, 1908), a division that practically every motif study of fantasy is obliged to follow.[7] Scholars of fantasy usually make a clear distinction between what they assume are the two principal motifs: secondary worlds and time travelling.

The so-called time fantasy undoubtedly is more preoccupied with time, including the very notion of time, its philosophical implications, and its metaphysical character. As to the construction of a magical universe and, as a direct consequence, the structure of the narrative, however, there are surely more similarities than differences in novels in which either a time shift or a secondary world is the dominant pattern.

Together with the established term "secondary world" (originally from J.R.R. Tolkien[8]) and the somewhat less established notion of "secondary time," I introduce in my study the concept of "secondary chronotope," that is, a magical world with its own specific time which contrasts with our primary world and time. This gives me the advantage of avoiding the division of fantasy novels into the two above-mentioned text types. Time and space relations are in fact identical in both secondary-world fantasy and time fantasy, and we can discern the particular features of the genre and its evolution much better if we refrain from the division.[9]

A close investigation of the narrative structure of various texts reveals that the principal feature of time fantasy, time distortion, is also present in the secondary-world fantasy. For instance, the most important "rule" of time traveling introduced in *The Story of the Amulet* and used by practically all writers of time fantasy novels is that primary time stands still while the characters are away in the other chronotope. This "rule" is also observed in *The Lion, the Witch and the Wardrobe* and many other secondary-world texts. On the other hand, what is believed to be the principal pattern of the secondary-world fantasy, the passage between the worlds, is most tangible in time fantasy. The passage is often connected with patterns like the door, the magic object and the magic helper (messenger). A real or symbolic door between the worlds is assumed to be the most common way of connecting the two worlds. We discover it in secondary-world texts such as *The Lion, the Witch and the Wardrobe* or Alan Garner's *Elidor* (1965), but also in time fantasies like *The House of Arden*, Alison Uttley's *A Traveller in Time* (1939), Philippa Pearce's *Tom's Midnight Garden* (1958) or Barbara Sleigh's *Jessamy* (1967). These are merely two examples of similarity, both of them quite eloquent.

When we examine the evolution of the fantasy genre we discover that there is a prominent general tendency in all types of fantasy novels towards fluid boundaries between reality and the magical world or secondary time, and towards psychological depth. Also, the changes within different text types very clearly influence each other.[10]

The most important feature of the fantasy chronotope is thus its multiplicity: a series of different times and places. Obviously, most often only two chronotopes or time-space dimensions—primary and secondary—are involved. However, some texts imply the possibility of an infinite number of chronotopes. They can be situated in a chain, one after another, as in C.S. Lewis's *The Last Battle* (1956) or Astrid Lindgren's *The Brothers Lionheart*, thus creating "tertiary" chronotopes. Or they can exist parallel, as in many of Diana Wynne Jones's exciting novels, probably the most explicit case being *The Homeward Bounders* (1981) and *The Lives of Christopher Chant* (1988). A universe structured to include an infinity of parallel worlds is quite in keeping with the modern scientific view of the world. Historically, however, the primary and the secondary chronotopes in literature reflect the fundamental division between the sacred and profane space in the early human comprehension of the world.

THE "CLASSICAL" (EPIC) CHRONOTOPE

As I have stated earlier, the chronotope as such is not typical of fantasy. Typically, fantasy utilizes a multiple chronotope, while other literary modes have their own time-space structures.

The epic, or "realistic," children's novel is characterized by the foremost features of epic narrative—a concrete, sometimes also clearly limited space and a relatively long time of action with a beginning and an end. The time is a definite or indefinite past, near or far away. The epic children's book does not use the narrative present tense. *The Secret Garden* (1911) and other books by Frances Hodgson Burnett would seem to be suitable examples.

One Swedish essay on narrative differences in books for boys and books for girls stipulated that male time is linear, while female time is circular.[11] I would like to develop this idea and examine the male and the female chronotope, since time in books for girls and in books for boys is closely connected with place. Not only is male time linear, but male space is open, as books for boys take place outdoors, sometimes far away from home in the wide world. Male narrative time is structured as a series of stations where an adventure is experienced, a task is performed, a trial is passed. Time between these stations practically does not exist. The text can say something like "after many days full of hardships they reached their destination . . . " The male chronotope is thus corpuscular, discontinuous, a chain of different separate time-spaces ("quants") which are held together by a final goal. These separate chronotopes may also correspond to chapters in adventure books: each chapter is self-contained, even if some threads can run from one chapter to another. It is easily observable in classic stories such as Mark Twain's *The Adventures of Tom Sawyer* (1876) or Robert McCloskey's *Homer Price* (1943).

The male chronotope is also expandable, meaning that both time and place can proceed farther and farther away from the starting point (although in practice the protagonist most often returns home between adventures). The male chronotope is determined by the basic premise of the genre, that is, the protagonist's primarily superficial maturation. Male time involves a relatively simple evolution: a child grows up or an adolescent becomes sexually mature in a movement from birth to death.

The chronotope in books for girls is completely different. The space is closed and confined. The action mostly takes place indoors, at home (alternatively at school). Time is cyclically closed and marked by recurrent time indications: ("It was spring again," "It was Christmas again"). Three classical girls' books, *Little Women* (1868), *Anne of Green Gables* (1908) and *Little House in the Big Woods* (1932), are very good illustrations. Any gaps in time can be easily filled by the reader, who knows that it takes time for plants to grow or for snow to thaw, that the school year is full of homework, that housework is the same year in and year out. Female narrative time is often extended to several years with certain recurrent points. The chronotope is continuous both in time and space. Spatial movement in girls' books means merely a change from one confined space to another likewise confined one—for instance, from the parents' home to a boarding school, from the heroine's childhood home to her husband's home, to "the doll house," an image often used by contemporary writers trying to break this pattern; one example is Maud Reuterswärd's *A Way From Home* (1979), the Swedish title of which is "The Girl and the Doll House."

The female narrative chronotope is also based on our conceptions of male and female nature (whether these conceptions are true or false is another question). Female time is circular, follows the cycle of the moon, and consists of recurrent, regular events of death and resurrection, seasonal changes, and so on. This is primitive, primeval time, nature's own time: "to every thing there is a season and a time" (Eccl 3:1). Linear male time is a product of enlightenment and is the spirit of action and progress.

In girls' books development occurs in inner space and affects the spiritual maturity of the protagonist. This inner movement is more difficult to discover, whence the charge that books for girls are totally static. Compared to the action-packed male chronotope, books for girls are apparently less dynamic in the sense of "less eventful." However, certain feminist literary scholars have revealed this inner type of dynamism, which is governed primarily by woman's and nature's cyclical time.

I do not mean that every book for boys and every book for girls corresponds to these two models. Like any model, they are merely abstractions or ideal images, in this case of the time-space organization of the two book types. In concrete texts we find many deviations, which we sometimes apprehend as a breaking of genre norms and sometimes as welcome experiments. As in all other areas, in chronotope structures of children's books of the past ten to twenty years there is also a merging of male and female, a disintegration of the epic chronotope, and some bold innovations.

THE CHRONOTOPE IN PARALITERATURE

Among the many features which characterize paraliterature ("side-literature," commonly called popular or mass literature) for children it is often underscored that the characters never grow up. For instance, William in Richmal Crompton's series is still eleven after thirty books; and Nancy Drew is forever young, although her age actually was changed from sixteen to eighteen to comply with driving licence regulations in different American states. Another feature of paraliterature is that the action often takes place during summer vacations. Although this may not be true of every book, we can still agree that time in paraliterature is static; it simply does not exist. Everything that is changeable—and which therefore leads to existential questions unimportant to paraliterature— is banished. The tokens of time in settings are also rare, and we can still read certain series from the 1930s without noticing that they belong to another epoch.

Unlike the chronotope in books for girls, which is also static, at least superficially, there is no cyclical movement in paraliterature (for instance, there are no seasonal changes) and no inner development in the protagonists. There is seldom any chronological order in the stories, so that every book and sometimes even every chapter can be read separately in any order. It is interesting to observe, therefore, that while certain features of paraliterature have been fruitfully used by contemporary children's writers, as I have shown in a previous chapter, nobody seems to be inspired by the static chronotope of paraliterature. I regard this as yet another confirmation of the genre character of the chronotope; generally speaking, what is significant about paraliterature is its chronotope structure rather than its motifs, characters or (absence of) issues.

My discussion of paraliterary texts has naturally been very general, and there may be a number of examples which contradict my points, since any particular text can deviate from the general trend. It is also easy to define more precisely chronotopes of different paragenres such as the adventure, the detective story, the romance, or science fiction.

THE SOPHISTICATED CHILDREN'S BOOK

The disintegration of the epic chronotope in children's literature coincides with the emergence of polyphony. The plot in children's books becomes a short, cut-out period in a child's life without any logical beginning or end. Very seldom does the action take longer than one year; often it is much shorter. The arbitrariness in the construction of the plot may be concealed by writers of contemporary socially engaged novels, who choose to start or end the book with the beginning or end of the school year or school vacation, or with Christmas or a birthday party. From the point of view of composition this may seem logical, but it is not necessarily psychologically plausible. Such festive occasions offer an excellent means of introducing characters or bidding them farewell (once again a "carnival procession"), but it is not sure that the protagonist's dilemma is solved exactly at these points. They do not have the same function as weddings in fairy tales or romances, where marriage is a logical solution and rewards the protagonists for their trials.

Note also the composition in fictitious diaries: the plot starts merely because the protagonist has bought or received as a present a notebook to keep a diary in; when the notebook is full the story ends, sometimes quite abruptly, to create an illusion of authenticity.

The closer we come to our own time the more we encounter arbitrary temporal dimensions in children's novels. The title of the Swedish writer Per Nilsson's "Between Waking Up and Going to Sleep" (1986) is a good illustration of this tendency. It emphasizes that for a child, even this very short period of time can contain important, sometimes decisive events. I think we can see parallels to the modernist novels of Joyce among others.

Space in contemporary children's literature is open but limited. It seldom involves going out into the wide world, but is instead restricted to an investigation of nearby surroundings. The Swedish author Barbro Lindgren has described this in a very subtle way in her books about the little girl Sparvel (1976–79): in the little child's perception, the world ends beyond the nearest hill. Moving into a new house, one of the most common motifs in children's literature, does not bring a radical change of chronotope, but merely substitutes a new environment for the old one.

The specific setting in contemporary children's novel is very often a big city. It was first introduced in the young adult novel, and then slowly filtered down into novels for younger children (one Swedish example is "Pelle Jansson—a Boy in the Middle of the City," 1976, by Hans Peterson).

The contemporary young adult novel, which takes the adult book *The Catcher in the Rye* (1951) as one of its models, is characterized by a very compressed time and a big city as the setting. *The Catcher in the Rye* takes place in New York during a few days. The city represents the threatening world of adulthood. The compressed time emphasizes the marginal situation of the young person; the protagonist is in a transitional stage between childhood and grownup life. The majority of Swedish teenage novels take place in city settings, which offer temptations, the life of the gang, and the attractive yet frightening grownup world. In particular Harry Kullman, a one-time runner-up for the Andersen Medal, elaborated this chronotope, where space becomes still more precise and limited. In *The Battle Horse* (1977), for example, it is restricted to "East Side," a prestigious neighborhood in Stockholm. In Swedish books for younger children we can single out Stockholm novels, Gothenburg novels, and so on. The implication is that the place is not merely a background, but an important image or symbol in the text. In Gillian Cross's *Wolf* (1991), for example, London is portrayed as a city hostile to children and is the setting for cruelties. In American children's literature we can probably identify the New York novel (*Harriet the Spy*, 1964, by Louise Fitzhugh), the San Francisco novel and even more specifically, the Chinatown novel (Lawrence Yep's *Dragonwings*, 1975 and *Child of the Owl*, 1977).

Paradoxically, the big city chronotope is not as prominent in children's literature of the urbanized United States; what we seem to find instead is the opposite, small-town chronotope of, for instance, Katherine Paterson, Patricia MacLachlan or Jerry Spinelli. The chronotope of American children's literature is further evidence that the chronotope is a powerful instrument for revealing specific traits of certain groups of texts. Further, Gary Paulsen's very special chronotope, a combination of a limited natural landscape and a relatively short time (*Hatchet*, 1987, *The Island*, 1988), must be viewed as this particular writer's treatment of timespace, and a most welcome innovation. I am, however, disturbed by the chronotope in *Jacob Have I Loved* (1980) by Katherine Paterson: the combination of an isolated island and a prolonged time span does not, in my view, create the chronotope structure necessary to carry the psychological content of the novel.

A limited time of action is emphasized in titles like *Hilding's Summer* (1965) by Barbro Lindgren, *Summer of the Swans* (1970) by Betsy Byars, *Tulla's Summer* (1973) by Rose Lagercrantz, or *That Early Spring* (1974) by Gunnel Beckman. Such "seasonal" titles convey a sense of the rapid passage of time which is normally not characteristic of children's literature. The temporal pattern in all these texts is always used in combination with a specific spatial pattern, often a confined space.

Thus compressed time and a concrete, often limited place are the typical chronotope of a modern children's novel. It reflects the insecure, detached existence of today's children, but it also marks a change of point of view: writers more often take the child's side, and children are believed, to a higher degree than adults, to live "here and now," to have difficulties perceiving their existence in a larger spatial and temporal perspective.[12]

THE SECONDARY CHRONOTOPE IN "REALISTIC" NARRATIVES

We can apply the notion of the primary and secondary chronotopes to other texts than fantasy, that is, texts that lack supernatural elements. This may be superfluous when there are just a few flashbacks in the text and when the time shifts are clearly marked, for instance by a phrase like "Twenty years earlier, when I was a child. . . . " But as soon as more complicated temporal patterns are involved, the chronotope can be a useful instrument. In Peter Pohl's *Johnny My Friend* (1985) we are confronted by very intricate time shifts. There is a primary time, the present, where the first-person narrator Chris is talking to a police officer. This primary time takes probably an hour. The secondary time, the past, takes just over a year, during which Chris meets, gets to know and loses Johnny. There are no clearly marked temporal changes (the narrative alternates between past and present tenses), and at the end the two times merge.

Chris's secondary time is regular and exact. His first encounter with Johnny happens on 31 August 1954 at 18:32. Time is not only governed by Chris's pedantical interest in detail, but also by school rules, family habits and the boy gang's routines. The structure of the chronotope reflects the protagonist's individual life style. The primary time, by contrast, is blurred and confused, for it is governed by the unexpected event of Johnny's disappearance. The space is in both cases the same and very concrete: every place mentioned can be found on a map of Stockholm.

Further, Johnny apparently has a special time which does not pass at the same pace as Chris's. At certain points Johnny simply ceases to exist, vanishing into his own chronotope. A somewhat far-fetched but not altogether impossible interpretation of Johnny is that he is an "alien child," a creature from another, secondary world into which the door of a shop functions as a passage. My interpretation of Johnny's part in the story as a catalyst for Chris's development allows him to have such a background, and Chris's meditation on alternative worlds supports this idea.

Katherine Paterson's *Bridge to Terabithia* (1978) is an example of the secondary chronotope in a realistic text with a more pronounced spatial element. The possibility of the division into primary and secondary chronotope is once again the essential distinction between sacred and profane space. Terabithia is a sacred place for the protagonists, and the passage is as clearly marked and as dramatic as in most fantasy novels. It is natural that Terabithia should also have its own time, which allows the two children to be totally oblivious of the world around them. We assume that children can live a whole life in their imaginary world within a few hours. Helen Cresswell, the author of several children's novels involving time displacement, comments on the young readers' specific perception of time:

> They [children] have a different sense of time from ourselves, they have a different dimensional view of the world. When Johnny comes in late for dinner and we say "Where the devil have you been?" and he says "Nowhere" and we say "What on earth have you been doing?" and he says "Nothing," we get irritated because we feel here is some kind of subtle threat to our view of time and clockwork and timetables.[13]

It is surely this assumed ability of children to perceive time as either compressed or expanded depending on what they are doing which allows writers to venture on extremely complicated time patterns, both in fantasy and in what are generally believed to be realistic narratives.

In the classical historical novel (Walter Scott, Robert Louis Stevenson, Alexandre Dumas) the chronotope is very concrete. The real historical figures—kings, politicians, army leaders, etc.—make it easy for the readers to relate the events to history; most often there is also a clear indication of place, since the plot demands historically correct descriptions.

The contemporary historical novel for young readers, the emergence of which may be ascribed to Rosemary Sutcliff (*The Eagle of the Ninth*, 1954), has a totally different structure and other purposes. Very seldom does it contain great historical events such as revolutions, military campaigns and battles; even when it does, the primary focus is not on kings and heroes but on ordinary people. Paula Fox's *The Slave Dancer* (1973) can serve as an illustration. In particular, the masculine viewpoint of the earlier historical novel has been challenged by contemporary writers in favor of the "her-story." *Lyddie* (1991) by Katherine Paterson is among the most recent examples.

Because of this, the time and place of the modern historical novel for young readers become less prominent. Sometimes they are directly mentioned, sometimes suggested; we can get a glimpse of some well-known event or person which gives us some idea of the time and place of action, but it is of subordinate significance, since seasonal changes in nature influencing plowing and the harvest were more important to people than concrete dates and the linear progress of time. Space as well was limited for people earlier in history, and local place names were more important than distant cities and countries. The specific chronotope in modern historical novels for children is different from the classical one.

In two comprehensive volumes on the contemporary historical novel for young readers, the Swedish scholar Ying Toijer-Nilsson suggests a terminological distinction between the historical novel proper and what she calls the retrospective novel.[14] The distinction is consistent and very practical. We can define as historical such novels in which the time of action lies beyond the writer's life span (for instance, American frontier-life novels today), while retrospective novels describe the time beginning with the writers' childhoods and thus within their experience: for instance, *One-Eyed Cat* (1984) by Paula Fox or *Unclaimed Treasures* (1984) by Patricia MacLachlan. Among these, we can again single out more specific chronotopes such as the World War II chronotope in British children's fiction: *Fireweed* (1969) by Jill Paton Walsh, *Carrie's War* (1973) by Nina Bawden, *Blitzcat* (1989) or *The Kingdom by the Sea* (1990) by Robert Westall.

Ying Toijer-Nilsson does not make use of the chronotope notion, since she is interested in other aspects of the novels than purely temporal structures, but her arguments are fully in accordance with the idea of the chronotope as a genre category; the difference between two very similar genres depends upon the chronotope. Further, historical time in this view is relative rather than absolute, that is, independent of the time when the book was written. One very useful consequence of this distinction is that we avoid problems with older novels, such as Harriet Beecher Stowe's *Uncle Tom's Cabin* (1852), which were written about the writer's own time but are apprehended today as "historical."

In pseudo-historical novels such as Lloyd Alexander's Westmark trilogy, neither time nor place is indicated. We can guess about the historical epoch—the eighteenth century, the time of great rebellions in Europe—from temporal hints in the text, provided that we are familiar with them, but there is no concrete country where the rebellion described takes place, and the beggar queen Augusta/Mickle has no historical model. Literary space in the Westmark novels is a collective image of past Europe. In another pseudo-historical suite, the Vesper novels, Alexander chooses to give his places romantically sounding, half-mythical names such as Illyria, Drachenberg, El Dorado and Jedera. However, in *The Philadelphia Adventure* (1990), the suite is concluded at a concrete geographical spot, even though the events have the same adventurous tone as in the previous, wholly fictitious countries. Neither the Westmark nor the Vesper novels are fantasy merely because the chronotope is fictitious. Place has the same function as Yoknapatawpha in William Faulkner's novels.

Joan Aiken's pseudo-historical novels, beginning with *The Wolves of Willoughby Chase* (1962), present a different pattern. According to the writer's note, they take place in a "period of English history that never happened—shortly after the accession to the throne of Good King James III in 1832. At this time, the Channel Tunnel from Dover to Calais [had been] recently completed . . ." (p 6). This is a subjunctive chronotope, a "might-have-been," with a concrete geographical reality as its spatial component. The series is treated as fantasy in many reference sources, but it has such a clearly different structure that it is not easy to suggest a genre label. The "Gothic fantasies" proposed in *The Oxford Companion to Children's Literature* is not adequate either.[15]

John Christopher's *The Prince in Waiting* trilogy (1970–72) takes place in the future after World War III, and his world combines remnants of modern civilisation with a medieval social order and mythical thinking. This series has a more pronounced character of science fiction, or rather dystopia, than Peter Dickinson's *Changes* novels (1968–70) with which it is sometimes compared. In Dickinson's texts, the magical aspect of the chronotope is much stronger.

The three series—Alexander's, Aiken's and Christopher's— illustrate three different hypothetical chronotopes involving the uncertain past, the alternative past and the possible future, which, to my mind, cannot be described as fantasy, and here the notion of the chronotope enables us to see the genre boundaries more distinctly and to evaluate more adequately the individual writer's special treatment of time and space.

PICTUREBOOKS

How do time and place indications function in visual communication? Our orientation in time and space is based primarily on *indexical* semiotic signs, which are mostly verbal—that is, words like "here," "there," "right," "left," "on," "under," "behind," "yesterday," "three hours later," etc. With the help of these signs time and place can be marked in literary works.

The visual sign system is in fact incapable by itself of indicating time. Not even in temporal visual languages such as film are there any direct ways to show the flow of time. This can be achieved either through verbal messages such as "three years later," or through the characters' dialogue in remarks like "Tomorrow we are going . . . " often followed by a fadeout. The flow of time can be indicated visually through pictures of clocks or of sunrise and sunset. Maurice Sendak's *Where the Wild Things Are* (1963) is often used to illustrate the different perception of time by children and adults. In Max's imaginary time he travels "through night and day and in and out of weeks and almost over a year" and then back "over a year and in and out of weeks and through a day and into the night" (verbal indication!), while his mother's time stands still, and when Max comes back he finds his supper warm and waiting for him. But the visual signs question the mother's (or the adult co-reader's) "objective" time. There is a new moon in one of the first pictures in the book and a full moon in the last, which means that some time has also passed in the mother's "real" world.

In order to convey movement and thus the flow of time picturebooks must resort to a sequence of pictures. If the same figure is first depicted under a tree and in the next picture in the tree, we read this as meaning that the figure has climbed the tree, which we know from experience takes some time. The sequence thus conveys the flow of time.[16] If this is in addition explicitly stated in the verbal text, information becomes redundant, which weakens its overall impact. Many wordless picturebooks make use of sequences to convey temporal relations; here may be mentioned Jan Ormerod's *Sunshine* (1981) and *Moonlight* (1981).

The Wild Baby—*circular time; illustration by Eva Eriksson*

Another means of depicting the flow of time in a static picture is through the simultaneous principle, which was often used in medieval art. A good example is the first page in *The Wild Baby* (1980) by Barbro Lindgren, illustrated by Eva Eriksson, where the baby is depicted six times in a wild circular motion corresponding to the verbal text: ". . . he always disobeyed her, he was reckless, loud and wild."[17] The circular composition emphasizes that the events depicted here are repeated again and again over a long period. If a single linear movement must be conveyed, the solution can resemble Sven Nordqvist's in his books, where Mercury the cat moves rapidly in a wild trajectory across the page and is shown at several stages of the movement.

Festus and Mercury—linear time; illustration by Sven Nordqvist from Pancake Pie

On the other hand, picturebooks are naturally well suited to the description of the spatial aspects of the chronotope, including both indoor scenes and landscape, the mutual spatial relations of figures and objects, their relative size, position, and perspective.[18]

The picturebook chronotope is thus characterized by the dominance of the spatial aspect and limited possibilities of expressing time. Many picturebooks from the 1960s and 1970s are clearly anchored in the "here-and-now," while later and more imaginative picturebooks explore new and exciting chronotope solutions. One such solution is the parallel actions in John Burningham's *Shirley* books (1977–78), which once again reflect the dual address of modern children's books.

TOVE JANSSON'S CHRONOTOPE

To illustrate the discussion above, let us examine how individual writers construct their chronotopes.

Like many other modernistic children's books, Tove Jansson's Moomin novels are extremely difficult to assign to any specific genre. One can choose to single out a dominant genre in each text,[19] but this will simply stress the unique character of each novel and blur the features they have in common. Such an approach will in any case not provide insights into the specific way in which Tove Jansson treats time and space. This problem arises if we unconditionally want to define Moomin novels as fantasy. The Moomin world is closed and self-contained, without the contact with the primary world which is presupposed by the definition of fantasy. It can be apprehended as "high fantasy," that is, a mythical world, but unlike Tolkien's Middle Earth, Ursula Le Guin's Earthsea or Lloyd Alexander's Prydain, with few exceptions (for example, the magic hat in *Finn Family Moomintroll*, 1949), the Moomin world contains no magic.

The primary world which in other "high fantasies" lies beyond the text is also present in Tove Jansson's novels. There is quite obviously another, "ordinary" world beyond the Moominvalley, and the inhabitants of this ordinary world are humans. There is one text in the Moomin suite which describes direct contact between the primary and the secondary world: the picturebook *The Dangerous Journey* (1977). This book dispels any doubt that the Moominvalley is a secondary world like Narnia or Elidor, a world that ordinary humans can reach through magic, in this case with the help of magical eyeglasses. The Swedish scholar Boel Westin has observed the circular composition of the first page— a round, framed picture which on the next page is opened and transformed into an endless Moomin landscape, but then limited again in the circular picture on the last page.[20] I also regard this round picture as a window for us who are outside the Moomin world and merely allowed to look into it. Susanna, however,

A window into Moominvalley—from The Dangerous Journey

is granted the privilege of entering it. The implication is that the Moomin world is open to those who possess the magical key. Some Swedish critics prefer to define only this book as fantasy,[21] whereas I see *The Dangerous Journey* as a confirmation of my interpretation of the whole chronotope structure of the Moomin novels. There are two more pieces of circumstantial evidence, both of them extra-literary and one something of a curiosity, which support this conclusion. In a hotel lobby in the Finnish town of Hamina there is a mural painted by Tove Jansson. It is a realistic seashore landscape, but in the foreground are some miniature Moomin figures. The other indirect evidence is television films not based on any of the Moomin novels but written by Tove Jansson. In one of them a Swedish king is viewing Moominvalley (situated, supposedly, in Finland) through a telescope—a parallel to Susanna's eyeglasses, or a transformation of the archetypal magic crystal.

As to the "reality" of the Moomin world, we are given a clue at the end of the picturebook: "She never learned whether everything really happened, but as far as I understand it does not matter." Exactly as in so many contemporary fantasy novels, readers are allowed to choose their own interpretation model ("real" or "dream"), but it does not change anything in the essence of the book, which is still about conquering your own bad temper and your own fears.

The temporal aspect of Moomin novels is also special. As in traditional paraliterary adventure books, time stands still. Moomintroll and the other characters do not grow up, and nothing ever changes in the Moominvalley. We learn from the very first book, "The Little Trolls and the Big Flood" (1945; not available in English), that Moominpappa has not always lived in the Moominvalley, and from *The Exploits of Moominpappa* (1950) we know that pappa once was young and unmarried (consequently, Moomintroll did not exist at that time). But this is also another chronology—memory time, secondary time—which is marked off from the neverending present beginning with the arrival in Moominvalley, the point zero of Moomin history.

The Moomin chronotope is static, and what little time movement there is is cyclical—an eternal summer interrupted by winter hibernation. Winter is allowed to enter the story temporarily, with all the fun and threat that Moomintroll experiences in *Moominland Midwinter* (1957). The Groke invades the summer idyll with her abominable coldness as a reminder of winter and the flow of time (which is implied to be moving towards the end, towards death). A sudden snow storm is also depicted in *The Dangerous Journey*. Incidentally, storms are a recurrent image in Tove Jansson's adult prose. Still, winter is far away and forgotten in the timeless summer paradise of the Moominvalley.

In *Moominvalley in November* (1970) time suddenly starts moving. Autumn is the time of withering, decay, and farewell, which, however, is necessary to prepare for the coming winter (death) and spring (resurrection). The Moomin family is absent in this novel, and at the end of the book they are on their way—back home, or just passing by the horizon to take a last glimpse of the childhood idyll before leaving it forever?

This can be interpreted as an awakening from the eternal enchantment, a return to reality. *Moominvalley in November* is the last full length Moomin book, but I disagree with W. Glyn Jones, who in his book on Tove Jansson states that it represents a definite step towards "real" adult authorship.[22] Moominvalley is not a paradise-like place of escape, and Tove Jansson does not abandon it but goes through the valley and on into another, no less distorted and carnivalized world in which the same characters appear in new disguises.

At the risk of sounding far-fetched, I would venture to state that Tove Jansson's adult novels are additional evidence of the existence of human reality beyond Moominvalley in her universe. I view her novels as periphrases or rewritings of the Moomin novels containing the same themes, character types, style and tone. Much as we catch a glimpse of the primary chronotope behind Moominvalley, we can see Moominvalley in the periphery of adult prose, just a few creeks away.

ALAN GARNER'S CHRONOTOPE

Alan Garner is one of the few writers who have managed to unite magical secondary worlds with a real landscape which can be found on a map. In his comprehensive study "Visits to British Children's Books Landscapes"[23] the Swedish scholar Göte Klingberg discusses the two places in Cheshire of overall importance in Garner's works, or at least in his *Red Shift* (1973): the folly on Mow Cop and the church in the village of Barthomley. Klingberg and other scholars point out that all of Garner's novels except *The Owl Service* (1967), which is set in Wales, take place within the very limited area where Garner himself was born, grew up and is still living.

Garner's first two novels, *The Weirdstone of Brisingamen* (1960) and *The Moon of Gomrath* (1963), are connected to Alderley Edge, a giant cliff in the middle of a rather flat landscape which is one of the main natural attractions in Cheshire. The inhabitants of the nearby village of Alderley Egde often go there on quiet Sunday outings, and children love to play in the exciting caves and tunnels of abandoned copper mines. Some of the attractions, like the "Druid Stones" or "The Wizard's Well," were commissioned by a romantically minded landowner and built by no other than Garner's grandfather, a mason portrayed in *The Stone Book* quartet. They are thus not genuine cult places, but in Garner's chronotope in *The Weirdstone of Brisingamen* they acquire a magical atmosphere. Alderley Edge is a natural place for Susan and Colin's magical adventures when the jewel in Susan's bracelet proves to be a powerful amulet coveted both by good and evil forces.

The landscape in *The Weirdstone of Brisingamen* is depicted so carefully that the action can be followed on an ordinary tourist map. There is also a map in the book, which, unlike most maps in books of fiction, represents a really existing landscape. The magical world of Garner's books is projected upon the real world, and the boundary between the two is practically non-existent.

The novel begins with the Legend of Alderley, a typical local legend which is connected with the landscape but at the same time using the wandering motif of knights sleeping in a cave. The legend is set at Thieves' Hole, a deep crevice on Alderley Edge. In the vicinity there is a pub called "The Wizard" whose signboard carries an illustration from the legend. In the novel, Susan and Colin discover the pub and the sign during their first walk on the cliff. They also see The Wizard's Well and read the incantation carved in the stone. In reality, the inscription was carved by Garner's grandfather; "wizhard" is therefore spelt with the "noble and romantic letter h," although the word has never been written this way, not even in Old English:

> Drink of this
> And take thy fill
> For the water falls
> By the wizhards will. (p. 23)

The children escape from the svarts, who are eager to get hold of Susan's bracelet; they run up a steep hill and see a figure between two enormous stones: this is The Iron Gate, a passageway into the underground cave, and the figure is the wizard Cadellin himself, the protector of the sleeping knights. Every detail in the magical landscape corresponds to real ones. Garner did not have to invent his magical country, for all the exciting landscape features were there waiting to be used: the Druid Stones (fake, as we know, but still excellent in a book), where Grimnir the giant takes the bracelet from Susan; The Castle Rock, where the children meet the wizard again; but especially the caves through which they run and crawl with no hope of ever seeing daylight again.

In this novel as in the sequel there is a clear sense of Garner's obsession with his native district and its numerous grave-mounds, standing stones and churches oriented according to sunrise on the vernal equinox. These details are woven so subtly into the story—especially in *The Moon of Gomrath*—that they often hamper the reader in following the plot. It is probably for this reason that Garner has expressed dissatisfaction with the two books. They were planned as a trilogy, but the third novel never appeared. Instead, a slightly new chronotope was introduced in *Elidor* (1965). The novel begins in the ruins of a church in the outskirts of Manchester. According to Garner himself, the setting was inspired by the ruined Coventry Cathedral. Today there is a new, modern building beside the ruin, and on one of the walls there is a suggestive statue of St. Michael. It became a model for the wizard Malebron in *Elidor*, a most ambivalent figure who is prepared to sacrifice anything for the good of his country. He entices the four siblings into the magical world which, incidentally, is the only Other World in Garner's novels—that is, another world beyond the ordinary British landscapes, beyond all time and space. The connections between the chronotopes are places of ruin and devastation where the boundary has been destroyed or weakened. Characteristically, the street where one of the passages emerges is called Boundary Lane.

When the children return to reality, they carry with them the four treasures of Elidor, which they bury in their garden. But the magical powers of the treasures (or their radioactivity, according to Garner's own half-rational explanation) enables the enemy in Elidor to trace them in the primary world. Because of Roland's fatal mistake, the front door of the house can serve as a passage from Elidor into the security of the real world. The threat from evil forces here is felt much stronger than if it had remained in the secondary world, as in Narnia books. The threat becomes still stronger from the knowledge that Garner is describing his own childhood home in Alderley, and the door that resists the evil forces from Elidor is the very same door that he himself has passed through thousands and thousands of times. The evil thus intrudes right into our own lives.

In contrast, the land of Elidor itself is very vaguely described and is something of a dream realm, especially as compared to the colorful magical world of *The Weirdstone of Brisingamen*. It is easy to imagine Elidor existing not only in another spatial but also in another temporal dimension. Here there is a link from Garner's first books over *Elidor* to *Red Shift*, a novel about the continuity of time and the simultaneous existence of all times. This thematic thread corresponds to a direct connection in the real landscape: Mow Cop, the important landmark in *Red Shift*, can be seen in clear weather from Alderley Edge like a dream castle in a haze. This is the prototype of the magical castles in *Elidor*.

The *Stone Book* quartet (1976–78), Garner's latest work except for several collections of folktales, were initially four related stories which many critics have praised as Garner's best and regarded as his final conquest of realism. At that time "realism" in children's literature was still a measure of quality. Superficially these are indeed realistic stories about several generations of the Garner family, but it would be a mistake to view the quartet as everyday realism. Everything that is typical of Garner as an artist, including his interest in the mystical and the inexplicable and the legends, rites and landscapes of his childhood, is present in the four stories and plays a most significant role. Here the real and the magical landscapes are intertwined. In the first part, *The Stone Book* (1976), there are at least two events in the secondary chronotope: Mary rides the church weathercock and then enters a cave where she discovers the stone book of the title—a picture of a bull and an imprint of a hand, identical with her own. This is a motif developed from the short story 'Feel Free.' The real church is in the middle of the village of Alderley (called Chorley in the book), very close to the door to Elidor. The cave, Engine Vein, is situated on the same cliff where the whole action of *The Weirdstone of Brisingamen* takes place. Like the other caves, it is not natural but a remnant from an old mine, but in the context of Garner's magical landscapes just a little imagination is needed to see a whole world of mystical creatures inside.

The sequels also have connections to both magical and real landscapes. The skillful stonemason Robert, Mary's father—in reality Alan

Garner's grandfather—had a mason's mark representing an arrow which can still be found on some stones in a stone wall north of the village. When this wall is built in *Granny Reardun* (1977), Joseph realizes that he does not want to become a mason, but a smith. Finally Robert, Joseph's son, discovers in *The Aimer Gate* (1978) his great grandfather's mark and their common name high up in the roof beam of the church tower—that is, the same church in Alderley where Mary once rode on the weathercock. Everything is skillfully connected in the quartet, and the landscape is the mystical link to everything in a way that reminds of Garner's earlier, more overtly fantastic books.

While place is of overall importance for Garner and the same magical landscape superimposed on the real appears in all of his books, time is negligible, in the sense that his protagonists move freely between different historical periods. The time of action is always the present, however, and therefore the banal formula of "here and now" is the most adequate description of Garner's chronotope.

THE CHRONOTOPE AS A SEMIOTIC SIGN

Chronotopes are abstract constructions, models that we use to investigate how space and time relations are manifested in concrete literary texts. In semiotic terminology, chronotopes are signs which signify something else. They are *iconic* signs, which are based on the similarity between the signs and the reality behind them. The various chronotope models which translate verbal into visual signs can be represented as shown in Figs. 5–8.

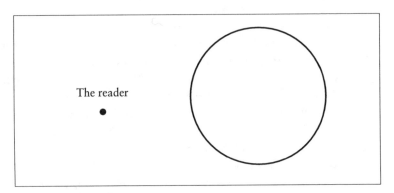

The reader

Fig. 5. The folktale chronotope

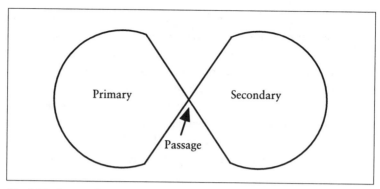

Fig. 6. *The fantasy chronotope*

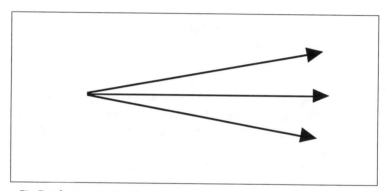

Fig. 7. *Adventure "male" chronotope*

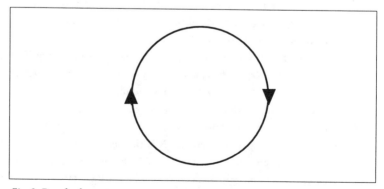

Fig. 8. *Female chronotope*

These figures are examples of the *first degree of iconicity,* meaning that the signs are directly connected with the things they signify.

There is also *a second degree of iconicity* in semiotics, in cases where the connection between the sign and the signified is indirect, or metaphorical. It is extremely difficult to discover second-degree iconicity in literary works, and as far as I know this has only been done on a very modest scale on small literary forms, like poetry. Some idea of second-degree iconicity can be gained, for instance, from *Winnie-the-Pooh* (1926), where the graphical layout of the text indicates Kanga's jumping or Pooh's fall from the tree (see Fig. 9).

	this				take		
"If	is		shall		really	to	
		flying I		never			it."

Fig. 9.

I have discovered one striking example of a chronotope as a second-degree iconic sign. In Alan Garner's novel *Red Shift* (1973) three plots are developed during different times. Time and eternity are the central images of the novel, and these are expressed in symbols such as fossils, the light from faraway stars, and so on.[24] This novel, however, has another, extremely interesting aspect of the chronotope structure. The two outermost plots take exactly nine months each. The Roman episode starts with the young priestess being raped by Roman soldiers, and at the end of the book she is about to give birth to her child. In the present time, nine months pass from the first conversation between Jan and Tom by the side of the M6 highway and their farewell at Crewe railway station. Yet the middle episode, the seventeenth century, takes just a few hours. Is this accidental? Alan Garner's own explanation, which is a brilliant illustration of a writer's conscious work with signs and symbols, is that this temporal structure represents a giant hourglass with a narrow passage in the middle, through which time can slowly flow back and forth (see Fig. 10).

This is an excellent example of second-degree iconicity. The temporal structure in *Red Shift* is reinforced by the global spatial structure, where the three plots take place within a huge equilateral triangle with its corners at the church in Barthomley, the folly at Mow Cop and Alan Garner's own house near the Jodrel Bank telescope. Mow Cop with the fake ruin has a very important spatial function: "It is the netherstone of the world. The skymill turns on it to grind stars" (p. 64). From Mow Cop the axis of the universe goes to the star Delta Orionis, which is the intersection of time and space in the novel.

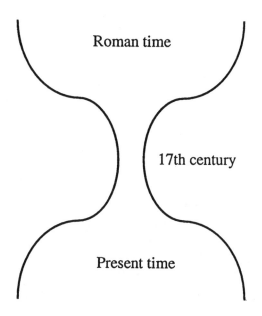

Fig. 10.

THE TOKENS OF OUR TIME

The various chronotope structures in literary works are based on our concepts of time and space, which are historically and culturally determined and therefore changeable. Since they are concepts, they belong to the category we defined earlier as mental culture. In other words, chronotopes in literature are *mentifacts*. One important feature in the chronotope of contemporary children's literature, however, consists of the many recurrent images which are clearly dated and contribute to the formation of time and space of the novel. These are concrete expressions for chronotope structures and function on a different level; that is, they are *artifacts*, material objects associated with this or that chronotope. Magic amulets, swords, invisibility capes, flying carpets and other magical objects in myth, fairy tale and fantasy are artifacts of the magical chronotope. Modern chronotopes have their own artifacts.

The Russian critic Mikhail Epstein has suggested a notion that seems to be extremely useful in children's literature research. The notion is *kenotype*, a term coined by Epstein from the Greek "kainos"—"new" and "typos"—"image."[25] In the system of cultural concepts kenotype should be seen as an opposition to *archetype*.[26] Unlike archetypes in Jungian philosophy and Jung-inspired literary criticism, kenotypes have no analogies in the prehistorical unconscious. Epstein argues that they are cognizable structures from modern history, primarily the twentieth century. Among his examples from world literature is Thomas Mann's *The Magic Mountain*, where the mountain itself is an archetypal image while the tuberculosis clinic is a kenotype reflecting a new system of human notions and experiences. Another example, which occurs in many works of fiction, is the sea and the beach. The sea and the seashore are archetypes that have been analysed in numerous critical essays dealing with both children's literature and adult texts.[27] But the beach as a place of recreation and human activity is a kenotype, an expression of man's exploitation of nature, commercialization and ambivalent progress, serving as a warning to humanity that paradise on earth is impossible. Thus according to Epstein, in different metaphysical contexts one and the same physical place can function on both the archetypal and the kenotypal level.

Epstein explains that it is necessary to introduce the notion of kenotype because of the profound abuse of such terms as "archetype" or "mytheme" in modern literary criticism, where these concepts have come to denote any universal textual element with or without connection with the collective unconscious. The primary difference in the nature of these two typological patterns is that the archetype is static, conservative and protective, while the kenotype is variable, self-creative and dynamic. Epstein stresses that the notion of the kenotype does not in any way reject Jung's theory of the unconscious, since Jung himself allowed for sudden changes foreboding historical shifts. Because I think that children's literature research has also recently been invaded by a wave of "archetypal" terminology, I believe the notion of kenotype can help us to put some things into their proper places.

With no ambition to be comprehensive, I would like to discuss some examples of kenotypes in children's literature. First, there is the subway. Here I foresee arguments to the effect that the subway is of course nothing but a modern variant of a cave and as such an obvious archetype. But remember the seashore. It is not the material form of the universal pattern but its function that defines its typological affiliation. The hollow caves of the subway in a modern big city are not the archetypal realm of death and eternal peace, but the locus of human crowds and throngs, motion, activity, contact and conflict. In the Swedish author Gunnel Linde's "Dingo—Robber Without Cops" (1981), the hero, a runaway orphan boy, takes refuge in the Stockholm subway among crowds of people who take no notice of him. The overcrowded modern cave becomes a symbol of hostility and alienation and the helplessness of the child in the world of adults; it is a visible token of our busy and crazy time.

Another noticeable kenotype in children's literature is the bicycle. Here again there are clear parallels with the horse archetype. The horse is the necessary attribute of a mythical or folktale hero and has its origin in totem animals. The bicycle cannot have such a source. It is not alive and cannot play the role of a friend, helper and advisor, as the horse—often a talking horse—does in myth and folktale. In quite a few modern Swedish books the bicycle is in the center, and conflicts around it constitute the plot itself; this is the case, for instance, in a book by Gunnel Linde significantly entitled *Bicycles Don't Grow on Trees* (1979). Also, in many novels bicycles become important images, status symbols and tokens of membership in some particular group. In *Johnny My Friend* (1985) by Peter Pohl skill on a bicycle enables a girl disguised as a boy to establish herself as a rightful member of a boy community. In another recent Swedish junior novel, Mats Wahl's "Maj Darlin" (1988), which has obvious intertextual links to Peter Pohl's book, bicycles function as a source of freedom for the characters, a means of achieving independence from adults, an indispensable part of their lives. It is significant that in both cases the bicycle is depicted on the cover, as the protagonist's central attribute. Both books are retrospective, set in the 1950s, when bicycles were both expensive and desirable gadgets for young Swedes. In modern British and American junior novels the image is transformed into a motorcycle (for instance, in Aidan Chambers's *Dance on My Grave*, 1982) and, further, into a car. One can also recollect similar kenotypal patterns of racing boats or skateboards. Most junior novels with sports as the central motif are definitely kenotypal.

Various modern means of communication are important kenotypes in children's novels. One essay regards telephones as transformations of mirrors, a mirror being one of the most important archetypes.[28] I think, however, that here the critic makes the very mistake that Epstein warns against, which is to perceive archetypal patterns in images that cannot have any connection with the prehistorical human experience. Telephones are modern appliances that enable us to overcome space and time in a way our forefathers could not imagine. But a telephone can equally become a source of separation and anguish, especially when replaced by a telephone answering machine, as in *Red Shift* by Alan Garner. Jan's parents are psychiatrists and have an answering machine because their patients prefer talking to it rather than to living people. In their busy life, the parents and the daughter communicate through the machine as well—it becomes a powerful symbol of total alienation.

Another electronic device depicted in *Red Shift* is the tape-recorder, a clear kenotype which here as well is used as a symbol for misunderstanding and loneliness. Tom's parents give him a tape-recorder for his birthday, but they forget cassettes to play on it. Tom puts on the ear-phones and listens to silence, shutting himself off from the world outside. One of the earlier occurrences of this image is to be found in Ray Bradbury's science fiction novel *Fahrenheit 451*, where the main character's neurotic wife goes around with her ears constantly plugged with miniature ear-phones. It is quite astonishing that since 1954, when Bradbury's novel appeared, this science fiction kenotype has become part of our everyday life, for now we see people of all ages running around with their walkmans.

The typewriter has recently become an interesting kenotype in children's literature. Epstein has a separate section on the typewriter in his book in which he discusses the revolutionary development of creativity and the authorial mentality in our time of typewritten and more and more frequently word-processed fiction. In fact Epstein believes the transition to the typewriter to be as crucial typologically as the transition from oral to written culture.[29]

In children's literature the imitation of the typewritten (or word-processed) narrative creates an atmosphere of credibility, especially when typing errors become prominent stylistic devices, which reflect, for instance, the character's agitated state of mind, as in Gunnel Beckman's *Admission to the Feast* (1969).

In a Swedish series about the girl Mimmi by Viveca Sundvall, the typewriter is an important symbol of inner maturity, a status gadget—and a means of beginning the narrative in a diary form. In the first book, "The Diary of a First-Grader" (1982), Mimmi finds an old typewriter in a garbage bin. Almost at once she feels important:

Today I have become a typewriter-owner. A typewriter-owner is a person who owns a typewriter, and that is what I do.

That the typewriter is more a symbol than an object can be seen in the fact that Mimmi typewrites her diary in a yellow notebook. She does not care to explain how she manages to squeeze the notebook into the typewriter. In the Mimmi omnibus volume (1986) the typewriter is shown on the cover as the character's most essential attribute.

The journey is a major archetypal pattern, but we can clearly see its kenotypal levels in some modern children's novels. Cynthia Voigt's *Homecoming* (1981) is by no means a traditional story of wandering. The children do not go into archetypal woods, mountains or deserts. Their itiner-

VIVECA SUNDVALL

MIMMIS
BOK

Typewriter—a kenotype. Cover by Eva Eriksson to "Mimmi Omnibus"

ary lies through busy and densely populated areas, they follow highways, make stops at camping sites and gasoline stations. The mother disappears in a department store instead of being carried away by a dragon. The department store, perhaps the most striking kenotype in modern culture, is described in *Red Shift* as follows:

> Woolworth's is a toolshed; Boots, a bathroom; The British Home Stores, a wardrobe. And we walk through it, but we can't clean our teeth, or mend a fuse, or change our socks. You'd starve in a supermarket.

The material plenty of a modern department store is not the same as the treasure of the fairy-tale cave; it is hostile and destructive, and like many other kenotypes suggests estrangement and spiritual hunger. A few modern American novels take place entirely in a mall; it would be difficult to invent a better kenotypal image of the world today. See, for instance, Richard Peck's *Secrets of the Shopping Mall* (1979). It is also used parodically in Terry Pratchett's trilogy *Truckers* (1989), *Diggers* (1990) and *Wings* (1990).

Quite a special use of kenotypes is the appearance of modern gadgets as magical objects in fantasy novels: trains taking characters into the past, elevators going straight into other worlds, the flying bed in Mary Norton's *The Magic Bed-Knob* (1945) or the flying rocking chair in Barbara Sleigh's *The Kingdom of Carbonel* (1960).[30] These patterns are transformations, or better still, deconstructions, of archetypal narrative elements such as horses, boats, flying carpets—that is, traditional means of transportation in myths and folktales. However, the modern material form of these objects creates a comical effect in a clash between the archetypal function and the kenotypal expression. As in all postmodern literature, these texts have a strong parodical impact. It is also true of the rich variety of wish-granting objects in contemporary humorous fantasy: walking sticks, umbrellas, jackets, or *The Magic Finger* (1966) by Roald Dahl. One of the earliest examples of such a parodical deconstruction is 'The Magic Fish-Bone' (from *The Holiday Romance*, 1868) by Charles Dickens, a text that abounds in kenotypes: an office, payday, an errand-boy and measles, all clashing perfectly with kings, princesses and fairy godmothers. This use of kenotypes is also marvelously developed by Edith Nesbit in her short tales portraying elevators, Lee-Metford guns, diving bells and the complete works of Dickens and Thackeray in an otherwise traditional fairy-tale surrounding.

What, then, is the point of applying the concept of kenotype in literary research? First, as earlier stated, it is important to make a terminological distinction between archetypes and elements which cannot have any archetypal connections. Second, kenotypes have a clear postmodern tone in texts and are often norm-breaking; in contrast to archetypes in earlier literature, they are tangible tokens of our time. It is essential to realize that kenotypes are precisely tokens built up by time and space structures at once, not simply time-determined signs or elements of modern surroundings. Kenotypes are parts of chronotope structures and can therefore be related to certain genres (for instance, jeans in so called "jeans prose") and carry a strong symbolic charge. An examination of kenotypes in children's literature must therefore be a significant part in the study of chronotopes.

SUMMING UP

A chronotope—the unity of time and space in the text—is a formal category, an instrument to be used for text analysis. Once again, I see its primary advantage to lie in the idea of a chronotope as a genre category, for this enables us to discern specific features of certain text types, especially those that are very difficult to define on the basis of conventional genre categories. I have tried to show this in the distinction I draw between fairy tale and fantasy, between male and female texts, "quality" books and paraliterature, historical and retrospective novels. On the other hand, the conventional categorization of texts as "fantasy" and "realism" can be questioned when similar chronotopes are found in both.

Further, studying the evolution of time-space relations in children's literature allows us once again to state that narrative structures are becoming more and more complicated. From relatively simple structures with a concrete place and a logically arranged, chronological action in epic stories, the chronotope develops into an intricate network of temporal and spatial relationships, which better reflect our own chaotic existence. The merging of genres outlined in the previous chapter naturally has an effect on the writer's construction of time and space. The concept of kenotypes, or "new-images," contributes to the description of contemporary chronotopes in children's books. Last but not least, a particular writer's chronotopes can be seen more clearly.

NOTES

1. Bakhtin, 1981, p. 84.
2. Ibid.
3. Rebecca Lukens, one of the few scholars who discusses literary categories in children's literature, has a section on "setting," but not on time (Lukens, 1992, pp. 102–199). Edström (1982) has two separate chapters on time and place.
4. Bakhtin, 1981, p. 85.
5. Among many interesting studies of the origins of folktale I would mention a less known companion to Vladimir Propp's *Morphology of the Folk Tale*: his "The Historical Roots of the Wonder Tale" (1946), partly translated into English in Propp, 1984.
6. Bakhtin, 1981.
7. See, e.g., Cohen, 1975; Klingberg, 1980; Lynn, 1983; Swinfen, 1984.
8. See Tolkien, 1968.
9. See Nikolajeva, 1988, pp. 66, 79, 88f.

10. For a more comprehensive analysis of time shift patterns see Nikolajeva, 1993.

11. Åhmansson, 1992.

12. I find it fascinating to compare this belief to what we know about the Australian aborigines' perception of "here and now"; however, I have no possibility of pursuing this idea here.

13. Cresswell, 1971, pp. 32f.

14. Toijer-Nilsson, 1987; Toijer-Nilsson, 1989.

15. Carpenter and Prichard, 1984, p. 10.

16. Cf Nodelman, 1988, pp. 158–192. Nodelman pays surprisingly little attention to the temporal issues in picturebooks.

17. The quotation is from the American translation. In the British edition, a whole stanza is added to the wordless Swedish page, repeating *verbally* the visual text—a typical case of redundance and overinterpretation.

18. For a more detailed discussion of this aspect see Moebius, 1990.

19. Such a treatment is present in the most profound study of Tove Jansson's work, by Boel Westin (1988a).

20. Westin, 1985, p. 240; Westin, 1991, pp. 55f.

21. Westin, 1985, p. 237.

22. Jones, 1984.

23. Klingberg, 1987.

24. For some interpretations of *Red Shift* see Chambers, 1973; Gillies, 1975; Philip, 1981, pp. 86–109; McVitty, 1981; Klingberg, 1982; Watson, 1983; Nikolajeva, 1989; Mählqvist, 1992.

25. Most dictionaries also offer spellings of the Greek morpheme as ceno-, caino- and caeno-. I prefer keno- because it is less ambiguous to the ear and more usable in different languages.

26. Epstein, 1988, pp. 388–392.

27. See for instance a discussion of the sea as archetype in Tove Jansson's *Moominpappa At Sea* in Rönnerstrand, 1992.

28. Timenchik, 1988.

29. Epstein, 1988, pp. 393f.

30. For a more detailed discussion see Nikolajeva, 1988, pp. 90f.

6 INTERTEXTUALITY IN CHILDREN'S LITERATURE

Among the most prominent features in contemporary children's books may be noted such as irony, parody, literary allusions, direct quotations or indirect references to previous texts—everything which in recent years has been included in the notion of *intertextuality*, or, if we prefer the original term of Mikhail Bakhtin, *dialogics*.

The notion of intertextuality was introduced in the West by Bakhtin's Bulgarian-born French disciple, Julia Kristeva. Nowadays, Bakhtin's *The Dialogic Imagination* is well known in the West in translation.[1] "Intertextuality" is by no means unambiguous, as literary terms preferably should be, and the intertextual method has given rise to enthusiasm as well as skepticism. While many scholars welcome intertextuality as a revolution in literary criticism and in views on literature as a whole, others are quite suspicious and wonder whether intertextual analysis is merely a new label for the old tried and true comparative method. Indeed, in both approaches texts are treated in juxtaposition to each other. Both the goal and the implication of the intertextual method, however, differ radically from traditional comparativism.

Comparative studies usually focus on the matter of influence. Even today, the great majority of histories of children's literature or author studies offer a "comparison" between texts or evidence of one author being "inspired" by another.

As stated above, Bakhtin himself does not use the term intertextuality; instead he speaks of "dialogics." What he means by this is that literature and art are created in a continuous conversation ("dialogue," "discourse") between creators, in which each new piece of art or literature is a new line in the conversation. Of all the variations on the notion of intertextuality I think this is the most fruitful. The meaning of the text is revealed for the reader or researcher only against the background of previous texts, in a clash between them and the present text.

Obviously, this is not a question of literary influence, as in traditional comparativism. Texts opposed in a comparative analysis are set in a causal relation to each other, the assumption being that one author has been influenced by reading another author. Two texts in an intertextual analysis are equal and are not necessarily presumed to have any direct connection. The relation between them, in contrast, is essential to the origin of the present text. According to the adepts of intertextuality, no artistic texts can be produced without an intertextual confrontation. Unlike comparativism, intertextuality is dynamic, since every line in the dialogue of texts not only looks back at previous texts but forward towards new, yet unwritten texts. Intertextuality does not view literature as a static system of completed texts, but as a movement in which the creation of a text is the crucial moment. While the comparativist is bound by evidence and proof, that is, literary or non-literary sources, the intertextualist builds his argument on the "codes" present within the text.

The notion of dialogics also emphasizes the intention of writers and their active role in the act of writing. We no longer simply state that two or more texts are similar, but try to see what the later writer does with the pattern from the previous text, what transformation the pattern has undergone, and possibly why. We abandon the idea of one author "borrowing" from another, but instead are intent on discovering hidden echoes and latent links. It is characteristic that a study by the Danish scholar Torben Brostrøm, dealing with transformation of folktale patterns in literature, should bear the title "Modern Use of the Folktale, or What the Writer Does" (the title itself is an allusion to the tale by H.C. Andersen: 'What the Father Does is Always the Best').[2] Brostrøm resorts to the intertextual method to show how contemporary writers create their texts *in dialogue* with traditional stories. Folktale as intertext has recently become the object of many exciting studies, from student papers to thick volumes, although not all scholars overtly adhere to the intertextual creed; this area of study has its roots in many different methods.

Some scholars also propose to distinguish between *dialogics* where the relation to a previous text is conscious, and *intertextuality* where it can be both conscious and unconscious.[3] Although this distinction is somewhat vague and often difficult to prove, it is worth contemplating. Further, it has been stressed that, unlike traditional comparativism, intertextuality has proceeded from the examination of what one individual author has borrowed from another individual author.[4] Naturally, such tasks are much more demanding than the traditional comparativist's; many of the hidden echoes in texts are inaccessible, but on the other hand intertextual studies can yield much more exciting results.

Regretfully, children's literature research has a tendency to lag behind general literary theory, and in many reference sources we still find "comparisons" between two texts or read that an author has been "influenced" by another author. Yet intertextual links are often more evident in children's texts than in mainstream literature. John Stephens, who has a chapter on intertextuality in his study *Language and Ideology in Children's Fiction*, suggests that "literature written for children is also radically intertextual because it has no special discourse of its own" but rather "exists at the intersection of a number of other discourses."[5] I would protest against the assertion that children's literature lacks a discourse of its own, but as I am sure is obvious in the chapters above, I certainly agree that contemporary children's literature has found inspiration in various discourses, literary as well as extra-literary. John Stephens discusses some interesting cases of intertextuality in poetry, fractured fairy tales, and fantasy. Perry Nodelman, without overtly using intertextual terminology, also treats children's literature within the context of childhood, popular literature, general literary experience, myth, culture, etc, that is, precisely at the cross-roads of different discourses.[6] In our striving to free children's literature research from purely educational applications, these approaches seem both exciting and fruitful.

Although I myself have also tried to study children's literature in a broader cultural context—for instance, by viewing contemporary fantasy for children as part of the twentieth-century natural science discourse—below I will focus on more specific literary aspects of intertextuality, that is, on the links of literary texts to other literary texts.

OPEN AND HIDDEN DIALOGUE

I will begin with examples of "open" and "hidden" dialogue in children's literature. *Neverland* (1989) by Toby Forward is a modern rewrite of *Peter Pan*, which is written intentionally so that readers recognize the original setting, the characters and the plot pattern. However, one important modern detail is introduced into the text: a computer. The children's adventures in Neverland are determined by outside forces: the father's actions at the computer have immediate consequences for his children within the game.

Staging the story of Peter Pan as a computer game enables the author to pose some essential moral questions. The issue of adults' responsibility, which is negligible in Barrie's story but is especially poignant in our own time, emerges in Forward's text because of the computer intertext. The critic who is tempted to accuse Forward of exploiting a famous plot, therefore, must ask: what is the intention? What does the author make of the plot? Does he add anything essential or simply imitate the old story? Given the scope of criticism on Barrie's portrayal of child psychology,[7] Forward's book is certainly a most interesting fictional contribution to this polemics.

Russell Hoban's *The Mouse and His Child* (1967), one of the most underestimated masterpieces of children's literature, has no direct models. But if we look for latent echoes we will in the first place discover Hans Christian Andersen both in the very idea of using toys as protagonists and in the story of the strange journey and homecoming of the little tin soldier. Present in Hoban's book is Andersen's melancholy refrain "gilding will fade," meaning that all toys sooner or later become broken and are thrown away, as in the tale of the Ball and the Top. The figures that the two toy mice meet in Hoban's book are similar to Andersen's characters: the greedy slave driver Manny Rat, the unreliable Frog, the cunning thinker Muskrat, the self-centered poet Serpentina the turtle. As in Andersen's tale, the toys encounter a great deal of treachery and evil, but also loyalty and unselfish courage. During their adventures and bitter defeat the two mice sustain their Andersenian longing for a home and childish Andersenian hope for a happy ending. There is in fact a happy ending of a sort, at least from the very young reader's viewpoint, but adults cannot but notice its deeply tragic undertones. Nothing will ever be again the same—the toys can never become new again, just as humans cannot become young again. This duality of address to both children and adults is also an Andersenian feature in Hoban's text, but the notion of intertextuality does not oblige me to prove that Hoban has been indeed directly influenced by Andersen.

There are also other literary allusions in Hoban's book, primarily on the adult level, namely to French existentialism and the theater of the absurd in the section where the crows' Art Experimental Theater Group stages "The Last Visible Dog." An empty can of dog food is the central symbol of the story, which would be quite daring in an adult novel as well. Most of these elements are probably forever hidden for the average reader, but together they create a peculiar choir of voices, echoes, and associations which makes the book a remarkable reading experience for both young and old. Intertextuality here functions on a variety of levels.

Intertextual studies show that children's literature is more complex than was earlier believed, and suggest that genres and the works of individual authors can be reexamined.

MYTH AS INTERTEXT

Many children's books use mythological subject matter, and reading becomes more rewarding if the reader is familiar with mythical intertexts. These do not necessarily have to be concrete mythical sources, however, but can consist of mythical thinking, manifested, for instance, in a myth-like organization of time-space relations or a use of the narrative components of myths.

Susan Cooper's *The Dark Is Rising* pentalogy, the first volume of which is *Over Sea, Under Stone* (1965), is partially based on Celtic mythology, and the texts contain many patterns which Anglo-Saxon reader will easily recognize. However, it is more a variation on a theme than a direct insertion of myth into the story. Unlike writers such as Alan Garner or Lloyd Alexander, whose books are based on the Celtic collection of myth *The Mabinogion*, in Susan Cooper's novels there are no concrete mythical sources, and as far as we know she has not done any research for the books. However, myths are part of her general cultural heritage (she studied English literature at Oxford and had J.R.R. Tolkien and C.S. Lewis among her teachers).

In *Greenwitch* (1974) Cooper describes a ritual in which the women of the village make a giant female figure with leaves and branches ("hazel for the framework, hawthorn for the body, rowan for the head"—all trees have magical implications in folk beliefs) and sacrifice it to the sea to ensure good fishing. Although it sounds very authentic, no such ritual exists, and Susan Cooper has simply made it up. Or more precisely, she describes a kind of amalgamated image of many different rites that have existed or still exist at various places in the British Isles.

Cooper's other books similarly lack any direct basis in myths or legends. She makes use of mythical material very freely, blending, reworking and transforming it in a creative and conscious literary method. The most prominent layer is the Arthurian cycle. Merriman the wizard, better known as Merlin, is its central character; he is the only figure who appears throughout the suite and thus holds it together. When Susan Cooper continues the tale and describes the arrival of Pendragon in today's England, she does not violate the original material, since certain versions do mention Arthur's son. However, the name Bran she gives to this mystical person transported from the time of Arthur to our own days comes from another legend.

There are many mythical figures involved in the suite: the Sleepers who will awake when time is ripe; the enigmatic Lady who appears in different shapes and represents the progenitor, the fertility goddess; the horned Hunter; the wise bard Gwion, better known as Taliesin; the evil Grey King. But these figures do not always have the same implications as in original myths.

The magical objects are recognizable too. The grail that is sought, found and lost again in the suite is important in Arthurian legends. However, Susan Cooper emphasizes that her grail is not The Holy Grail. It is illuminating to know that the grail is found in Welsh mythology in the form of the Horn of Plenty together with a sword, a lance and the jewel of wisdom. The combination will be immediately recognized by anyone who has read Alan Garner's *Elidor* (1965). Something similar, a magical cauldron, is central to Lloyd Alexander's Prydain suite.

The Lost Country in *Silver On the Tree* (1977), the last book of the pentalogy, leads our thoughts to the Celtic notion of Annwyn, the realm of death (also described in Alexander's books). But it can also be traced back to the well-known myth of Atlantis, which sank to the bottom of the sea. A variation of this motif has appeared already in *The Wonderful Adventures of Nils* (1906) by Selma Lagerlöf.

The legend of silver mistletoe in an oaktree also comes from Celtic and Norse mythology. But Susan Cooper has interwoven different stories, blended figures and objects from different legends, and, in particular, connected them with modern England. For this reason they acquire a stronger impact than, for instance, C.S. Lewis's Narnia books, in which the struggle takes place in a faraway magical country. This effect is felt especially in *The Dark Is Rising* (1973), where the everyday is very tangible and the threat feels strong and real. The last two books become more and more lost in the mystical and the symbolic. Were it not for the Drew siblings, there would be no links with reality at all in *Silver On the Tree*.

Interestingly, Susan Cooper also adheres to another tradition than the Celtic when she explains the meaning of the six magical signs which are the quest objects in *The Dark Is Rising*. They are representations of the old Indian mandala, "a very ancient kind of symbol dating back to sunworship and that kind of thing—any pattern made of a circle with lines radiating outward or inward" (p. 94). It is not mentioned, however, that the Celts too used the same symbol. The Thetis myth in *Greenwitch* also stands out from the Celtic tradition, but it is interwoven so subtly that Thetis represents just another incarnation of the First Mother.

As John Stephens proposes, children's literature with Arthurian and similar motifs can be intertextually related to something he chooses to call *medievalism*, or medieval discourse.[8] This can be applied to Cooper's books, although it is not necessary to recognize mythical allusions to appreciate them. Swedish children, who do not possess the Anglo-Saxon reader's familiarity with Arthurian legends, can still enjoy them, but the reading experience is doubtless strengthened by such knowledge, and Susan Cooper is aware of the fact. In contrast, when the Swedish writer Gunila Ambjörnson offers her Swedish readers a novel based on the Arthurian cycle—"Thin As Gossamer" (1990)—she apparently miscalculates her Swedish reader's capacity to relate her literary text to its mythical model. The unreasonable number of allusions almost seems ostentatious. The title, incidentally, refers to a phrase from Edith Nesbit.

The key figure of modern fantasy, Edith Nesbit, is a gratifying object for intertextual studies, partly because her works magnificently summarize earlier children's literature, and partly because they pave the way for many English-language children's writers. When she started writing (like the majority of her contemporary women writers, mostly for economic reasons), English children's literature had been for many years dominated by Victorian views on childhood and children's reading; the most popular writers of the time were Mary Molesworth and Juliana Horatia Ewing, who are today not nearly as famous as Nesbit. Their didactic books portray nice, well-behaved children who dutifully live up to Victorian morals. The most appreciated books around the turn of the century, however, were *The Golden Age* (1885) and *Dream Days* (1898) by Kenneth Grahame—the writer who would soon become world-famous for *The Wind in the Willows* (1908). *The Golden Age* was a book for adults about childhood written from the adult point of view, but it was still an attempt to reconstruct the child's way of thinking and seeing the world. This attracted Edith Nesbit's attention, and she was probably one of the first British writers to take the part of the child and use the child first-person narrator endowed with a penetrating and genuine childlike view.

Dream Days, also a novel for adults, contained a separate tale entitled 'The Reluctant Dragon,' a *mundus inversus* tale about a romantically minded dragon with poetic aspirations who does not want to fight St George. This little gem of a tale became a favorite at once, but it would hardly have given rise to the lively "dragon dialogue" still going on today had it not been for Edith Nesbit's enthusiastic contribution. Her dragon tales, first published in magazines, are collected in *The Book of Dragons* (1900). They are very obviously Grahame-inspired, although they develop rather than merely repeat his plot. Nesbit "borrows" the very idea of turning a traditional tale upside down, which also can be traced back to Lewis Carroll and his nonsense worlds. Dragons in Nesbit's tales have nothing against being tamed, princesses are clever and often can save their less intelligent male deliverers from trouble.[9] The essentially new feature in Nesbit's tales, compared with Grahame or George MacDonald, was that she introduced tokens of her own time, such as elevators, telephones, diving bells or cars, into traditional fairy-tale settings. All these details can be apprehended as violations of the genre norms.

'Melisande' is rich in allusions. The first model one thinks of is naturally Lewis Carroll, since princess Melisande grows tall and then returns to normal again. She also cries "a pool of tears," but remembers her *Alice in Wonderland* and stops crying at once. Here Nesbit promptly acknowledges

A line in the dragon dialog; illustration by Eric Blegvad from Edith Nesbit's The Last of the Dragons

the Carroll allusion, but there are others too, for instance to *Gulliver's Travels*, in the episode where the giant princess fights the enemy's navy. Her hair doubles in length every day, arousing associations with Rapunzel and her enormously long hair. Thus every "line" in Nesbit's tale becomes an answer to an earlier text, and this makes her own text all the richer in nuances.

Nesbit's dialogic link to her various predecessors is probably seen best in her full-length fantasy novels, starting with *Five Children and It* (1902). British scholars have pointed out various sources for this text. One is Mary Molesworth's *The Cuckoo Clock* (1877), where a wooden cuckoo plays the part of a good fairy for the child, but there are also two adult novels by F. Anstey: *Vice Versa* (1882) and *The Brass Bottle* (1900). In the first book, father and son in London change places through a magic wish, whereupon the father in his son's image endures the humiliations of a boarding school, while the son is forced to take upon himself the responsibilities of a grownup. *The Brass Bottle* depicts a young London architect who by chance sets free a genie. The genie tries hard to grant his deliverer all his wishes, but everything turns into a big mess. The absurd idea of letting magical figures and objects appear in modern London, and the inability of modern humans to make use of magic are thoughts which appealed to Nesbit, and this is what all of her children's books are based on.

Following Anstey, Nesbit "deconstructs" folktale patterns. Naturally, young readers lack a significant layer of meaning in Nesbit's texts if they are not familiar with folktales. The type of fantasy Nesbit has created is sometimes (quite wrongly, I think) labeled "humorous fantasy" or even "nonsense." The humorous effect depends on the reader having folktales as intertext. In addition to its literary models Molesworth and Anstey, *Five Children and It* refers to the well-known folktale about three wishes in which the third wish must be used to eliminate the devastating consequences of the first two. In the novel, five ordinary British children find a strange creature in a sand-pit, a Psammead, or Sandfairy, who can grant wishes. But whatever the children wish for, something is bound to go wrong. They wish to be "beautiful as the day"; then they have to go without lunch because the nurse does not recognize them. They wish for money and get a sand-pit full of old coins which cannot buy anything. Much like the folktale hero, the children waste magic wishes and do not become happier. Finally, they themselves refrain from asking for the Psammead's magical help.[10]

In *The Enchanted Castle* (1907), one of Nesbit's later fantasy novels, there are links with the Niebelung legend, in which a magic ring confers endless power upon its bearer but at the same time corrupts him. There is, however, a major difference between these two examples. Readers are supposed to be familiar with the folktale, and their appreciation of the novel is determined by the interaction between the two codes of folktale and fantasy, which produces a "deconstructed," or "fractured" tale. The ring motif may or may not be familiar, and appreciation of the text does not directly depend on recognition of the legend. Nesbit herself was probably not aware of the link. But it is important for a scholar to view the motif in a broader cultural context, since it provides a seemingly simple text a deeper psychological and symbolic meaning.

When Nesbit wrote her first fantasy novels for children she had few models to which she could turn. What she knew well were science fiction novels by her contemporary and close friend Herbert George Wells. *The Story of the Amulet* (1906), classified as the very first book of its kind ever written for children,[11] was definitely inspired by H.G. Wells's *The Time Machine* (1895). It is not a children's book, and it is doubtful that it was at that time included in young people's reading to the same extent as science fiction is today. Both in *Amulet* and in other novels, therefore, Edith Nesbit's refined dialogues with Wells lie within adult codes.

Although the idea of time travelling is similar in both texts, there is an essential difference in the nature of fantasy and science fiction, with regard to both purpose and the treatment of irrational events. Unlike science fiction, Nesbit has no intention of foreseeing the future. She wants to introduce children to history in a new and entertaining manner, so that her time travels return to exciting epochs of the past in places such as ancient Egypt and Babylon, Roman Britain and legendary Atlantis.

In Wells's *The Time Machine* the instrument of time travel is a gadget constructed by a scientist. Although the novel does not explain how the machine works, the point of departure is a rational explanation of a technically conceivable phenomenon. The amulet in Nesbit's story is a kind of time machine, but, unlike the science fiction gadget, it does not need any rational explanation. Nesbit's notion of time, however, is quite close to the modern scientific view of the world, which is expressed in *The Amulet* by the daring statement: "Time is only a mode of thought."

The most important law introduced by Nesbit is that magic adventure does not take any "real," primary time. The children come back from their journeys in time at exactly the same moment they went through the arch of the amulet. Primary time stands still in their absence. Their magical helper, Psammead the Sandfairy, explains that it would be wrong to mix up the present and the past or to cut bits out of one to fit into the other. This is a very convenient way to solve the time paradox and also build up the narrative without having to explain why the characters in the book are not

Mabel is invisible, but not her shadow. Illustration by H.R. Millar to The Enchanted Castle

missed by the grownups while they are away traveling. In Wells's novel the primary and the secondary time are parallel. His Traveler does not have to be home in time for tea.

When Nesbit's children arrive in ancient Egypt in 6000 B.C., readers can expect them to have problems with communication. Nesbit dismisses these by saying magic also allowed the children to talk and understand other people even in the most distant epochs. Wells's adult novel does not admit of such explanations. His Traveler must take pains to learn the language of the secondary time he enters. We can wonder whether these side addresses towards Wells are conscious on Nesbit's part, and of course there is no definite answer to this question. Obviously she was consciously trying to articulate rules for magical travels. More were to come in her later novels with time shift motif such as *The House of Arden* (1908) and *Harding's Luck* (1909).

Quite a different example of Nesbit's dialogue with Wells on the adult level is found in *The Enchanted Castle*, where one of the motifs is invisibility. The idea most probably comes from Wells's novel *The Invisible Man* (1897), although it is a common motif in folktales. The protagonist in Wells's novel has made himself invisible by scientific means. Therefore only his body, living matter, is invisible, but not his clothes. At one point Griffin is trying to escape from his pursuers and takes off his clothes that give him away. There is an allusion to this episode in *The Enchanted Castle* in a scene describing an invisible girl going to bed. She has been made invisible by magic, and her clothes are invisible too. When she takes off her clothes the dress becomes visible: first one arm appears out of thin air, then another, then the hem, and finally the whole dress comes flying through the room. For Nesbit's purpose it is both logical and convenient to suppose that clothes worn by an invisible person are invisible. Most of her followers using this motif have also accepted this principle.

If there is evidence of Nesbit's "polemics" with Wells in the close friendship of the two writers, in many cases the links can only be guessed. Still, studies of children's books with adult fiction as intertexts can help us explore the nature of children's literature and provide insights into the intentions of the writers.

IN DEFENCE OF EDWARD EAGER

The impact of Edith Nesbit on English-language fantasy cannot be overestimated. As Marcus Crouch puts it in a volume characteristically entitled *The Nesbit Tradition*: "no writer today is free from the debt to this remarkable woman."[12]

Among Nesbit's most ardent disciples we find the American writer Edward Eager, who pays tribute to her in his essay "Daily Magic."[13] Scholars, however, probably should not pay too much attention to writers' self-evaluations. It may be of some interest to know that Eager admired Edith Nesbit, but it explains very little of what it was in Nesbit's works that fascinated Eager and why. For intertextual purposes, it is more interesting to note that all of Eager's seven fantasy novels contain direct references to Nesbit's books, which his characters read. But this, too, is merely an amusing detail.

Most critics have read Eager's books as direct imitations or adaptations of Nesbit's texts. They point out that Eager's *Knight's Castle* (1956) uses the same idea as Nesbit's *The Magic City* (1910), that *The Time Garden* (1958) develops the motif of time travel, and that *Magic or Not?* (1959), like Nesbit's *The Wonderful Garden* (1911), plays on the hesitation of the characters and reader as to whether the events should be explained as magic or coincidence.

Other novels by Eager are perhaps more original with respect to plot, but there as well critics have discovered "loans" from Nesbit, especially her magical wish-granting creatures the Psammead and the Mouldiwarp. Eager has a toad in *Magic by the Lake* (1957) and a Natterjack in *The Time Garden*. Both are by nature and temperament true heirs of Nesbit's figures. Many of Eager's magical objects resemble Nesbit's. However, it is wrong, as many critics do, to call Eager a helpless imitator—I expressed such a mistaken view in an earlier essay myself. Although Eager doubtless had Nesbit as a model, he has in his own texts done much more than simply played variations on her tunes. What he does is to throw lines to Nesbit's ingenious figures and events. Against the background of her texts, this makes his own inventions stand out as even more clever, for they almost demand that the reader be familiar with them. A closer look at the magical patterns in Eager's novels will reveal this very clearly.

The most important principle that Eager takes from Nesbit is her intricate way of introducing magic into the story. Magic in Nesbit's novels is never omnipotent, but must obey certain rules. In one respect it makes the narrative easier to handle, and it also facilitates the unexpected turns upon which comic effects are based. For instance, in Nesbit's texts magic always stops at sunset. Often this limitation creates complications for her characters, and this is precisely her purpose: to show that magic is tricky and does not really suit our modern times.

Eager's characters have read Nesbit, so they are prepared for magic to stop at sunset—"it is supposed to be so in books." However, Eager does not merely repeat Nesbit's idea, but develops it dialogically. In an episode in *Magic by the Lake* magical adventure begins at night, which leads the characters to guess that it will be over by the time the moon sets. This is not simply borrowing, but an excellent example of a creative use of loan which is also handled with distance and irony.

Another magical detail that Eager unreservedly takes from Nesbit is to place limits on magic, which in Nesbit's books often is a compositional device, as in *The Phoenix and the Carpet* (1904). Here the flying carpet is wearing out and its magic becomes weaker and weaker. It is only partially effective. When the children take a priest from London to a desert island, half of the priest is on the island and the other half back in London. Finally, the children fall through a hole in the carpet, and their adventures come to a natural end.

Eager enthusiastically borrows this idea in his first novel *Half Magic* (1954), but he also develops it and creates his entire plot around the peculiar qualities of the magic coin, which is so old and worn out that it only grants half of a wish. The children wish for a fire, and there is half a fire, in a playhouse. Their mother, who takes the coin by mistake, wishes she were home from a boring visit and suddenly finds herself halfway home on a lonely road. The children wish for the cat to start talking, and it starts half-talking. The iron dog on the gatepost becomes half-alive. But the best example is when Mark wishes he were on a desert island and finds himself in the Sahara. His sister explains that he has gotten half his wish: "Desert, yes. Island, no." As soon as the children have realized how magic works they gain full control of their wishes by articulating them correctly: "I want to go home, only twice as far." In the end, as in Nesbit's book, the magic object gets so worn out that all its magical powers disappear. But Eager goes a step further and lets his children watch the coin picked up by a new owner, whereupon it regains its magic.

If the coin is in a way a variation on Nesbit's wish-granting motifs, many other of Eager's inventions are much more original, although they, too, bear traces of Nesbit's influence. In *Seven Day Magic* (1962) the children borrow a book from a library (it is stated explicitly that it is a book by Edith Nesbit), which proves to be magic, but only remains magic for a week, the period of the library loan. Thus here the principle of limiting magic acquires very concrete dimensions. In *Magic by the Lake* the motif is even more clever. The children in the story discover a signboard on their summer house saying "Magic by the Lake," which they interpret as "Magic adventures happening by the side of the lake" and wish that it were true. But the wish-granting toad interprets the phrase as "A whole lakeful of magic," and spitefully produces a lake full of all sorts of magical creatures.

Here as well Eager enters into a dialogue with Nesbit, who shows repeatedly in her books how deceitful magical formulas can be in everyday speech. Many critics have stressed that magic in Nesbit's works is essentially verbal, and that the conflict is based on the contrast between the magical, or ritual, meaning of the words and their everyday usage. "I wish" no longer means in an everyday situation "I want to utter a wish to be granted."[14] Eager similarly plays with the ambivalent meanings of words, even in his titles;

besides *Magic by the Lake*, there is *The Time Garden*, which involves a play on the homophones "time" and "thyme"; and *The Well-Wishers* (1960).

Eager's puns are definitely inspired by Nesbit, but instead of copying her, as some critics state, he gives witty replies to her ideas. Intertextual studies of particular authors like Eager who have been accused of epigony can help us to re-evaluate them and appreciate the creative approach they have taken to the ideas of other authors.

THE DIALOGUE CONTINUES

There are a number of English-language writers besides Eager who have acknowledged their debt to Edith Nesbit. One of these is Pamela Travers, whose Mary Poppins is a true heiress of the Psammead. Another is Mary Norton, who in *The Magic Bed-Knob* (1945) and sequel *Bonfires and Broomsticks* (1947) describes travel in time and space by means of an ordinary bed which has been enchanted by a nice lady who takes a correspondence course in black magic. The children first fly to London, where they are arrested for disorderly conduct in public—that is, the unmade bed in the middle of the street. Then they go to an island in the Pacific where they are very nearly eaten up by cannibals. There is a similar episode in Nesbit's *The Phoenix and the Carpet*. The bed has the same function as the carpet, and Miss Price—the helper and adviser—plays the same role as the Psammead or the Phoenix. The only difference is that Nesbit uses a magical object commonly found in folktales, whereas the bed in Norton's stories is a violation of the "norm," a deviation apprehended as irony or parody even if its function in the plot is similar. Norton does not mechanically repeat Nesbit's patterns, but goes further in "deconstruction" away from the common and the expected. Since flying carpets are as "normal" in folktales as in Nesbit's novel, it is not necessary for the reader to be familiar with Nesbit's text to appreciate the "deviant" bed. It can have both Nesbit and the folktale as intertext, but a magic bed in everyday life is definitely a line in a dialogue with Nesbit.

We can similarly analyse the episode in C.S. Lewis's *The Magician's Nephew* (1955) which in many reference sources is quoted as a direct imitation of Nesbit. In this scene the evil witch Jadis arrives in London from another world. It has many parallels with the chapter in *The Story of the Amulet* where the queen of Babylon visits the modern capital of England. The similarities are apparent, and there is evidence that C. S. Lewis had read Nesbit. Comparative analysis would probably be satisfied by this statement, but it is absolutely essential to see the principal difference between these two episodes to understand C.S. Lewis's "loan" from Nesbit. In her books time travel consists of amusing adventures, and the fluent visit of the Babylonian queen to London is just one merry prank among many. The episode is humorous and even nonsensical, based on the total puzzlement of the queen as she confronts an unfamiliar society. There is a similar episode with a similarly light tone in Mary Norton's *Bonfires and Broomsticks* where a young man from the epoch of Charles II is amazed by water pipes, cars and other wonders of our time.

The wicked witch in C.S. Lewis's novel comes to Earth from another world as an uninvited guest and presents a horrible threat. She is so powerful that one word is enough to destroy the planet. There is nothing humorous or nonsensical about her visit to London, and the episode is gruesome and frightening. Even if Lewis consciously proceeds from Nesbit's story (which is itself debatable), the scene he creates has quite a different atmosphere and significance, and his story is therefore something else than merely a variation on Nesbit.

The most interesting aspects that are unveiled in intertextual studies, however, are not superficial similarities in plot, motifs, characters or attributes between Nesbit and her followers. More exciting are the hidden echoes from Nesbit which are exposed through serious examinations of the entire genre of fantasy in which she did most of her work. Such studies help us to appreciate Nesbit's enormous contribution to the evolution of fantasy and can provide insights into what this evolution actually involved.

Because Edith Nesbit was the first to develop a "theory" of magical time travel it was she who more or less created this specific subgenre of fantasy. It was developed further in works by many later writers in Britain and other English-speaking countries. All these writers, without referring to Nesbit, accept her "rules" for magical travel in time as if these rules really existed: primary time stands still while the travelers enter other chronotopes; travelers cannot carry objects between chronotopes; travelers have no difficulty understanding and speaking foreign languages; and most important, travelers can in no way interfere with history. Nesbit chooses this principle because the purpose of her time adventures is to present history in an exciting manner; she does not want to get involved with the consequences of such an interference. The confidence of young readers in the permanence of the universe must not be shattered. Tragic events such as the Gunpowder Plot or the execution of Anne Boleyn in *The House of Arden* (1908) must therefore take place, even if the children try hard to prevent them. Likewise, Penelope in *A Traveller in Time* (1939) by Alison Uttley cannot save Mary Queen of Scots even if she knows about her tragic fate. Some other time travelers cannot participate actively in the epochs they visit either; most often they are merely passive observers and, as in the case of Tom in Philippa Pearce's *Tom's Midnight Garden* (1958) or Tolly in Lucy M. Boston's *The Children of Green Knowe* (1954), are apprehended as ghosts by those around them.

Not until the 1980s do writers of fantasy venture to contradict Nesbit in this long dialogue. Yet in Ruth Park's *Playing Beatie Bow* (1980), the whole purpose of time displacement is to change history, which naturally also affects the protagonist's own time. The challenge of this violation of the norm only becomes evident if we use as intertext the whole fantasy genre headed by Edith Nesbit. Similarly, the total absence of innovation in certain texts is more obvious if we contemplate the genre as intertext. Gunila Ambjörnson's "The House of Silvercrona" (1992) alludes in title and in plot to Nesbit's *The House of Arden*. The book is a helpless, bleak imitation of Nesbit, with the story transposed from England to Sweden; the writer totally ignores the contemporary evolution of fantasy towards deeper psychological and ethical dimensions and writes as if nothing has happened in the genre since Nesbit. However, as scholars we need to be familiar with the evolution to realize the derivative nature of Ambjörnson's text.

DIALOGUES IN *The Root Cellar*

One recent line in fantasy dialogue is Janet Lunn's *The Root Cellar* (1981), a Canadian fantasy novel that has been awarded a number of prizes. It is illuminating to investigate an intertextual connection between this book and traditional British fantasy. Since the main pattern in *The Root Cellar* is a time slip it is natural to regard Edith Nesbit's and other novels about time travel as background texts. The comparative approach would then compel a scholar to prove or at least assume that Janet Lunn has read such writers as Edith Nesbit's, Alison Uttley, Lucy M. Boston and other British masters of time fantasy. If we take an intertextual approach we are primarily interested in the use Janet Lunn makes of time travel motifs, and the question we want to answer is whether her novel represents a new contribution to the genre or merely copies old models.

The protagonist of *The Root Cellar* is the twelve-year-old orphan Rose, and the story told through her reflects deep penetration into her thoughts and feelings. In contrast to the "adventure" fantasy of the past, this approach is typical of a more recent trend in time fantasy that might be called psychological fantasy. The novel *Playing Beatie Bow* mentioned above is another example. Unlike traditional comparativists, we need not speculate whether Janet Lunn has read Ruth Park and been influenced by her novel. Instead we can state that both texts belong to the same paradigm shift in the typological pattern of the fantasy genre.

Rose's first experiences of the past are presented as visions, and the figures of the past may as well be ghosts—as in fact they are assumed to be by the rest of the family. This pattern appears very early in British fantasy, in *A Traveller in Time*. While time travelers in Edith Nesbit's novels not only were perfectly aware of their transference but could choose their destination, Penelope in *A Traveller in Time* has difficulty believing that she has arrived in another historical epoch.

In *The Root Cellar* we meet the common figure of the *messenger*, that is, a person that in some inexplicable magical manner is able to wander through time. The are numerous variations on the figure in traditional fantasy—from the mysterious old nurse who appears in different historical epochs in *The House of Arden* to Dame Cecily in *A Traveller in Time* who duplicates Penelope's Aunt Tissie in the present, to Granny Oldknow in Lucy M. Boston's *Green Knowe* series (1954–76), who is grandmother to children from different times. Most often the function of this figure is to support the lonely child protagonist who is displaced in time, provide him or her with a sense of security, and to serve as a link back to the primary chronotope. Not so in *The Root Cellar*. That there is something queer about Mrs Morrissay is obvious; she says herself that she "shifts," that is, she is transferred in time. Rose also wonders whether Mrs Morrissay has come to fetch her into another historical epoch. As it turns out in the end, Mrs Morrissay is in fact Susan, one of the central characters in the secondary chronotope. The author lets her protagonist meet Susan not as a young girl but as an old woman, probably to suggest that at the end the two different times are separated forever. The shock of realizing that the old lady is her friend Susan is hard on Rose—harder than Lucy's and Edmund's shock in *The Voyage of the Dawn Treader* (1953) when they meet prince Caspian as an old man, and probably equal to Tom's shock in *Tom's Midnight Garden* when he becomes aware that old Mrs Bartholomew is his secondary chronotope friend Hatty. An encounter of this kind in a fantasy novel makes heavy demands on us as readers, compelling us to ponder the nature of Time.

The most common device of passage between chronotopes in fantasy is a door of some kind, real or symbolic. In *The Root Cellar* the door is quite tangible, leading into a cellar which sometimes but not always can lead Rose into secondary time. She is forced to make several attempts to figure out the mechanism of the opening, and here the author reverts to a more traditional pattern of passage: Rose can consciously and voluntarily enter another time. From now on her time travels are well prepared and comfortable: she can even bring along her overnight bag! She can make use of modern information services to find out about the past. She passes neatly between chronotopes, carrying all the knowledge and experience of the twentieth century with her. Here the author makes things too easy for both the character and the reader. However, at the end of the novel the cellar is destroyed by a storm, which means that Rose cannot go back to say farewell to her friends. The separation of chronotopes is definite and irrevocable.

Rose enters secondary time repeatedly, in a "loop," which naturally creates the problem of correlating the two chronotopes. Like most time fantasy authors, Janet Lunn chooses to let primary time stand still while Rose is away. But when she is back in primary time, the two times pass at different paces. When she comes back after three primary weeks, it turns out that two years have passed in secondary time. Her friends Susan and Will have grown older, but not she—a dilemma that Tom encounters in *Tom's Midnight Garden*. Rose discovers a way of preventing temporal incongruence: another unnecessary "rationalisation," or rather a concession to a more traditional pattern. There is no visible or even hidden "time machine" in Janet Lunn's novel, but the amulet which Rose gives Susan ensures that secondary time will not pass too quickly.

Thus we see that as far as the narrative structure is concerned, *The Root Cellar* displays a high degree of sophistication, some daring solutions and original patterns that stimulate the reader's imagination. In this respect the novel is indeed innovative and fresh. However, the central question of modern psychological fantasy is how the magical adventure affects the protagonist. In Edith Nesbit's novels the time adventure was sufficient in itself, offering readers entertainment plus some practical knowledge of history. The characters of C.S. Lewis do not seem to be affected at all by their involvement with Narnia. For Abigail in *Playing Beatie Bow*, her visit to secondary time implies maturity which enables her to cope with problems in her own time. This is also the case with Rose. Unhappy and unwanted, she is determined in the beginning of the story to stay in secondary time. By and by she realizes that everyone belongs to their own time, and that the very purpose of the time shift has been to make her strong enough to face her own reality. At one point Rose suddenly feels that she longs for "home," that strange farm in Ontario, and the strange half-crazy family she lives with. This is the beginning of her acceptance of her own situation. The chapter in which she comes back to her own chronotope is called "Home." The memory of primary time and the sense of belonging to it, which at the beginning seemed a primitive device and a concession to more traditional fantasy, suddenly appears in a new light. Rose's journey is not an escape into a world of dreams and ghosts, but a journey home, towards a full and conscious awareness of reality. There is no evidence of her having visited the past, except for the Christmas dinner served by Susan/Mrs Morrissay instead of Rose's failed attempt at cooking, which is more a humorous epilogue than an indispensable part of the narrative. Indeed, many fantasy authors insert some such evidence in the story—like Penelope's clothes smelling of herbs from the garden in the past in *A Traveller in Time*. Obviously, Janet Lunn does not think that her readers need any evidence.

The consequences of Rose's experience are all the more apparent as compared to Penelope in *A Traveller in Time*, who tells the whole story long after the events and still bears her maiden name. Involvement with the past and her impossible love for Francis Babington have broken Penelope, who is never able to be reconciled with her own time. Rose, like Abigail in *Playing Beatie Bow*, has developed in a positive direction, and because Rose's life has acquired a meaning, the open ending is a promise to the reader.

I see *The Root Cellar* as belonging to the recent trend in English-language fantasy (although we see some features of it as early as 1939 in Alison Uttley's novel), where authors are more interested in the character's psychological development than in the magical events as such. The impact of this kind of fantasy is apparently much stronger than traditional forms involving abstract distant worlds or times. It is also sometimes stronger than in strictly realistic young adult novels.

We have seen that the intertextual method allows us to discover the merits of *The Root Cellar* where the comparativist most probably would have stated that motifs, figures and images from previous texts have been used, presumably under the influence of earlier authors. Intertextuality makes it possible to recognize a creative development where the comparative method suggests mechanical repetition. Not only can we in this manner do full justice to a particular text or author, but we can reject the common accusation that fantasy is stale and stagnated, a mere variation on a limited number of patterns. Analyzed with proper instruments, novels like *The Root Cellar* show that the fantasy genre is vital and able to produce new and original texts.

IN DEFENCE OF MICHAEL ENDE

A text extremely rich in intertextual links is *The Neverending Story* (1979) by Michael Ende. The different literary patterns and motifs are so abundant in this novel that one critic called it "banal, pretentious, derivative and mind-numbing."[15] My immediate reaction to this evaluation is that this scholar has failed to recognize the author's intentional use of patterns and clichés to parody well-known fantasies.[16]

The novel falls very clearly into two parts, the first of which is "a story in a story" where Bastian is reading a book. The book has all the features of a fairy tale, or probably rather traditional fantasy, where every sign is supposedly recognized both by the narratee—Bastian—and the actual reader.

The Neverending Story is quite a unique text which introduces the reader into the narrative. Bastian is sitting in a school attic, reading a fantasy novel of a very conventional type, something on the order of Tolkien, about a closed mythical world without any contact whatsoever with our own world. Michael Ende is clever enough not to describe his imaginary world at one go, but attentive reading yields quite a vivid picture of Fantastica. It is populated by every possible kind of mythological creature, from dragons, gnomes, unicorns, fauns, sprites and salamanders to less familiar rock chewers, bark trolls, flimflams, sassafranians, shadowcamps and so on. It appears that every folk has its own kingdom and its own local tongue, although high Fantastican is used as a common language, and they are all united under the rule of the wise and ageless Childlike Empress. The dimensions of Fantastica seem to be enormous; it evidently has no boundaries, which in addition to being in accordance with the modern scientific view of the universe is, of course, a beautiful symbol.

From the folktale this "story in a story" has both its system of characters and plot—the *sequence of functions*, to use Vladimir Propp's terminology.[17] Atreyu is the typical so called "low hero" of the fairy tale, an orphan of unknown parentage. The Childlike Empress is the princess who has to be saved from evil, while she is at the same time the donor who presents the hero with a magic object. Cairon the centaur is the dispatcher, who tells Atreyu about his mission and sends him on his quest. Falcor the luckdragon is the helper who assists Atreyu and provides for his spatial transference. Finally, the Nothing is the villain, the unuttered evil force threatening the princess and the whole country.

The sequence of functions in the first part (or "move" in Proppian terminology) is quite close to that of the traditional fairy tale. It develops from villainy through mediation, counteraction and departure into a series of trials, where the hero encounters different donors, that is, characters who through advice, a magic agent or in some other way assist him on his journey. In fairy tales these encounters are usually repeated three times (the magical number of three); in Ende's novel there are at least six.

When Atreyu's mission is completed, he returns to the Ivory Tower. Here, in the middle of the novel, the closed world suddenly opens, and the reading boy is drawn into it. Some hints of the coming contact are spread over the narrative, first in the form of insertions describing Bastian in his attic and his reaction to the story he is reading. Incidentally, these insertions, marked by a different color of print, are much more numerous than most readers would guess. When asked, people say twelve to fifteen. There are actually forty-eight of them. I find this fact worth mentioning because it shows how skillfully Michael Ende has interwoven the two seemingly independent stories. The two direct instances of contact are when Atreyu meets the monster Ygramul and hears Bastian's cry of aversion, and later when he sees Bastian in a magic mirror. When Atreyu returns to the Ivory Tower, the frontier between the two worlds is almost gone: Bastian no longer reads the story, he sees and feels it.

The second part of the novel develops according to a different pattern, and by this means Michael Ende shows how folktale elements are transformed (or deconstructed, if that term is preferred) when creatively used. Bastian has now entered the story he has been reading. He is the hero and Atreyu his helper ("squire"). There is no villain, and the Childlike Empress is a dispatcher and donor, who presents Bastian with a magic amulet and sends him off on his adventures. Bastian also receives a magic sword from Grograman the lion, a magic jewel from the inhabitants of the Silver City, an invisibility belt from Xayide the enchantress. Bastian abuses all these magic objects in the same way as the false hero in fairy tales, the character who lays false claim to the hero's role and demands his rewards. Bastian draws the sword from the scabbard by force, uses the stone to satisfy his vanity, eavesdrops while invisible on his friends, and in all cases brings grief to himself and the whole country. Unlike the traditional fairy tale, in which the hero is changed from fool into prince, Bastian reverts from the superman he has become in Fantastica back into his own self.

Bastian is by no means privileged in his involvement with Fantastica, as humans seem to have been visiting this world from time immemorial—at one place a certain Shexper is mentioned, for example. The book dealer, Mr Coreander, also admits having been to Fantastica. Quite a few humans who have not been able to come back live in the Town of Old Emperors. The purpose of Bastian's visit is thus to recreate the fantastic world and then return to his own. The latter action he is reluctant to perform until he realizes its necessity. In more senses than one, the way back lies through his wishes, since at the end the wish-granting amulet AURYN itself turns into a magic door. The price Bastian must pay for his omnipotence and the endless string of granted wishes is the loss of memory of his own world.

The second part of the novel takes place in an open world, that is, a magic secondary world in tangible contact with the primary world of our own reality. Contact between the two worlds is maintained through a magic talisman, which is another common motif borrowed from folklore and familiar from other works of fantasy. The most important talisman in *The Neverending Story* is the book itself, since it exists in both worlds. Bastian is reading it in the primary world, while in Fantastica the Old Man of Wandering Mountains is writing it. When Bastian is within the secondary world he tries to send a message to his own world, probably to someone reading the neverending story, probably to us readers. When Bastian comes back the book is gone, which suggests that someone—perhaps we, the "real" readers—has found it and will read it next.

The other amulet that exists only in Fantastica is AURYN, the magical jewel. When carried by Atreyu it gives protection and guidance, but in Bastian's hands it turns into a powerful magical agent. By and by it enslaves and corrupts its bearer, much like the ring in Tolkien's trilogy or, which is probably more interesting considering Ende's German heritage, the ring of the Niebelungs. Only through the amulet can Bastian get home, and remarkably, he bears the door with him through his entire journey in Fantastica.

The door, the gateway, the passage is an important narrative element in folktale and fantasy. It also occurs when Atreyu has to go through the three magical gates into the oracle and when Bastian wanders in a maze of doors trying to find and articulate his next wish.

Yet another motif familiar from other fantasy literature is the relativity of magical, secondary time. It is active during Atreyu's journey to the Southern Oracle—seven days pass, while to him it seems only one. This anticipates Bastian's travels in Fantastica, which may have taken years or even centuries of Fantastican time—at one point it is mentioned that he has been there for many thousands of years—while a single night has passed in his own world.

The importance of names is prominently stressed in *The Neverending Story*. The reader is initiated into the magic of names when Bastian Balthazar Bux and Carl Conrad Coreander are introduced. To save Fantastica from the Nothing, a new name must be given to the Childlike Empress. It is emphasized that what threatens the Fantasticans is their inability to invent new stories and new names. To create the new Fantastica, Bastian has to give names to things: the forest Perilin, the desert Goab. To possess magic objects he must name them: the sword Sikanda, the stone Al Tsahir, the belt Ghemmal. It is well known that in old witchcraft, learning the true names of things, animals or people grants unlimited power over them.[18] When Bastian ultimately loses his name as the price for his last wish, he loses his identity as well; he is no longer Bastian, but a boy without a name. He is known as such until he is back in his own world.

All these patterns are easily recognized. The whole of Part Two—Bastian's adventures in Fantastica—is a series of narratives, each of which draws on a well-known story: the myth of creation, the myth of death and resurrection (in the image of Grograman the lion, which is also an obvious parallel to C.S. Lewis and his lion Aslan). Biblical allusions appear in the presentation of Bastian as the Savior, and the wise mule carrying him is, of course, a direct quotation.

Further, we find chivalrous romances as well as the medieval motif of the contest of bards. The dragon Smerg immediately reminds us of Tolkien's Smaug; the evil enchantress Xayide may again be a line in a dialogue with C.S. Lewis, as are the battle for the Ivory Tower and the apocalyptic vision of the end of the world, as described in C.S. Lewis's *The Last Battle* (1956). Images such as the Three Wise Men, or the City of Fools, or the mysterious picture mine, and last but not least the Water of Life, all have their origins in myth, folktale or earlier works of literature.

The question may arise whether Michael Ende is a helpless imitator who is not able to invent a story of his own and is simply borrowing the ideas of others. This is what some critics have charged. This is obviously not the case, for if it were, it would be difficult to account for the enormous appeal of the book. The author deliberately provides his readers with recognizable patterns and images in order to stimulate reflection around them. His use of clichés is conscious and skillful and ultimately serves the message of the story. All of Bastian's adventures are products of his imagination inspired by books. As long as he does not understand the goal of his quest, it is he who is the slavish copyist.

C.S. Lewis's British biographer Roger Llancelyn Green has on one occasion defended him against a similar charge of uncritically borrowing a mixture of Antique, Celtic, Christian and other mythology in his Narnia. Green points out that the use of the various patterns is intentional, that literary echoes are part of the narrative structure, that the encounter with familiar figures is meant as a meeting with old friends, and above all that the whole experience of Narnia is planned as a rediscovery rather than a new discovery.[19]

In his adult novel *Perelandra* (1943) C.S. Lewis advances an argument which supports Green's interpretation: on meeting mythical characters on the planet Venus, the protagonist wonders whether all creatures that are perceived as myth on Earth are in fact scattered throughout other worlds of the universe as real beings. The land of Narnia can exist as long as its inhabitants believe in Aslan; here C.S. Lewis shows how mythical thought works. In Ende's Fantastica as well it is a matter of creating and preserving the world of images which are perceived as myths and folktales on Earth, images that belong to our common cultural heritage—or, if you prefer, to the collective subconscious.

A DIALOGUE WITH ONESELF

Sometimes intertextual analysis is absolutely indispensable in order to obtain a reasonably relevant interpretation of a difficult, multidimensional text. One of many cases in which this approach can produce exciting results concerns the intertextual connections of writers to themselves, that is, the connection between an individual text and the author's entire *oeuvre*. I do not here mean cases such as the clearly ironical references Edith Nesbit makes to her earlier works. Thus in *The House of Arden* the characters Edred and Elfrida receive a book entitled *The Story of the Amulet*, that is, Nesbit's own earlier published book, although she does not mention this fact. It is from this book that Elfrida gets the idea of traveling in time, saying that "unlikelier things happened in *The Amulet*."

This is an amusing and original narrative device, but what I mean by intertextual links to oneself is something more subtle that does not always lie on the surface but can remain hidden until we are for some reason forced to unveil it. Contemplating the writer's whole production while analyzing a concrete text can sometimes help illuminate it or simply help us arrive at a possible interpretation.

In Lloyd Alexander's *The First Two Lives of Lukas-Kasha* (1978) a boy is sent away by a wandering sorcerer to another world, where he meets with different adventures and matures both in body and in spirit. The title of the book is sometimes interpreted to mean that when Lukas returns to his own world he will start a new life as a better human being. This is a plausible interpretation, but it is not the only possible one. If we look for intertextual background in Alexander's own earlier works, we will discover *Time Cat* (1963). It is based on the famous saying about cats having nine lives, and the writer allows his character and the magical agent, a cat, to literally live nine lives in nine different countries and epochs. From this viewpoint, the title and the meaning of the later book allow the additional interpretation that Lukas will possibly go on to have more magical adventures in more secondary worlds.

A more complicated example is *Red Shift* by Alan Garner, a text I have already discussed on several occasions above. This enigmatic novel has been analyzed from many different perspectives ranging from the meaning of the landscape or the parallels between its Roman episodes and the Vietnam War to feminist apologies for the female protagonist, Jan.[20] Critics have also highlighted the intertextual links of the novel to, in particular, *King Lear*.[21] But *Red Shift* has so many dimensions that it can be discussed by taking yet another point of departure. Let us consider the male protagonist, Tom, and his dilemma, which also constitutes the core of the intricate narrative structure of the novel: why all this fuss? Why three levels of action that seemingly have nothing in common but the geographical location in which they take place?

My interpretation, which is shared to some extent by other critics, is that the two historical layers of the novel, the Roman time and the seventeenth century, are used to deepen and illuminate Tom's and Jan's relations in the present.[22] This interpretation is reinforced by the fact that despite their fantasy motifs, all of Garner's novels deal with our own time and our own reality. Other times and alternative worlds are present there only insofar as they relate to the people of today and their emotions. Although the subject matter of *Red Shift* is inspired by history and legend, it is a story of modern young people, of our own problems, of loneliness in the midst of our busy and fast-moving lives.

A key to the understanding of *Red Shift* may be found in Garner's short story 'Feel Free,'[23] which can be regarded as an early étude for the novel and therefore an obvious intertext. The story depicts a young boy trying to draw a Greek vase in a museum for a school project. When he holds the vase he experiences a sense of connection between himself and the ancient pottery master. He also finds a thumbprint which coincides with his own but for a little scar.[24] When Brian later tears his thumb on a nail and disappears into a cave in an amusement park attraction, we guess that the two times have merged: Brian and the unknown potter become one; he enters the depth of time or timelessness.

Brian's direct connection with the potter is naturally more primitive than the subtle links between the three male characters of *Red Shift*. Brian can be interpreted as the reincarnation of the potter. Tom, on the other hand, lives simultaneously in all three times where he—or his twin—is captured in the same painful relation to a woman. The behavioral patterns that we see on the two historical levels stand in sharp contrast to Tom's actions in the present. Because he actually lives outside time, he feels unreal and shadowlike.

The ambiguous ending of the novel is the consequence of Tom's problems. It ends with the letter that Tom has written to his girlfriend Jan in a secret code, the so-called Lewis Carroll cipher, or Vigenaire, which is very difficult to decipher. If we as readers guess what Tom is trying to convey to Jan at their last meeting, namely, that the key phrase is "Tom's a-cold" (a seemingly meaningless Shakespeare quotation which echoes throughout the novel), and take the trouble to decipher the letter, we realize that Tom is going to commit suicide, since his relation with Jan has come to a dead end. Nor is this information stated explicitly—Tom simply says that he is going to the church tower in Barthomley and will feel the smell of Jan's hair in his face. This is a reference to the recurrent image of Jan's hair blown by the wind into Tom's face; it produces an immensely strong sensation comparable to flying. What Tom is trying to tell Jan is that he intends to fly, that is, jump from the tower.

The letter also says that it is too late to correct the wrong that has happened between him and Jan. What has actually happened is a most banal case of jealousy. Before Tom and Jan fell in love, Jan had been an au pair in Germany and slept with her German employer. Tom cannot forgive her. But he himself is too scared and emotionally immature to have a sexual relationship with Jan, and when he eventually does try, it has a catastrophic effect upon their otherwise pure and elevated love. Incidentally, their intercourse is conveyed in the form of a pause between Jan's two lines, and only a keen eye can discover it.

Tom cannot forgive Jan's unfaithfulness, although she explains that this brief affair has made her love for Tom possible. ". . . he let me become what you felt the day I got home. . . . He made us possible. What we have was never before" (p. 113). But this is more than Tom is able to comprehend and forgive. He is not like Macey of the Roman episode who takes care of the raped and pregnant girl. He is not like Thomas who sees his wife being raped by an old rival. "If you are, I'll be proud," he says, referring to the possibility that she might get pregnant. Jan is probably pregnant at the end of the novel, and although the baby can only be Tom's, he will never be able to accept it. There is a solution for both Macey and Thomas. The half-wit Macey eventually buries the cursed axe and becomes free. Thomas is going to live a happy life with Margery in their own house on Mow Cop. So the two historical levels suggest that there is hope for Tom as well. Or is it the other way round? Is the author contrasting our own ruthless time with the past, where blood was shed but people had peace at heart?

One can turn to Garner's earlier books to find an answer. Tom's letter of farewell contains a feeble hope of a last positive solution for the two young people. If Jan cares enough to decipher and read the letter, if she wishes to get involved in Tom's inner struggle once again—remember that she is training to be a sister of mercy—then she probably can save him. Tom does give her hints in the letter about where and when he intends to take his life.

What solutions are there for us the readers in this open ending? Does the writer want us to understand that Jan indeed makes this last endeavour to save Tom? In Garner's previous books there are several keys that help to interpret the ending of *Red Shift*. In *The Owl Service* (1967) there is a story of a curse upon generation after generation which makes three young people play again and again the roles in the legend of the flower woman who became an owl. In this book the characters break out of their predestined roles and escape the curse. Tom, on the other hand, has broken the pattern of reconciliation and forgiveness described on the two historical levels.

Another key is probably hidden in the ending of *Elidor* (1965), where, at least according to Garner's own interpretation, the final scene forebodes Roland's insanity. This is the price he has to pay for interfering in Elidor's struggle for power. In *Red Shift* Tom is raving on Mow Cop, going mad as punishment for irresponsibly playing with the sacred, represented here by the stone axe. Against this background there is no hope whatsoever for Tom, and the ending of *Red Shift* is definitely pessimistic.

ALLUSIONS — TO ONESELF OR OTHERS

Another writer whose entire *oeuvre* can facilitate an adequate interpretation of an individual text is the Norwegian H. C. Andersen medal winner Tormod Haugen. For instance, his young adult novel "Winter Place" (1984) is a realistic rewrite of his earlier symbolical fairy tale "The White Castle" (1980). But it takes a keen eye of a scholar to discover this connection.

However, allusions can also be quite obvious and meant to be recognized by children. In Haugen's novel "The Day That Disappeared" (1983) the main character meets the hero from his own childhood reading, Peter Pan. Ignoring the reader's knowledge of Peter Pan as an adventurous and carefree Disney figure, Haugen dwells on the tragic element in the image of Peter Pan: his endless loneliness and his bitterness towards the adult world. Haugen's Peter Pan wants to take revenge on his parents by enticing children to following him to Never-neverland. Unlike Wendy and her brothers, Haugen's character Willem cannot learn how to fly, for he is too heavily burdened down with sorrow and anguish. Comparing Haugen's text with *Neverland* by Toby Forward, discussed above, we see more clearly how, depending on intention, a writer can take up different threads from the same intertext.

There are other intertextual links in "The Day That Disappeared" that are not as explicitly presented. These include above all connections with Tove Jansson's short story 'The Invisible Child' (from *Tales from Moominvalley*, 1962) and Maria Gripe's *The Glassblower's Children* (1963), but also Haugen's own book "The White Castle." Invisibility as a sign and consequence of oppression is sharply contrasted to the same motif in folktales or in early fantasy, as in Edith Nesbit's *The Enchanted Castle* (1907), where it is used for the purpose of adventure and entertainment.[25] While the image of Peter Pan requires a previous knowledge, invisibility is instead part of the "anonymous rush of voices."

Allusions can also consciously be used so that they escape the primary addressee, the child. It is remarkable that at least four Swedish young adult novels from the 1980s should make use of the motif "girl disguised as boy": four books as different as Peter Pohl's *Johnny My Friend* (1985), a psychological novel in 1950s urban setting; Maria Gripe's modern Gothic novel, the so-called Shadow tetralogy (1982–88); Ulf Stark's "The Nuts and the No-Goods" (1984), a comedy of mistaken identity in a contemporary school setting and "Anna-Carolina's War" (1986) by Mats Wahl, which is a straightforward historical novel. This may of course be a coincidence. The wide generic and thematic diversity of the books precludes direct influence. All four of them, however, seem to actualize a well-known character from Swedish literature—the androgynous figure of Tintomara from the novel by C.J.L. Almqvist *,The Queen's Diadem* (1834). Allusions to Almqvist belong to the adult code, for not many young readers in Sweden today are familiar with Tintomara. It is possible that in referring the adult co-reader to an established literary source, the writers are trying to legitimize their own writing and raise the status of children's books. Parallels with Tintomara have been noticed by Swedish critics in the case of Carolin, the heroine of Maria Gripe's novels which clearly display Romantic traits, but not in the other texts which lack such features. But the allusion is naturally still there. The fact that the Tintomara image suddenly becomes relevant in the 1980s can be contemplated against the background of the emergence of feminism and feminist literary criticism in Sweden, which have put the life circumstances of women in a male-dominated society into the limelight. The phenomenon of transsexuality has also been given some attention in the media during the previous decade.

There are many examples of allusions and quotations in children's books that are based on adult codes. One case of purely literary allusions is to be found in *The Church Mice and the Moon* (1974), a picturebook by Graham Oakley, where a charming vegetarian cat mumbles something about it being elementary, dear Watson, to a mouse whose name he knows very well is not Watson. Since the picturebook very clearly is addressed to small children, the allusion is a wink at the adult co-reader, unless the writer is merely playing a game for its own sake.

In the novel "The Backwards Life" (1990) by the Swedish writer Per Nilsson there are nameplates in an apartment house with the names of

Stoican, Holmér and El-Sayed. The three names belong to three very notorious political figures of the late 1980s in Sweden. It is a non-literary allusion on the adult level which is moreover culturally determined and bound to be lost in translation, and short-lived, since within a few years these names will lose their significance and become simply three in a row of other names on the same plate: Lakatos, Hämäläinen, Gonzales and Christapopulos. At that point they will no longer be an allusion, and the sign will become part of the child code, leading the contemporary Swedish child to conclude that, since these are all non-Swedish names, the setting must be a district in which many immigrants live.

Further, Per Nilsson's protagonist mentions a book title that he thinks would suit him perfectly: *The Idiot*. Child readers most probably do not know that there really exists a well-known book with this title, and they know still less about the connotation it arouses. At the same time, however, this reference is Nilsson's allusion to himself, to his earlier book "Between Waking Up and Going to Sleep" (1986), where the boy buys *The Idiot* for his aunt, not yet aware what it is about.

Precisely as with Alan Garner, using Per Nilsson's other novels as intertexts can contribute to an interpretation of "The Backwards Life." In this case, however, I would state that the explanations we can extract from earlier books considerably diminish the mystical charm of the novel. Bible quotations such as "Why have you forsaken me," which supposedly reinforce the character's relation to Gert Oscar Davidson (G.O.D.), are an "overcodification" of the message to the child.

It is rewarding to treat intertextual elements such as allusions and quotations semiotically. In semiotic terminology, quotations are *iconic* signs, while allusions are *indexical* signs. Let us recall that the notion of *icon* in semiotics denotes a sign that is related to the signified through similarity. Repetitions in a text, that is, self-quotations, are also iconic. *Index* is a semiotic sign related to the signified through a reference. This distinction in Peircian semiotics is based on trichotomy, as well as on a hierarchal relation between the different sign types. For instance, all indices are also icons. That means that allusions are also iconic signs related to the signified through similarity. Analyzing quotations and allusions as semiotic signs can, among other things, help us to understand better the not always simple relationship between text and intertext.

DIALOGUE AROUND A WARDROBE

It is often tempting to study a concrete motif or image occurring in the works of different writers. Such occurrences are usually treated as conscious borrowing. I do not mean, of course, the use of archetypal figures or objects such as horses, swords or shadows, but more concrete images which are also not kenotypal. For instance, a central element in fantasy is the door leading into the secondary world, and in several texts this door is represented very concretely, as a wardrobe, cupboard or closet. The first text that springs to mind is *The Lion, the Witch and the Wardrobe* (1950) by C.S. Lewis.

Several scholars have discovered different sources for this quite peculiar passage between reality and the magic world. C.S. Lewis's biographer Roger Green refers to Edith Nesbit's short story 'The Aunt and Amabel' (from the collection *The Magic World*, 1912), in which a railway station on the way to a magic realm is called BIGWARDROBEINSPAREROOM.[26] Rosemary Jackson, who is above all concerned with fantasy for adults, sees the sources of the wardrobe in George MacDonald's adult novel *Phantastes* (1858),[27] which is not at all impossible, given the admiration C.S. Lewis felt for MacDonald and his vehement denial of any influence by Nesbit. MacDonald may have been inspired in turn by his great German predecessor E.T.A. Hoffmann, who in *The Nutcracker and the Mouse King* (1816) allows his protagonist to enter the magical kingdom through a closet. C.S. Lewis may also have remembered Hoffmann's tale.

After Lewis, the wardrobe appears in at least two English-language texts. In *Jessamy* (1967) by Barbara Sleigh the time shift occurs when the character locks herself in a wardrobe. In *A Castle of Bone* (1972) by Penelope Farmer a wardrobe functions both as a peculiar time machine and as a passage into another world. Both writers could hardly avoid being familiar with C. S. Lewis.

Ignoring the totally uninteresting question of who has borrowed the idea from whom, and focusing instead on the use these different writers make of the motif, we can discover both similarities and dissimilarities. In all these texts the wardrobe symbolizes something alien and even frightening and threatening, which forebodes the encounter with the Other World. In both Lewis's and Barbara Sleigh's novels the wardrobe is located in an unfamiliar house visited by child characters during school holidays; in Penelope Farmer's book the wardrobe has been recently purchased by the family. All wardrobes bear a pronounced resemblance to a gateway. In Hoffmann's story, however, the wardrobe plays a subordinate role in the plot and may simply go unnoticed by the reader. The same is true about MacDonald's book. The wardrobe in C.S. Lewis's novel is central, appearing in the title together with the two main rival powers in Narnia.

The land of Narnia is not situated inside the wardrobe, although Lewis mentions in passing how clever Lucy was not to shut herself in the wardrobe so that she is able to return. As a narrative device the wardrobe has the same function as in Hoffmann's and MacDonald's texts, but it attracts much more attention. It is in fact unnecessary for Lewis to after-rationalize the magical qualities of the wardrobe in a later text, *The Magician's Nephew* (1955). He explains in *The Lion, the Witch and the Wardrobe* that there are many gateways to Narnia, and that it is not necessary and sometimes not even possible to take the same way again. The wardrobe is just one of these many gateways.

In Barbara Sleigh's book the wardrobe leads the protagonist, Jessamy, into another time. She is not transposed into another world, and the first time shift occurs unintentionally. Otherwise the function of the wardrobe as a magical passage is amazingly similar to its use by Lewis. Jessamy's second visit to the past is conscious, just like Lucy's second visit to Narnia. But it is clearly understood that the door is not open always or for everybody. In Jessamy's case the marks and dates inside the wardrobe give her clues.

The Pevensie children in Lewis's text pass through the wardrobe into Narnia three times—thereafter the gate is closed for them. Lewis does not mention this fact, but it reflects the usual magical number of three in folktale. Jessamy is also given three chances to enter the past, but the last time she fails. A grownup—typically!—has wiped off the marks inside the wardrobe. Sleigh shows how magical powers can be destroyed by everyday interference. This is a daring intrusion into the magic code.

Finally, in Penelope Farmer's novel the wardrobe has a dual function. It works as a sort of time machine that transforms everything into its original form: a brass button into ore, a leather wallet into a live piglet. One of the main characters accidentally goes back in time and becomes a baby. In order to save him, his friends must voluntarily enter the wardrobe, whereupon they find themselves in another world. It is not a matter of fighting evil forces in a magical realm of the Narnia type, however, but of investigating one's own fears, entering one's one psyche—symbolized by the wardrobe. The novel is a complicated psychological quest, and the narrative structure centering on the wardrobe is much more sophisticated than in the earlier examples. Even if Penelope Farmer has indeed "borrowed" the wardrobe from C.S. Lewis—which is not at all implausible—she has made it into something much more exciting than the model.

JONATHAN LIONHEART SEAGULL

I would like to conclude the intertextual argument with an example which may seem far-fetched but which once again confirms that any direct connection between two texts is not at all necessary. It is natural to discuss Astrid

Lindgren's *The Brothers Lionheart* (1973) in the context of children's literature: as a subversive, imaginative book in the midst of the then dominant social realism, as I have done above; as a part of the Swedish and world fantasy tradition; or as a milestone in Astrid Lindgren's *oeuvre*. The book is doubtless "ambivalent," in the sense that it contains easily discernible children's and adult codes. The differences between these are so manifest that some critics have proposed two totally separate interpretations, a "subjective" one from the child's viewpoint and an "objective" or "adult" reading.[28] Personally I think it is irrelevant whether we see the transference of the two brothers to Nangijala, and later to Nangilima, as "real" or as Rusty's feverish fancies or his sorrow after the loss of his brother; whatever the interpretation, the book still depicts the inner maturation of the protagonist.

What I think is worth discussing is the chronotope of the novel in its intertextual relations. The universe of *The Brothers Lionheart* is presented as a chain of worlds: the Earth—Nangijala—Nangilima (and theoretically further into infinity) where every new world is supposed to be better and more perfect than the previous one. The first association this may suggest is the end of C.S. Lewis's *The Last Battle* (1956), in which the characters pass from reality to Narnia and then farther to a "new" and more genuine Narnia. As in Astrid Lindgren's text, death is the ultimate gate between the worlds. The new Narnia, however, which like Nangilima is never described but only mentioned, represents the third and final stage in the classical Platonic triple world of ideas. Besides, Lewis's children have in no way shown themselves worthy of proceeding into an even better world. They have of course fought for the best of Narnia, but afterwards they could return comfortably into the security of their own reality, regressing from clever and wise sovereigns into young children totally unaffected by their experience. It is probably only Edmund, the traitor, who has really gone through the trials which made him worthy of a death leading into a better world.

In *The Brothers Lionheart* it is above all physical and spiritual trials which precede death and a transference into another world. With its endless multiple worlds this model of the universe is neither Platonic nor Christian but Buddhist. As a possible intertext, therefore, I venture to suggest Richard Bach's *Jonathan Livingston Seagull* (1970), a book which is probably unexpected in the context of children's literature but which was very significant as an inspiring cult book when it appeared. I am not intimating that Astrid Lindgren is a Buddhist or that her text must necessarily be interpreted in terms of Buddhism. If there is any influence, it is entirely indirect. But is it mere coincidence that the name of Astrid Lindgren's hero is Jonathan?

Intertextuality is one of the most prominent features of postmodern literature for adults, and critics have proclaimed it both welcome and indispensable. In children's literature most intertextual links are often approached as imitative and secondary. However, the growing intertextuality of contemporary children's literature, which is often apparent in allusions, irony and the fracturing of well-known patterns, demands that these narrative elements be reevaluated.

With the help of the intertextual method we can often reach the dimensions of texts that are overlooked by other approaches. Viewing each text in a dialogue with previous texts or relevant discourse can lead us to new conclusions. Especially fruitful is the examination of hidden dialogue, of latent echoes and connections.

Studies of children's books drawing on mythical sources show that some writers have skillfully used and others mechanically applied this subject matter. Studies of children's texts in dialogue with adult literature reveal certain traits specific to children's literature. The apologies of Edward Eager and Michael Ende that I have offered make use of intertextuality to show that these writers are using creative irony rather than blatantly imitating previous models. Intertextual studies of particular motifs can help us understand the writers' intentions, messages and individual style. Intertextual studies within the works of an author can often lead to more adequate interpretations of "difficult," multidimensional texts. The extensive use of both literary and extraliterary allusions enriches children's texts and also allows writers to operate on both the child and adult code levels. This latter feature is probably most prominent in recent texts, and, precisely like other postmodern features of children's books, it will probably increase in significance in the near future.

In trying to visualize the future of children's literature research, two strategies can be proposed. First, looking backwards, we can most probably discover more intertextual links between texts than are imaginable today. Personally I think the most exciting line of study is purely typological, that is, discovering similarities in texts that definitely have no generic links. How can three writers, obviously independently of each other, use elevators as a means of passage into the secondary world? We must assume that their intertext is the extraliterary development of technology.

Secondly, we must be prepared for children's literature to display an increasing degree of intertextuality in the near future. Children's writers are undoubtedly becoming more and more aware of their own intertextual connections, literary as well as non-literary, and many of them consciously work with a vast range of intertextual links manifested in parody, allusions, and so on. Also, as contemporary children's literature crosses the boundaries into mainstream literature, it participates to an increasing extent in the "postmodern" discourse.

NOTES

1. Bakhtin, 1981.
2. Brostrøm, 1987.
3. Espmark, 1985, p. 25.
4. Ibid.
5. Stephens, 1992, p. 86.
6. Nodelman, 1992.
7. See, e.g., Rose, 1984.
8. Stephens, 1992, pp. 122ff.
9. Although they seldom acknowledge their debt, contemporary "fractured" feminist tales owe much to Nesbit.
10. Cf. John Stephens's analysis of *Five Children and It* as "carnival," that is, a questioning ("interrogating," in Stephens's terminology) of societal norms (Stephens, 1992, pp. 125–132).
11. Cameron, 1969, p. 83.
12. Crouch, 1972, p. 16.
13. Eager, 1969.
14. Cf. Buckley, 1977, pp. 14f.
15. Philip, 1984.
16. This parodical tone is totally absent from the film version, which, to my mind, accounts for the evident failures of the film.
17. See Propp, 1968. The terms used in the discussion of the system of characters and the sequence of functions are taken from Propp. The English translation is not always adequate, but I prefer to use it to avoid confusion. It is also possible to analyze the text with the help of A.J. Greimas's so-called *modalities*, which are much better known in Western literary criticism but are a development of Propp's model (Greimas, 1966).
18. This is superbly described in Ursula Le Guin's short story 'The Rule of Names' in her collection *The Wind's Twelve Quarters* (1975).
19. Green, 1957, pp. 34f.
20. Cf. note 27 to chapter 5.
21. Mählqvist, 1992.
22. Cf. Aidan Chambers's suggestion: "Garner means them to be co-plots, the function of which is not simply to support the top tune, but to add variation to the main theme" (Chambers, 1973, p. 495).
23. See Philip, 1981, pp. 110f.
24. There is an echo of the thumbprint in *The Stone Book* (1976), where Mary discovers in a cave a print of a palm that is identical to her own. In Garner's work images wander from one book to another as self-allusions.
25. On the invisibility motif in Haugen's books see Metcalf, 1992.
26. Green, 1957, p. 36.
27. Jackson, 1981, p. 147.
28. See Törnqvist, 1975; also Edström, 1982, p. 55; Edström 1992a, pp. 217–221.

METAFICTION IN CHILDREN'S LITERATURE

We have focused on the text itself—on its codes and its relationship to other texts. We have thus ignored the links in both directions of the communication chain to the writer (sender) and the reader (recipient). However, in contemporary children's literature these links are steadily growing more complex, which leads us once again to the question of realism in children's books. It is only and exclusively the relation between the writer's reality, the reality of the text (the fictitious reality) and the reader's reality that can serve as a basis for the question whether children's literature is "realistic," that is, whether it depicts a concrete, tangible world that the reader can recognize.

Why did Alfred Hitchcock always allow a glimpse of himself in every film he made? Was he trying to create an illusion of reality, or on the contrary, did he want to destroy it? If a creator can enter his own created world—is it the world or the creator who is fictitious? One is immediately overwhelmed by metaphysical questions.

One of many problems that young readers (and sometimes even grownup readers) encounter when reading novels is to distinguish between fiction and reality. This sounds simple, but it is quite possible, for example, to treat literary characters as if they were living people of flesh and blood; their behavior and their moral values are interpreted from these premises instead of upon the writer's intentions ("John Silver is a bad guy. His mother must have maltreated him when he was a child"). Sometimes we discover such statements in literary analyses which are reminiscent of medical journals in that they treat figures in novels as if they were indeed patients ("Rusky goes through a psychic crisis with the following symptoms . . ."). Many a critic today seriously questions reading fiction mimetically, as if there were a reality behind the words. In mimetic reading the first-person narrator in a novel is identified with the writer. Realism as a literary device is confused with credibility or verisimilitude. However, unlike documentary or journalism, fiction is not a direct *reflection* of reality but an artistic *transformation* of it.

As various reception studies have pointed out, in any work of art there is a relationship between the author, the text and the reader. The notions of *the implied writer* and *the implied reader*, the *narrator* and the *narratee* are of general significance for our understanding of the nature of children's literature. More and more children's books consciously pose questions about the relationship between the writer, his creations and his readers. Such texts have been named *metafiction*, books about books and the writing of books, books which somehow explain themselves, investigating the essence of writing by describing the creative process itself.

The diversity of metafictional levels we can observe in literature today is a feature of its postmodern phase, although it can be found in texts from much earlier periods. Still, it is only recently that literary critics have both become aware of this fascinating device and started examining it. A study by Patricia Waugh, *Metafiction. The Theory and Practice of Self-conscious Fiction*, is wholly devoted to this subject.[1]

Patricia Waugh defines metafiction as "fictional writing which self-consciously and systematically draws attention to its status as an artifact in order to pose questions about the relationship between fiction and reality" (p. 2). The cornerstone in the metafictional view of literature is a rejection of the old attitude to literature as a reflection of reality, and to language as an instrument used in this reflecting process. "Language," Patricia Waugh states, "is an independent, self-contained system which generates its own 'meanings.' Its relationship to the phenomenal world is highly complex, problematic and regulated by convention" (p. 3). What she means is that language basically allows writers to write anything, whether or not it makes sense. If writers most often choose to be understood, it is probably because they have something to communicate. Language itself, however, does not automatically presuppose that there is any meaning behind words, much less any concrete "reality."

Waugh points out that "meta" terminology is necessary to investigate the relationship between the arbitrary linguistic system and the world to which the system pretends to refer. In other words, the terms of metafiction allow us to describe a relationship between the world *within* fiction and the world *outside* it. This has become more necessary than ever in our time, when so many writers deliberately violate logic and use language for its own sake.

Patricia Waugh's material is literature for adults, in particular complex authors such as Jorge Luis Borges, Vladimir Nabokov, John Barth, John Fowles, Muriel Spark and Kurt Vonnegut. Waugh states that although metafictional tendencies are theoretically present in any novel, metafiction as a literary device is a relatively new phenomenon in Western literature, perhaps only about twenty years old. Most of the examples that I have discovered in children's literature are quite recent, primarily from the 1980s and 1990s. The notion of metafiction first appears in English language literary criticism during the early 1970s.

Patricia Waugh presents two principal types of metafiction: that which exposes the writing process and that which for the purpose of parody comments on a well-known work of literature. Her notion of metafiction also includes the specific organisation of space, alternative worlds, which I have explored in the chapter on the chronotope. It also includes many cases of intertextuality manifested in parody and irony, which I have discussed in the chapter on intertextuality. As I mentioned above, metafictional levels are found in any work of fiction, but in certain texts they become more palpable. Patricia Waugh's definition of metafiction is very broad, but I would like to concentrate on just one part of it, namely, that which focuses on texts that in some way or other consciously discuss the art of writing and their own existence. These may be texts which have fiction as their subject matter, "a novel within a novel." They may be texts which examine the origin of fiction and often leave the reader in hesitation. Or we may have to do with texts which state that the world itself is a fiction.

As postmodern literature, metafiction is highly involved in experimental devices. But it would be essentially wrong to evaluate metafiction as mere formal experiment. Metafiction is not only a means of exposing the essential narrative structure to the reader, but is above all a confirmation of the postmodern view of the world as something artificial, constructed, manmade. Aidan Chambers's novel *Breaktime* (1978), mentioned above in connection with experimental narrative techniques, is also an example of a metanovel.

On the other hand, metafiction is by no means a subgenre but is instead a trend *within* the novel genre. Since modern children's literature is drawing closer and closer to the novel in the full meaning of the word in its evolution from epic to polyphony and dialogics, it is no wonder that as prominent a trait as metafiction should also appear in books for young readers. Polyphony itself may be considered a metafictional feature.

Among Patricia Waugh's basic terms we find "frames" and "frame-breaking," notions that belong in semiotics. However, the point of departure in Waugh's theory is the postmodern view of the world as a construction of frames and boundaries. What is the boundary that delimits fiction and reality? One clear attitude becomes apparent in the tendency in modern literature to start and end texts arbitrarily, to tell a story without a chronological order, and so on.

Other boundaries that can be crossed in metafiction are those between the subject and object of the text. One possible way to approach metafictional structure in a text is to depart from the relationship between the different subjects, objects and addressees within and outside the text: the writer, the implied writer, the narrator, the protagonist, especially the first-person protagonist, the narratee, the implied reader and the real reader.

Metafiction in children's novels has not yet been studied thoroughly, although reviewers occasionally notice this aspect in individual works. However, metafiction can assume many different forms and need not be a central and obvious motif. It is all the more exciting to detect metafictional features in books that seemingly lack them, but I have chosen more obvious cases for the sake of clarity.

Patricia Waugh sets forth a number of features as typical of metafiction. I do not wish to overload my analysis with repetitive references to her book, but most theoretical arguments in this chapter are based on her comprehensive study. It is essential, however, to emphasize the particular difference between metafiction in children's and adult literature. Metafictional levels in books for young readers exist within two separate semiotic systems or groups of artistic codes: that of the adult and that of the child. Some of the metafictional structures in children's texts are obvious and belong to both codes, while others may be hidden and addressed only to the adult co-reader. Since metafiction always involves a game with the reader which is based on previous experience, it can be expected that metafictional elements will more often be found within the adult code. Precisely where the boundary goes is impossible to say; the crossing of boundaries is the most essential feature of recent literature.

Mimmi, the seven-year-old heroine of Viveca Sundvall's novel "The Diary of a First-grader" (1982), has found a typewriter in a trash container and uses it to write her diary. At the same time she tells us that she is writing in a yellow notebook, and hastens to add:

> Now, some of you may wonder how I manage to put my yellow notebook into my type-writer. Go ahead and wonder.

Rational grownups will probably continue to wonder over this not very convincing detail—the only metafictional element in Viveca Sundvall's novels about Mimmi, while young readers will accept this convention and not give it much thought. But what is its implication? Is the text we are reading supposed to be a published version of an authentic diary written by a seven-year-old girl in a yellow notebook? But we are informed that Mimmi has typed her diary, that is, she has done something totally impossible, and this calls into question the whole narrative and the process by which it came into being.

The paradox with the notebook and the typewriter may well have been detected by a reader (for instance, a diligent editor) in the manuscript stage, a little inconsistency which the writer has not noticed. More probably, however, it is a conscious device used to draw the reader's attention to the conventions of writing. Mimmi is imaginary, is what the author is telling us, as are her notebooks and her typewriter, her friends and her parents, her whole world. The question "Has this really happened?" which children often ask in their letters to writers (including Viveca Sundvall), is thus totally irrelevant.

WRITER—PROTAGONIST—READER

One of the most elementary problems of metafiction is precisely whether the characters have really existed. A metafictional hint is found as early as in Astrid Lindgren's *Emil and His Pranks* (1963), which is said to be based on Emil's mother's notes. This information is seldom perceived as metafiction. On the other hand many readers, young and old alike, have been tricked by the statement in the preface to Mats Wahl's historical novel "The Master" (1985) that the book is merely a publication of an authentic manuscript. As any observant reader will notice, the illusion is shattered very early in the novel. The text is very definitely constructed as a novel rather than as an authentic diary or autobiography. Also, the text is much too modern in its view of history. The preface is merely a gimmick to entice the reader.

Similar devices are well known in mainstream literature. For instance, in Alexandre Dumas's *The Three Musketeers* (1844) the author states in the preface that he has discovered and edited an authentic document. Before the novel became an accepted literary genre, such stratagems were necessary to justify publication. In Mats Wahl's case, however, the reason is quite different.

IMPLIED WRITER AND PROTAGONIST

One way to call into question the narrative and its truthfulness is to let the protagonist at the end of the book start (or contemplate) writing precisely the book we have just read. In *Freaky Friday* (1972) by Mary Rodgers the first-person narrator begins her story by saying that nobody in their right minds would believe her, but at the same time she assures us that it is definitely true. The described events are indeed hard to believe.

On waking up, Annabel finds that she has turned into her mother. In an amusing, ironical manner the story explores Annabel's experience of discovering her own identity through one day "in her mother's shoes." Among her many worries is a school composition that she is supposed to write and turn in. We learn that she did write it after all, that it was 145 pages long, and that her teacher gave her a low mark because its basic premise was utterly fantastic. Annabel adds that she was not surprised by this reaction, because she had predicted it. Then she herself poses the question: "When did she predict that"? And explains, turning directly to the real or implied reader (the implied reader or narratee may be her newly found friend Boris):

> Way back on page one, silly. You're not a very careful reader. Don't you remember page one? The story begins:
> "You are not going to believe me, nobody in their right minds could possibly believe me, but it's true, really it is."
> And the story ends the same way. (p. 145)

There are 145 pages in the book, and the story turns out to be Annabel's school composition. The credibility of the plot, which we as readers accept as part of the genre, is completely undermined. From Mary Rodgers's correspondence with her editor we learn that the metafictional idea of *Freaky Friday* was a late afterthought, used as a last resort because the manuscript would not hold together.[2] At the time the book was written metafiction was not yet established as a literary device, least of all in children's books. It was a daring idea indeed to explain Annabel's experience as a product of not merely her imagination but also her creativity.

In the 1980s this sort of thing becomes more common. In the Norwegian writer Per Knutsen's "Black Eye-Liner" (1989), the reader is more or less ready for the revelation, since the first-person character Jonny has throughout the novel been practising creative writing. Shall we interpret the ending to mean that Jonny is now going to describe what has actually happened to him? Or is the text we are reading in fact a product of his writing? The issue of the book—homosexuality—is quite controversial, and we can easily believe that the whole story merely takes place in Jonny's imagination.

A similar variant of hesitation is found in the last chapter of Vivien Alcock's novel *The Cuckoo Sister* (1985). Who has invented the story? Has is actually happened or is it just writing exercises that the young first-person narrator Kate shares with her sister Emma? At a certain age imagining

oneself a foundling is a common fantasy, which serves as a means of finding one's own identity. Is it possible that Vivien Alcock adds this chapter to
emphasize that "this has not really happened"? Until this chapter we have
no reason to doubt the credibility of the narrative. But the psychologically
credible story can be merely a fantasy in which Kate indulges in her struggle
against her own feelings of rivalry and jealousy towards her sister. Note that
Emma does not protest against Kate's story as such but merely comments
on its artistic structure. Emma wants a traditional epic narrative, while Kate
has left the ending open. She feels obliged to provide an ending, but that
does not eliminate our hesitation.

Metafictional hints, however, may be much less prominent than this.
In *Our Snowman Had Olive Eyes* (1977) by Charlotte Herman the first-
person protagonist, Sheila, is at the end of the book given a notebook by
her grandmother. The novel is about Sheila's discovery of her grandmother,
and through her, of herself. On receiving the notebook Sheila decides that
perhaps she will write down grandmother's story. If we wish we can interpret the text we have just read as the result of Sheila's writing efforts.

On the other hand, metafiction can be as obvious and provocative
as in Chambers's *Breaktime*, where the narratee (and hence the reader) is
confronted by the disturbing question whether he exists at all otherwise than
as a fictitious character. The narratee (who is also a character in the story,
which complicates the patterns still more) makes the very mistake that I have
mentioned earlier, namely, he identifies the first-person narrator with the
author and therefore believes that his friend's—the implied writer's—story
is true. The real reader may or may not make the same mistake, but in the
end will be left skeptical or even puzzled. Chambers has himself analyzed
his novel and the purpose for which it was written in his *Booktalks*.[3] There
he exposes the metafictional level of his novel and, in so doing, defends the
purpose of fiction challenged by the narratee.

WRITER, IMPLIED WRITER AND NARRATOR

The reader is sometimes signaled about the metafictional nature of the narrative from the very beginning, as in "The Backwards Life" (1990) by Per
Nilsson. The story as such, an exciting biography of a man who lives backwards, is a manuscript which the writer/first-person narrator receives in the
first chapter from a mystical deaf and dumb boy in the yard of his apartment house. Halfway through the book, however, the reader has probably
forgotten this detail (the suspense in the plot contributes to this) and may
start wondering about a couple of inconsistencies. For instance, what are
the time frames of the story? The events described take sixty years. But when

does the story begin? Does it take place in the future? Judging by the various temporal indications it seems as if real time stands still while the protagonist lives out his sixty years. As readers we may be slightly irritated at first; is the writer really so silly as to think we will accept this? But as soon as the narrator/writer has read the manuscript (and we are reminded that it was indeed a manuscript) he starts thinking about all the details that do not fit together. He comes to the rather trivial conclusion that there probably is "another sort of time." A literary work, of course, has its own time, which is different from real time, since fictitious time does not have to follow the same natural laws as real time.

Even when we have accepted the fact that we have read a story within a story, many questions still remain unanswered. Is the boy's manuscript an autobiography? Has this story, remarkable yet from the point of view of modern science not entirely impossible, really happened to him? Also, his story is told in the first person. Or has he written, that is, invented, this work of science fiction? It does remind us of the kind of stories that schoolchildren write. Is the novel about the first literary attempts of a young aspiring writer? In such a case the temporal inconsistencies are faults a keen editor would have noticed. Or is it even more complicated—perhaps the mysterious boy is also the creation of the narrator within the text?

If we read the novel against the background of earlier texts by Per Nilsson with the same protagonist, we get a somewhat clearer picture of the narrative structure, or, in Waugh's terminology, of the various frames of the text within the text. "Between Waking Up and Going to Sleep" (1986) is a "conventional" first-person narrative where the child narrator Nils Persson is identical with the protagonist. In "Important Things" (1988) Nils Persson keeps a diary. Thus we assume that in "The Backwards Life" he has written a science fiction novel and let the writer/narrator Per Nilsson read it. But who is this Nils Persson? Playing with the names of the writer and the protagonist is a common feature of metafiction.

There is also an essential difference between the function of the first person in conventional texts and in metafiction. The pronoun "I" can only be defined in a context. In most first-person narratives the narrator is undramatically identified with the literary character. In metafiction the first-person narrator is definitely separated from the character, even though the latter may also be referred to as "I."

Reader and Writer

In the novel *A Pack of Lies* (1988) by the British writer Geraldine McCaughrean the questioning of authorship and the origin of the story becomes very complicated. The title itself suggests that writing is an act of making up things. The main character, Ailsa, meets a mysterious young man who appears from nowhere, installs himself at the antique shop run by her mother, and helps her to sell a number of unsalable objects by telling exciting stories to the customers about each object. Sometimes they are sentimental stories, sometimes ghost stories, adventures or ballads, and every story is related to a book that the young Mr. MCC Berkshire happens to be reading. The stories are also perfect examples of the genre they represent: a concise course in creative writing. When Ailsa says indignantly that he is lying, Mr. Berkshire explains to her the difference between lies and fiction, or creativity.

But this is just one of the many metalayers in the book. It begins with Ailsa meeting the young man in the library, where she has just seen a catalogue card saying "A Pack of Lies, Oxford University Press 1988." The young man also states that he comes from Reading, pronouncing the word to rhyme with "feeding," not with "bedding," as the name of the town is pronounced. It is obvious that there is something mysterious about the man, but we never realize the meaning of his appearance until he vanishes, leaving behind a book called "The Man Who Came from Reading." When Ailsa starts reading the book, its first paragraph repeats the description of Mr. Berkshire in the beginning of the novel itself.

Ailsa and her mother decide that MCC Berkshire does not exist and has never existed. At the same time, all his stories appear to be true. This is an inexplicable paradox which Ailsa's mother summarizes as follows: ". . . if Mr. Berkshire doesn't exist but we know his stories for true, there is only one explanation" (p. 164). This last chapter in the novel is entitled "The only answer." What the answer is the readers must decide for themselves.

Because they exist as statements rather than substances, characters in metafiction sometimes behave illogically. There is nothing logical or reasonable in Mr. Berkshire's behavior. A couple of pages before the end of the novel we finally get an explanation. Michael Charles Christie Berkshire tears a sheet of paper from his typewriter and puts it aside—a young, beginning, unknown author in the midst of creative agony. His mother complains that her son never goes out, never meets a nice girl and naturally never earns a penny with his writing.

Michael contemplates whether it was right to abandon his story: "They got away from me. My characters. I lost control of them. You heard them: they were working it all out! They got too real for me!" (p. 167). He realizes—and this is another sign of a writer's despair—that he cannot go back into his own story. Or can he? "Of course I could always change the ending. . . . Perhaps it would work better if I just changed the last few. . . That's it! That's what I'll do! I'll do it!" (ibid.). He lunges towards his typewriter, and when his mother shortly afterwards comes into his room he is not there. She gazes at the sheet in the typewriter and says to herself that "A pack of lies" is not a very good title. Then she notices her son's eyeglasses on the desk and wonders where he could have gone without them.

A metaphor? A writer literally "absorbed" by his work, dissolved in it, starting to exist outside his own reality? But it is also a question of the writer's relationship to his characters becoming so intimate that they become living persons. In this situation the writer no longer exercises his own free will or power over the characters; on the contrary, they gain power over him. It is not writers who create books but books that create writers—one of the many paradoxical theses of modern reception theory. In this argument we have totally ignored the writer Geraldine McCaughrean's relationship with her colleague in the novel.

WRITER AND NARRATOR

Swedish critics have noted that the fourth part of Maria Gripe's so-called Shadow tetralogy, "The Shadow Sanctuary" (1988), is different with respect to narrative structure from the first three, in which the first-person narrator Berta tells the story, apparently several years after the fact. In the last part Maria Gripe gives the floor to Carolin, the enigmatic figure of the first three novels, whom we really never get to know. This change in perspective alone can be viewed as a comment on how fictitious persons are created and function.

The new narrative technique in "The Shadow Sanctuary," however, involves more than merely a change in point of view. More important is the mixed nature of the narrative, which consists partly of Carolin's first-person narrative and partly her letters to herself (in itself a metafictional element), as well as her drafts of dramas and screenplays, which in turn are based on the events of her real life and thus contribute to a better understanding of them.

At the same time these explicitly fictitious texts create a sense of doubt about the larger fiction, that is, the novel "The Shadow Sanctuary" itself. How much of what Carolin tells, describes in letters, and recreates in artistic form is true? Where is the boundary between reality and Carolin's imagination? In the previous books she is portrayed as an actress and pretender who creates a number of false roles and identities. She also has two names: Carolin and Saga (which in Swedish means both "saga" and "fairy tale," but also "lie") and leads two different lives under these names, sometimes even assuming the appearance of a man. How much can we trust her after this? We did not doubt the story told by the earthbound Berta, but do we believe Carolin's version? Is she not creating a world of her own? Here the notion of the unreliable narrator is driven to the extreme. Further, if we place "The Shadow Sanctuary" in a broader context, then who has written the three previous books? Maybe it is Carolin already there, but she lets Berta be her front to provide an air of credibility. Perhaps she simply lets Berta appear as "I" and refers to herself in the third person, which is a common trait in metafiction. The romantic, uncanny atmosphere of the stories does in fact permit the interpretation that they are all Carolin's invention.

Still, Carolin is even less identical with Maria Gripe than is Nils Persson with Per Nilsson (the stories are supposed to take place before Maria Gripe was born). If Carolin is the implied writer and Berta the narrator (at least in the three first novels), the boundaries between the real writer, the implied writer and the narrator become extremely flexible. Unlike Per Nilsson or Geraldine McCaughrean, Maria Gripe does not directly offer a metafictional interpretation of her texts. Especially in view of the overall importance of the creativity motif in her *oeuvre*, however, it is tempting to regard them from this perspective.

IMPLIED WRITER AND HIS WORLD

The novel *Fade* (1988) by Robert Cormier leaves us in no doubt as to who has written the text within the text. However, questions in the novel arise around the relation between fiction and reality. Cormier makes things a bit easier for the reader by very promptly singling out "the novel within the novel" and placing it in separate chapters. The first section resembles an exciting fantasy story with serious undertones, which become all the more serious when a murder is committed by the first-person character. Nothing in this section suggests that it should be a story after the fact, that is, that Paul Moreaux tells a story about himself at the age of thirteen long after events which have been filtered through temporal distance and adult experience. Nor is there anything which—within the genre frames of fantasy— would prompt the reader to question the plausibility of the story. The story is interrupted just when it is most exciting, however, and the question "Is it true?" is raised most pointedly. This first section appears to be a manuscript that is being read by the next first-person character, Susan Roger, and that seems to be written by her grandfather's deceased cousin, the famous writer Paul Roger. He is famous for realistic stories from his home town, Monument, Massachusetts. Although the settings are real and it depicts several real people and events, this posthumously discovered manuscript is distinctly unlike his usual style and themes. We can say that it is a roman à clef in which Paul Roger calls himself Paul Moreaux.

Together with Paul Roger's literary agent Meredith, Susan tries to find signs in the text that would enable them to establish whether the text is fiction or autobiography. Meredith has asked Paul's cousin Jules, Susan's grandfather, to read and comment on the manuscript. His comments are a very good example of a writer working on his characters, who are like but also unlike their real models. The events are also only partially real. There is no way to prove or disprove them. The divergence in details may be due to the failing memory of Paul or Jules or both. And then there is the writer's imagination:

> It is obvious that Paul again is demonstrating his talent for taking real people in a real place and transforming them into fictional charac-
> ters in an artificial setting. He seizes the truth and moulds those to the design he has in mind. His characters . . . appear to be real when seen from a distance but they are much different when viewed close up. (p. 171)

What leads Jules to dismiss the story as fiction is above all its supernatural element—Paul's ability to "fade" and become invisible. "To believe otherwise is to believe in the impossible," he ends his review (p. 181). Jules is an old, experienced and down-to-earth criminal inspector who is used to basing his investigations on facts. Susan, on the other hand, would like to believe the incredible, especially when she gets her hands on the sequel to Paul's manuscript. When we read the following section of the novel we already know that it is a novel within a novel, and so we see it in a new light as compared to the previous section. The narrator's presence is more evident here, and it is obvious that the story is retrospective, occurring in a specific time and with flashbacks into Paul's childhood—the time of the first section.

Then the story is interrupted again, and at first there is an uncertainty as to whether we are still reading Paul's manuscript together with Susan. It is now a third-person narrative about Ozzie, Paul's nephew and the next "fader." Not until twenty-five pages later does the narrative start alternating with Paul's notes in the first person—a definite metafictional sign. In the final chapter Susan contemplates the question why Paul should suddenly mix "I" and "he." The Ozzie chapter has an omniscient, empathetic narrator, which is an unlikely narrative device in an autobiographical text. Does this prove that the text is fiction, as Meredith believes? Unlike the previous sections, the setting of the Ozzie chapter is fictitious.

Here we are left with the final and crucial question of the fading itself, the invisibility. Is it possible? The author gives us the following clue to the mystery of creativity:

> On paper, between the first and last pages of a manuscript, nothing is impossible. But in the reality of sunshine on a carpet, furniture you can touch as you pass, faucets that spout water, headaches, loneliness on a Sunday evening, the illusion created by nouns and verbs and similes and metaphors become only that—illusions. Words on a page. And *fade* becomes, then, just another word. (p. 303)

Here is an excellent illustration of Patricia Waugh's statement about language being a self-contained system. The quotation underscores the fact that it is words which are the writer's material, and this leads us to interpret Paul Roger's manuscript as pure fiction, although Susan once again experiences doubt on the last pages of the novel.

But we can also try to take one more step along the axis "narrator—implied writer—real writer." Is Paul Roger a direct portrait of Robert Cormier, who has lived all his life in Massachusetts and is most famous for his realistic novels? Is *Fade* an autobiographical novel? If the question does not seem relevant it is only because of our reluctance as readers to accept the incredible events in the novel as "realistic." It is not accidental, however, that writers such as Mary Rodgers, Cormier, Per Nilsson or McCaughrean, who play with metafictional levels of their texts, use supernatural elements. It is these elements that evoke the characters' (and the readers') doubts as to the credibility of the stories, draw our attention to whatever seems incoherent, and, consequently, also stimulate reflections upon metafiction. The absence of magical elements in "The Shadow Sanctuary" makes it more difficult to view the work as metafiction. It is worth recollecting that the majority of texts analyzed by Patricia Waugh are by authors such as Vonnegut, García Marquez or Borges who make use of supernatural elements. Patricia Waugh also stresses, however, that metafiction does not break the conventions of realism, but instead reveals them. That means that metafictional features are by no means determined by the supernatural. They are on the contrary more important in "realistic" books but more difficult to discover there.

The crossing of boundaries, or frames, between reality and fiction is otherwise the dominant feature in the genre of fantasy. Books in which protagonists wander between "reality" (which in itself is a fiction) and a story within a story are often classified as fantasy. This is open to question, and adult literature enjoys a freedom for which children's literature still has to struggle. It is not "nice" to put labels on adult metafictional texts, whether these are novels or films; who would call Woody Allen's *Purple Rose of Cairo* a fantasy? The essence of metafiction, however, is to erase the illusion of a boundary between fantasy and reality, and in so doing it also questions the reality of "reality."

READER AND PROTAGONIST

This difficult dilemma can occasionally best be addressed within the fantastic genre. Michael Ende's novel *The Neverending Story* (1979), which I have already discussed in another context, is an example of a reader entering the fiction. But the reader—Bastian—also becomes a creator, or at least, a co-creator, of "The neverending story," a book written by The Old Man of the Wandering Mountain, which appears mysteriously in Carl Conrad Coreander's bookshop and then disappears to be read by others—why not by us? There are at least three levels of reality in this novel: our reality (outside the novel), Bastian's (in the novel) and the third within the book that Bastian is reading. The relations between reality and the two fictitious levels are rather complex and depend on the reader's interpretation.

A magic book in which the protagonists can read about themselves is a common motif in fantasy and is found, for instance, in Lloyd Alexander's Prydain suite (1964–68), or in Alan Garner's *Elidor* (1965). The magic frame does not, however, allow us to perceive metafictional features clearly enough. In *The Neverending Story* it is the protagonist's definite step into fiction that makes us aware of metalevels. The genre conventions make us accept it as part of the narrative structure.

REAL AND IMPLIED WRITER

In a book with totally "realistic" features, on the other hand, a writer will have to use other narrative devices to evoke the reader's doubts. It is often the writer's situation as such that serves this purpose. One recent children's novel that very clearly investigates the art of writing is the Norwegian Tormod Haugen's "A Novel About Merkel Hanssen, and Donna Winther, and The Big Escape" (1986). Significantly, the genre is stated in the very title, and it is also repeated several times in the text. This is indeed a complicated postmodern experimental novel in which the crossing of boundaries between the world of the novel and the world of the writer constitutes the story itself. ("The story!" exclaims the author from time to time. "I have forgotten the story. I have lost the line.") He allows us to view his pains of creation ("I've hoped that everything should be easier as soon as they began the escape,") to be present at his contemplations on how he is to relate certain episodes, how much he as a writer is supposed to know about his characters ("I always think I know so little,") how much he knows about the whole novel before he starts writing.

Haugen's crossing of the borders of fiction is superbly executed. The book begins dramatically with the nameless character standing on the outside edge of a balcony six stories up and just about to climb down to the balcony below. We are given a detailed description of his fears, doubts and determination. The third-person narrative is at one point interrupted by an inner monologue in italics: "*I don't want to tumble down, but I will!*" This has become a common technique in children's literature and is probably never noticed by the reader. When we read "I give up" several lines further on, we apprehend the phrase as the character's thought. Unlike what we saw in Geraldine McCaughrean's text, however, the very next phrase introduces a complete change without as much as a blank line to separate it from the preceding text: "Bitter and irritated I get up from my typewriter. I would like to tear the sheet out and forget the book. I can't make it the way I want to have it." The suspense is gone. The image of the boy on the balcony is "frozen" as if by the control panel on a VCR and will not return until the middle of the book—in a different form, since the writer (and the reader) by now know a lot more about the character. But already with this first crossing of the border the reader becomes aware of the writer's participation in the forming of the book.

During the whole novel we as readers are given a thorough course in creative writing. How do we start a story? How do we finish it? How is suspense created? How much should the reader know about the characters, the main character, the secondary characters? The writer complains of one of these that he does not know enough about him but still feels that he belongs in the novel about Merkel. How important are the different characters to the action? At one point the writer decides to eliminate Donna Winther, saying that she suddenly became too tiresome when he failed to fit her into Merkel's story. Is it imperative to relate events in chronological order? How does a flashback work? These are some questions that teachers ask their students, although perhaps in a slightly different form, when discussing texts in class.

The writer is omniscient and emphasizes his knowledge: ". . . I can at least tell the reader something that Donna doesn't know. It is I—the writer—who makes up the story and the characters." But he also confesses that the characters have a life of their own: "I don't know enough about Merkel. I am hardly acquainted with him at all." He stresses that when he states something about the characters he simply *thinks* that they thought or felt like that.

The writer is also present in the story and addresses the reader directly ("You probably understand that . . . "). Among other things, the reader is requested not to stop reading even if the story seems a bit slow. One recurrent device is to describe something by not describing it, for example: "I could have told you . . . but I won't"; "here is what the writer could have written, but as I say: I know too little about Torremolinos with its beach and esplanades and waves and pesetas and food." With brief hints Haugen allows the reader to fill in the missing details.

We learn about the meaning of dedications and prefaces. We are given insights on characterization, composition, and metaphors. The writer willingly comments on the use of certain words and expressions, especially stale clichés: "Quick as lightning (I couldn't think of a better wording) . . ." or "It is this sort of evening when nothing means anything and everything takes on a meaning (the writer liked this phrase because it looks so artistic)." He also emphasizes that he dresses his young characters' thoughts in a language that they cannot master:

> Still Donna knew that her gaze was visible, that her eyes looked like small, longing moons (these are the writer's words, because Donna didn't think exactly this way at exactly that time. But I guess it suits her to be thinking like that).

He comments further:

> This gives the writer a possibility of using the words he likes, for instance about what Donna is thinking. It is not certain that she would have used those words herself, yet the writer lets her use them. It happens especially when the writer feels a need to be poetic. (my translations)

This is a narrative device that we have discovered in Maria Gripe's books about Elvis and that has been developed by many modern Scandinavian children's writers. It permits writers to use the riches of language and at the same time enter into a young child's innermost thoughts.

It is clearly demonstrated that the writer is free to let certain things happen (he offers us two versions of the course of events, and he chooses one of them himself); yet he cannot let anything happen (for instance, allowing the father's girlfriend Julia to be absent during Merkel's encounter with his father would be an impossible and too simple solution). The characters and events must be subordinated to a certain logic so that we as readers can believe the whole story ("I am always afraid that I decide too much"). Merkel, Donna, their parents, Donna's sister Marylin and her boyfriend can only act within the scope of character that "the writer" has created for them. Sometimes "the writer" feels that they are beyond his control and "surprise" him ("The writer thinks that it is awfully exciting, especially because he is not so sure himself about what is going to happen"). He cannot undo what is done or make an utterance unuttered. He does not know how the story will end ("Naturally the writer can tell you where the mother is and what must happen next in order to give the novel a happy ending. But I simply cannot . . . ").

Who is the protagonist of Haugen's novel? Is it Merkel or is it the writer, the first-person narrator? Does the book tell us about Merkel's dramatic conflict with his parents (and Donna's as a parallel) or about the writer's impossible work of describing Merkel's feelings adequately? The writer's story is an important part of the novel. It has its own time and place. We learn something about the writer's habits, such as his taste for tea and red wine. We know that his typewriter is green, but that he sometimes uses a pen. For the sake of authenticity there are some misprints in the book at points where the writer is supposed to be tired—we remember this device from Gunnel Beckman's *Admission to the Feast* (1969). In other words, we know that the writer is a person of flesh and blood who must go out to the toilet at times. On the other hand, it is clear that "the writer" in the novel is not identical with Tormod Haugen. The fact that "the writer's" narrative also alternates between "I" and "he" is a typical metafictional feature corresponding to Carolin's portrayal of herself.

In Haugen's book we discover the whole chain that constitutes a metafictional text: the writer (Tormod Haugen)—the implied writer ("the writer" in the novel)—the narrator (the "I" of the novel)—the implied reader ("you")—the real reader.

But why should a writer reveal his anguish? Why does he bother to comment upon his characters and his writing method—something that most writers do in interviews or self-reflective essays? An important part of metafiction is the writer's dilemma: is it at all possible to describe reality, and then once again: what is reality? One Swedish critic stresses in a presentation of Tormod Haugen that he "demonstrates that realism and fantasy are equal expressions of a writer's creativity. A realistic story is also arranged, manipulated. A realistic novel is no more real than a fantasy novel. It is also an illusion."[4] Incidentally, in Haugen's novel there is a supernatural element that has a direct link to his other novels: Donna's mother becomes invisible when she is unhappy. Haugen's comment in the novel is as follows: "As long as anything can happen in a book it can also happen in real life, since it always happens more in real life." An idea parallel to Cormier's notion?

SUMMING UP

Metafiction has joined the disintegration of the epic plot, the growing complexity of the chronotope and the intertextual density of texts as one of the prominent features of modern children's literature. The number of expressedly metafictional texts on the order of those I have discussed in this chapter is still low, but less pronounced metafictional elements can be traced in many recent novels for children.

Because it interrogates our own existence, metafiction reflects the chaos and ambivalence of our life and the loss of absolute values and truths. Of all the polyphonic features in children's literature metafiction is probably the most daring and disturbing, but it also takes the most radical step away from convention and didacticism.

What I have not touched upon at all are the messages of the texts. I hope that even "a text within a text" has a meaning. Haugen's depiction of Merkel being exposed to the cruelty of the adult world is a direct continuation of his themes in other, non-metafictional novels. Cormier's book is as cruel and violent as his "realistic" young adult novels, and it contains a clear warning against the constant encroaching of violence into modern society.

Metafiction is not self-sufficient. Of all the texts discussed it is probably Haugen and Geraldine McCaughrean who deliberately use metafiction as a consistent narrative device. In the works of other writers it is merely a way to draw our attention to the essence of fiction.

NOTES

1. Waugh, 1984.
2. Kerlan collections, MF 680, folder 7.
3. Chambers, 1985.
4. Toijer-Nilsson, 1991, p. 176. My translation.

WHITHER CHILDREN'S LITERATURE?
BY WAY OF CONCLUSION

I have throughout this study tried to show that children's literature today is evolving towards complexity and sophistication on all narrative levels. This complexity is reflected in such phenomena as the disintegration of traditional narrative structure and the extensive use of different experimental forms, in the intricate use of time and space, in a growing intertextuality, in a questioning of conventional approaches to the relationship between text and reality.

I must, however, qualify my general argument. Everything that has been said obviously refers only to a very small portion of modern children's books, even a very tiny part of what is normally classified as quality literature. I would like to offer the following comparison. Modern film critics set up an opposition between *genre film* and *auteur film*. Like children's literature, film is a relatively young form of art which is now catching up with the other arts. Like children's literature, film was not at first perceived by critics to be a serious art form. While most films are, of course, genre films, we can today see a growing amount of auteur films; we speak of Bergman films, Fellini films or Tarkovsky films without thinking about which genre these masters use. At the same time, they often do use what may appear to be popular forms; this is the case, for instance, in Tarkovsky's use of science fiction in *Solaris* or *Stalker*.

It would seem that we can similarly speak of genre children's books and "auteur" children's books. The latter are becoming literary, sophisticated and complex. But there still is, and will and must always be, a vast number of genre or "epic" books. That implies not only paraliterature but so-called quality literature as well. However, Astrid Lindgren or Tove Jansson, Aidan Chambers or Alan Garner do not fit into genre categories. We apparently need new approaches to evaluate these texts.

Evidently auteur books are still limited in number, which accounts for the fact that the same titles reappear in different sections of my study. The reason is not my lack of imagination but the restrictions of the material itself.

Obviously, "literary" children's literature puts greater demands on the reader. Today we see that many writers are not afraid to do that. At the same time we see that many are still convinced that children need happy endings. And we can still encounter books written as if the entire contemporary evolution were not even taking place. Writers who venture to attempt complicated novel forms, however, have confidence in their readers. Have they reevaluated the young readers' intellectual capacity? Or have the readers actually become more mature and ready to accept difficult forms? Obviously both factors are at work here. Both processes will most probably continue in the near future, and the number of auteur books for young readers will grow in proportion to the general output. This also means that children's literature will *on the whole* come closer to mainstream literature. Already today we see a number of books crossing a frontier which twenty years ago was totally unpenetrable. I mean books which, unlike the children's "classics" that once and for all moved from mainstream literature into the children's literary system, exist freely in both.

It is essential that we grownups who provide children with books—writers, critics, teachers, librarians—be aware of the changes taking place in modern children's literature. Instead of hiding in a ghetto and demanding special treatment for our field, we must maintain its rightful place in society, in education, in literary criticism. Only then can children's literature become an important part of the world cultural legacy.

BIBLIOGRAPHY

PRIMARY SOURCES

Only the first title in a series is mentioned, unless individual books are treated separately. Original titles of non-English language books are given in parentheses. The English titles in quotation marks are approximate translations for books not published in English.

Afanas'ev, Aleksandr. *Russian Fairy Tales*. Tr. Norbert Guterman. New York: Pantheon, 1945.

Aiken, Joan. *The Wolves of Willoughby Chase*. London: Cape, 1962; New York: Doubleday, 1963—The first book in a pseudo-historical suite.

Alcock, Vivian. *The Cuckoo Sister*. New York: Dell, 1985.

Alcott, Louisa May. *Little Women* (1868). Harmondsworth, England: Puffin, 1953.

Alexander, Lloyd. *Time Cat*. New York: Holt Rinehart, 1963.

———. *The Book of Three*. New York: Holt Rinehart, 1964—The first of the five chronicles of Prydain.

———. *The First Two Lives of Lukas-Kasha*. New York: Dutton, 1978.

———. *Westmark*. New York: Dutton, 1981—The first of the three books in the Westmark trilogy.

———. *The Illyrian Adventure*. New York: Dutton, 1986—The first book in the Vesper series.

Ambjörnsson, Gunila. *Spindelvävsridån*. Stockholm: Bonnier, 1990. ("Thin as Gossamer").

———. *Huset Silvecronas gøta*. Stockholm: Bonnier, 1992. ("The House of Silvercrona").

Andersen, Hans Christian. *The Complete Fairy Tales and Stories*. Tr. Erik Haugaard. New York: Doubleday, 1974.

Anstey, F. *Vice Versa* (1882). Harmondsworth, England: Puffin, 1981.

———. *The Brass Bottle*. New York: Appleton, 1900.

Asbørnsen, P. C. and Jørgen, Moe. *Norwegian Folk Tales*. New York: Pantheon, 1982.

Babbitt, Natalie. *Tuck Everlasting*. New York: Farrar Straus, 1975.

Bach, Richard. *Jonathan Livingston Seagull*. New York: Avon, 1970.

Barrie, James M. *Peter Pan and Wendy*. London: Hodder & Stoughton, 1911; New York: Scribner, 1980.

Baum, L. Frank. *The Wonderful Wizard of Oz*. Chicago: George M. Hill, 1900—The first of many books about the land of Oz.

Bawden, Nina. *Carrie's War*. Philadelphia: Lippincott, 1973.

Beckman, Gunnel. *The Girl Without a Name*. Tr. Ann Parker. New York: Harcourt Brace Jovanovich, 1970 (*Flickan utan namn*, 1967).

———— *Admission to the Feast*. Tr. Joan Tate. New York: Holt, Rinehart & Winston. 1971. (*Tillträde till festen*, 1969; also as *Nineteen Is Too Young to Die*. London: Macmillan, 1971).

————. *A Room of His Own*. Tr. Joan Tate. New York: Viking, 1974. (*Försök att förstå* 1971).

————. *Mia Alone*. Tr. Joan Tate. New York: Dell, 1978. (*Tre veckor över tiden*, 1973; also as *Mia*. London: Bodley Head, 1974).

————. *That Early Spring*. Tr. Joan Tate. New York: Viking, 1977. (*Våren då allting hände* 1974; also as *The Loneliness of Mia*. London: Bodley Head, 1975).

Bellairs, John. *The House with a Clock in Its Walls*. New York: Dell, 1974—The first book in a fantasy trilogy.

Berg, Leila. *The Adventures of Chunky*. London: Oxford University Press, 1950.

Bergström, Gunilla. *You Are a Sly One, Alfie Atkins*. Tr. Robert Swindells. Stockholm: R & S Books, 1988. (*Aja baja Alfons Åberg* 1973)—One of many picturebooks about Alfie Atkins.

Beskow, Elsa. *Aunt Green, Aunt Brown and Aunt Lavendel*. London: Harper and Brothers, 1938 (*Tant Grön, tant Brun och tant Gredelin*, 1918)—The first book about the three aunts.

————. *Children of the Forest*. Tr. William Jay Smith. New York: Delacorte, 1969 (*Tomtebobarnen*,1910).

————. *Peter's Adventures in Blueberry Land*. Tr. Sheila LaFarge. New York: Delacorte, 1975. (*Puttes äventyr i blåbärsskogen*, 1901).

Blyton, Enid. *Five on a Treasure Island*. London: Hodder & Stoughton, 1942—The first book in the Famous Five series.

Boston, Lucy M. *The Children of Green Knowe*. London: Faber, 1954; New York: Harcourt, 1967—The first book in the Green Knowe suite.

Bradbury, Ray. *The Golden Apples of the Sun*. London: Rupert Hart-Davis, 1953.

Briggs, Katharine M. *A Sampler of British Folk-Tales*. London: Rutledge & Kegan Paul, 1970.

Brunhoff, Jean de. *The Story of Babar, The Little Elephant*. Tr. Merle Haas. New York: Random House, 1933. (*Babar*, 1931)—The first of many picturebooks about Babar.

Bødker, Cecil. *Silas and the Black Mare*. New York: Delacorte, 1978. (*Silas og den sorte hoppe*, 1967)—The first book in the series about Silas.

————. *Silas and Ben-Godik*. New York: Delacorte, 1978. (*Silas og Ben-Godik*, 1969).

————. *Silas and the Runaway Coach*. New York: Delacorte, 1978. (*Silas fanger et firspand*, 1972).

Burnett, Frances Hodgson. *The Secret Garden*. New York: Stokes, 1911.

Burningham, John. *Come Away From the Water, Shirley*. New York: Crowell, 1977.

————. *Time to Get Out of the Bath, Shirley*. New York: Crowell, 1978.

Byars, Betsy. *Summer of the Swans*. New York: Viking, 1970.

Caldwell, Erskine. *Georgia Boy*. New York, Avon, 1943.

Calvino, Italo. *Italian Folktales*. Tr. George Martin. New York: Pantheon, 1980.

Carpelan, Bo. *Bow Island*. Tr. Sheila LaFarge. New York: Delacorte, 1972. (*Bågen*, 1968; also as *The Wide Wings of Summer*. London: Heinemann, 1972).

Carroll, Lewis. *Alice's Adventures in Wonderland* (1865). New York: Knopf, 1988 and other editions.

————. *Through the Looking Glass* (1871). New York: Knopf, 1988 and other editions.

Cervantes, Miguel de. 1606–15. *The Adventures of Don Quixote de la Mancha*. New York: Knopf, 1951 and other editions.

Chambers, Aidan. *Breaktime*. London: Bodley Head, 1978.

————. *Dance on My Grave*. London: Bodley Head, 1982.

————. *Now I Know*. New York: Harper, 1988.

————. *The Tollbridge*. London: Bodley Head, 1992.

Christopher, John. *The Prince in Waiting*. New York: Macmillan, 1970—The first book in "The Prince in Waiting" trilogy.

Chukovsky, Kornei. *The Crocodile*. Tr. Babette Deutsch. Philadelphia: Lippincott, 1931.

———. *Wash'em Clean*. Tr. E. Felgenhauer. Moscow: Foreign Literature, 1962.

———. *Dr. Concocter*. Adapt. Richard Coe. London: Oxford University Press, 1967.

———. *The Telephone*. Tr. Marguerite Rudolf. New York: Bobbs-Merrill, 1971.

Ciardi, John. *I Met a Man*. Boston: Houghton Mifflin, 1961.

Cleary, Beverly. *Ramona the Pest*. New York: Morrow, 1968—The first book in the series about Ramona.

———. *Dear Mr Henshaw*. New York: Morrow, 1983.

Cleaver, Vera & Cleaver, Bill. *Where the Lilies Bloom*. Philadelphia: Lippincott, 1969.

Cole, Joanna, ed. *Best-Loved Folktales of the World*. New York: Doubleday, 1982.

Collodi, Carlo. *The Adventures of Pinocchio*. Tr. Marianna Mayer. New York: Macmillan, 1981. (*Le avventure di Pinocchio*, 1881).

Cooper, James Fenimore. *The Last of the Mohicans* (1826). New York: Scribner, 1973 and other editions.

———. *The Pathfinder* (1840). New York: Regents, 1973 and other editions.

Cooper, Susan. *Over Sea, Under Stone*. London: Cape, 1965; New York: Harcourt Brace, 1966.

———. *The Dark Is Rising*. New York: Atheneum, 1973.

———. *Greenwitch*. New York: Atheneum, 1974.

———. *The Grey King*. New York: Atheneum, 1975.

———. *Silver on the Tree*. New York: Atheneum, 1977.

Cormier, Robert. *The Chocolate War*. New York: Pantheon, 1974.

———. *I Am the Cheese*. New York: Pantheon, 1977.

———. *Fade*. New York: Pantheon, 1988.

Coster, Charles de. *The Legend of the Glorious Adventures of Tyl Ulenspiegel in the Land of Flanders and Elsewhere*. Tr. Geoffrey Whitwort. New York: McBride, 1918. (*La légende et les aventures héroïques, joyeuses et glorieuses d'Ulenspiegel et de Lamme Goedzak*, 1867).

Cresswell, Helen. *Up the Pier*. London: Faber, 1971; New York: Macmillan, 1972.

Crompton, Richmal. *Just William*. London: Newness, 1922—The first in a series of more than forty books about William.

Cross, Gillian. *Wolf*. New York: Holiday, 1991.

Dahl, Roald. *Charlie and the Chocolate Factory*. New York: Knopf, 1964.

———. *The Magic Finger*. New York: Harper & Row, 1966.

———. *The BFG*. New York: Farrar Strauss, 1982.

Defoe, Daniel. *Robinson Crusoe* (1719). New York: Norton, 1975 and other editions.

Dickens, Charles. *The Magic Fishbone* (1868). New York: Vanguard, 1953.

Dickinson, Peter. *The Weathermonger*. London: Gollanz, 1968; Boston: Little, Brown, 1969—The first novel in the "Changes" trilogy.

———. *AK*. London: Gollanz, 1990.

Druon, Maurice. *Tistou of the Green Thumbs*. Tr. Humphrey Hare. New York: Scribner, 1958. (*Tistou les pouces verts*, 1957).

Dumas, Alexandre. *The Three Musketeers*. Tr. William Barrow. New York: Pan Books, 1974 and other editions. (*Les trois mousquetaires*, 1844).

Eager, Edward. *Half Magic*. New York: Harcourt, 1954.

———. *Knight's Castle*. New York: Harcourt, 1956.

———. *Magic by the Lake*. New York: Harcourt, 1957.

———. *Time Garden*. New York: Harcourt, 1958.

———. *Magic Or Not?* New York: Harcourt, 1959.

———. *The Well-Wishers*. New York: Harcourt, 1960.

———. *Seven Day Magic*. New York: Harcourt, 1962.

Egner, Thorbjørn. *The Singing Town*. Tr. Evelyn Ramsden & Leila Berg. New York: Macmillan, 1959. (*Folk og røvere i Kardemomme by*, 1955).

Ende, Michael. *The Neverending Story*. Tr. Ralph Manheim. New York: Doubleday, 1983. (*Die unendliche Geschichte*, 1979).

———. *Momo*. New York: Doubleday, 1985. (*Momo*, 1973).

Ericson, Stig. *Jenny från Bluewater*. Stockholm: Bonnier, 1982 ("Jenny from Bluewater").

Ewing, Juliana Horatia. *The Brownies and Other Stories* (1870). New York: Dent, 1975.

Farmer, Penelope. *A Castle of Bone*. New York: Atheneum, 1972.

Fitinghoff, Laura. *The Children of the Moor*. Tr. Siri Andrews. Boston: Houghton Mifflin, 1927. (*Barnen ilrån Frostmofjället*, 1907).

Fitzhugh, Louise. *Harriet the Spy*. New York: Harper & Row, 1964.

Forward, Toby. *Neverland*. London: Simon & Schuster, 1989.

Fox, Paula. *The Slave Dancer*. Scarsdale, NY: Bradbury, 1973.

———. *The One-Eyed Cat*. Scarsdale, NY: Bradbury, 1984.

Frank, Anne. *The Diary of a Young Girl*. Tr. R.M. Mooryaart. Garden City, NY: Doubleday, 1952.

Garner, Alan. *The Weirdstone of Brisingamen*. London: Collins, 1960; New York: Philomel, 1979.

———. *The Moon of Gomrath*. London: Collins, 1963; New York: Philomel, 1981.

———. *Elidor*. London: Collins, 1965: New York: Philomel, 1979.

———. *The Owl Service*. London: Collins, 1967; New York: Philomel, 1979.

———. 'Feel Free.' In *Miscellany 4*, ed. Edward Blishen. London: Oxford University Press, 1967.

———. *Red Shift*. New York: Macmillan, 1973.

———. *The Stone Book*. London: Collins, 1976; New York: Collins World, 1979.

———. *Tom Fobble's Day*. London: Collins, 1977; New York: Collins World, 1979.

———. *Granny Reardun*. London: Collins, 1977; New York: Collins World, 1978.

———. *The Aimer Gate*. London: Collins, 1978; New York: Collins World, 1979.

———. *Alan Garner's Fairytales of Gold*. New York: Philomel, 1980.

———. *Alan Garner's Book of British Fairytales*. New York: Philomel, 1984.

———. *A Bag of Moonshine*. London: Collins, 1986.

George, Jean Craighead. *Julie of the Wolves*. New York: Harper & Row, 1972.

Grahame, Kenneth. *The Golden Age* (1895). New York: Garland, 1976.

———. *Dream Days* (1898). New York: Garland, 1976.

———. *The Wind in the Willows*. New York: Scribner, 1908.

Green, Roger L. *King Arthur and His Knights of the Round Table*. London: Penguin, 1953.

———. *The Adventures of Robin Hood*. London: Penguin, 1956.

———. *A Book of Myths*. New York: Dutton, 1965.

———. *Folk Tales of the World*. Boston: Ginn, 1966.

Greenwood, James. *The True History of the Little Ruggamuffin*. London: 1866.

Grimm, Jacob & Grimm, Wilhelm. *The Complete Fairy Tales of the Brothers Grimm*. Tr. Jack Zipes. Vols. I, II. New York: Bantam, 1987.

Gripe, Maria. *Hugo and Josephine*. Tr. Paul Britten Austin. New York: Delacorte, 1969. (*Hugo och Josefin*, 1962).

———. *Hugo*. Tr. Paul Britten Austin. New York: Delacorte, 1970. (*Hugo*, 1966).

———. *The Night Daddy*. Tr. Gerry Bothmer. New York: Delacorte, 1971. (*Nattpappan*, 1968).

———. *Josephine*. Tr. Paul Britten Austin. New York: Delacorte, 1973. (*Josefin*, 1961).

———. *Papa Pellerin's Daughter*. Tr. Kersti French. London: Chatto & Windus, 1966. (*Pappa Pellerins dotter*, 1963).

———. *The Glassblower's Children*. Tr. Sheila LaFarge. New York: Delacorte, 1973. (*Glasblåsarns barn*, 1964).

———. *In the Time of the Bells*. Tr. Sheila LaFarge. New York: Delacorte, 1976. (*I klockornas tid*, 1965).

————. *The Land Beyond.* Tr. Sheila La Farge. New York: Delacorte, 1974. (*Landet utanför,* 1967).

————. *Elvis and His Secret.* Tr. Sheila LaFarge. New York: Delacorte, 1976. (*Elvis Karlsson,* 1972).

————. *Elvis and His Friends.* Tr. Sheila LaFarge. New York: Delacorte, 1976. (*Elvis! Elvis!* 1973).

————. *Agnes Cecilia.* Tr. Rika Lesser. New York: Harper & Row, 1990. (*Agnes Cecilia—en sällsam historia,* 1981).

————. *Skuggan öven stenbänken.* Stockholm: Bonnier, 1982. ("Shadow Over the Stone Bench")—The first book in the "Shadow" tetralogy.

————. *Skugg-gömman.* Stockholm: Bonnier, 1988. ("The Shadow Sanctuary").

Harris, Geraldine. *Prince of the Godborn.* New York: Greenwillow, 1983—The first book in the tetralogy, *The Seven Citadels.*

Haugen, Tormod. *Slottet det hvite.* Oslo: Gyldendal, 1980. ("The White Castle").

————. *Dagen som forsvant.* Oslo: Gyldendal, 1983. ("The Day that Disappeared").

————. *Vinterstedet.* Oslo: Gyldendal, 1984. ("Winter Place").

————. *Romanen om Merkel Hanssen og Donna Winther og Den stora flykten.* Oslo: Gyldendal, 1986. ("The Novel About Merkel Hanssen, and Donna Winther, and The Big Escape").

————. *Night Birds.* Tr. Sheila LaFarge. New York: Delacorte, 1982. (*Nattfuglene,* 1975).

————. *Zeppelin.* Tr. David R. Jacobs. London: Turton & Chambers, 1991. (*Zeppelin,* 1976).

Hearn, Michael Patric, ed. *The Victorian Fairy Tale Book.* New York: Pantheon, 1988.

Hellberg, Hans-Eric. *Grandpa's Maria.* Tr. Patricia Crampton. New York: Morrow, 1974. (*Morfars Maria,* 1969).

————. *Maria and Martin.* Tr. Patricia Crampton. London: Methuen, 1975. (*Martins Maria,* 1970).

————. *I Am Maria.* Tr. Patricia Crampton. London: Methuen, 1978. (*Jag är Maria jag,* 1971).

————. *Ben's Lucky Hat.* Tr. Patricia Crampton. New York: Crown, 1982. (*Björn med trollhatten,* 1965).

Hellsing, Lennart. *The Pirate Book.* New York: Delacorte, 1972. (*Sjörövarbok,* 1965).

————. *Ägget.* Stockholm: Rabén & Sjögren, 1978. ("The Egg").

Herman, Charlotte. *Our Snowman Had Olive Eyes.* New York: Dutton, 1977.

Hoban, Russel. *The Mouse and His Child.* New York: Harper & Row, 1967.

Hoffmann, E.T.A. *The Nutcracker.* Adapted by Janet Schulman. New York: Dutton, 1979. (*Nussknacker und Mausekönig,*1816).

Holm, Annika. *Amanda! Amanda!* Stockholm: Rabén & Sjögren, 1989.

Jacobs, Joseph. *English Fairy Tales.* London: Bodley Head, 1968.

————. *Celtic Fairy Tales.* London: Bodley Head, 1975.

Jacobson, Gun. *Peters baby.* Stockholm: Bonnier, 1971 ("Peter's Baby").

Jacobsson, Anders. *Berts dagbok.* Stockholm: Rabén & Sjögren, 1987. ("Bert's Diary")— The first book in a series about Bert.

Jansson, Tove. *Smätrollen och den stora översvämningen.* Stockholm: Hasselgren, 1945. ("The Little Trolls and the Big Flood").

————. *Moominsummer Madness.* Tr. Elisabeth Portch. New York: Walck, 1961. (*Farlig midsommar,* 1954).

————. *Moominland Midwinter.* Tr. Thomas Warburton. New York: Walck, 1962. (*Trollvinter,* 1957).

————. *Tales from Moominvalley.* Tr. Thomas Warburton. New York: Walck, 1964. (*Det osynliga barnet,* 1962).

————. *Finn Family Moomintroll.* Tr. Elisabeth Portch. New York: Walck, 1965. (*Trollkarlens hatt,* 1949).

————. *Exploits of Moominpappa.* Tr. Elisabeth Portch. New York: Walck, 1966.

(*Muminpappans bravader*, 1950).

———. *Moominpappa At Sea*. Tr. K. Hart. New York: Walck, 1967. (*Pappan och havet*, 1965).

———. *A Comet in Moominland*. Tr. Elisabeth Portch. New York: Walck, 1968. (*Kometen kommer*, 1956).

———. *Moominvalley in November*. Tr. K. Hart. New York: Walck, 1971. (*Sent i november*, 1970).

———. *The Dangerous Journey*. Tr. K. Hart. London: Benn, 1978. (*Den farliga resan*, 1977).

Johns, W.E. *The Camels Are Coming*. London: John Hamilton, 1932—The first book in the Biggles series.

Jones, Diana Wynne. *The Homeward Bounders*. New York: Greenwillow, 1981.

———. *Archer's Goon*. New York: Greenwillow, 1984.

———. *Howl's Moving Castle*. New York: Greenwillow, 1986.

———. *The Lives of Christopher Chant*. New York: Greenwillow, 1988.

Jones, Gwyn. *Scandinavian Legends and Folk-Tales*. London: Oxford University Press, 1956.

Kästner, Erich. *Emil and the Detectives*. Tr. May Massee. New York: Doubleday, 1930. (*Emil und die Detektive*, 1928).

———. *The 35th of May*. Tr. Cyrus Brooks. New York: Dodd Mead, 1934. (*Der 35:e Mai*, 1931).

———. *The Animals' Conference*. Tr. Zita de Schausee. New York: D. McKay, 1949. (*Die Konferenz der Tiere*, 1949).

———. *Lottie and Lisa*. Tr. Cyrus Brooks. Boston: Little, Brown, 1951. (*Das doppelte Lottchen*, 1949).

Katz, Welwyn Wilton. *False Face*. Toronto: Douglas, 1987.

Keene, Carolyn (pseud). *The Secret of the Old Clock*. New York: Grosset & Dunlap, 1930—The first of the Nancy Drew series.

Kipling, Rudyard. *The Jungle Book* (1894). New York: Doubleday,1981.

Knutsen, Per. *Svart cayal*. Oslo: Capellen, 1988. ("The Black Eye-Liner").

Konigsburg, Elaine. *From the Mixed-Up Files of Mrs. Basil E. Frankweiler*. New York: Atheneum, 1967.

Krohn, Leena. *Ihmisen vaatteissa*. Helsinki: Werner Söderström, 1976. ("In Human Clothes").

Krüss, James. *My Great Grandfather and I*. Tr. Edelgard Brühl. New York: Atheneum, 1964. (*Mein Urgrossvater und ich*, 1959).

———. *The Happy Islands Behind the Winds*. Tr. Edelgard Brühl. New York: Atheneum, 1966. (*Die glückliche Inseln hinter dem Winde*, 1958).

Kullman, Harry. *Den svarta fläcken*. Stockholm: Rabén & Sjögren, 1949. ("The Black Spot").

———. *The Battle Horse*. Tr. George Blecher & Lone Thygesen-Blecher. Scarsdale, NY: Bradbury, 1981. (*Stridshästen*, 1977).

Lagercrants, Rose. *Tulla's Summer*. Tr. George Blecher & Lone Thygesen-Blecher. New York: Harcourt Brace Jovanovich, 1977. (*Tullesommar*, 1973).

Lagerlöf, Selma. *The Wonderful Adventures of Nils*. Tr. Velma Swanston Howard. Vols. I, II. Minneapolis: Skandisk, 1991. (*Nils Holgerssons underbara resa genom Sverige*, 1906–07).

Le Guin, Ursula. *A Wizard of Earthsea*. New York: Parnassus, 1968—The first book in the Earthsea suite.

———. *The Wind's Twelve Quarters*. New York: Harper & Row, 1975.

L'Engle, Madeleine. *A Wrinkle in Time*. New York: Farrar Straus, 1962—The first book in the suite about the Murry family.

———. *A Swiftly Tilting Planet*. New York: Farrar Straus, 1978.

Lewis, C.S. *Perelandra*. London: Lane, 1943; New York: Macmillan, 1944.

———. *The Lion, the Witch and the Wardrobe*. New York: Macmillan, 1950.

——. *Prince Caspian*. New York: Macmillan, 1951.

——. *The Voyage of The Dawn Treader*. New York: Macmillan, 1952.

——. *The Silver Chair*. New York: Macmillan, 1953.

——. *The Horse and His Boy*. New York: Macmillan, 1954.

——. *The Magician's Nephew*. New York: Macmillan, 1955.

——. *The Last Battle*. New York: Macmillan, 1956.

Linde, Gunnel. *The White Stone*. Tr. Richard & Clara Winston. New York: Harcourt Brace & World, 1966 (*Den vita stenen*, 1964).

——. *Eva-sjams land*. Stockholm: Bonnier 1967. ("Eva-Sham's Island").

——. *Eva-sjam och Lua*. Stockholm: Bonnier 1968. ("Eva-Sham and Lua").

——. *Eva-sjam och Nalle*. Stockholm: Bonnier 1968. ("Eva-Sham and Nalle").

——. *Om livet är dig kärt*. Stockholm: Bonnier, 1977. ("If Life Is Dear to You").

——. *Dingo—rymmare utan fasttagare*. Stockholm: Bonnier, 1981. ("Dingo—Robber Without Cops").

——. *Trust in the Unexpected*. Tr. Patricia Crompton. London: Dent, 1984. (*Lita på det oväntade*,1979; also tr. as *Bicycles Don't Grow On Trees*).

Lindenbaum, Pija. *Else-Marie and Her Seven Little Daddies*. Adapted by Gabrielle Charbonnet. New York: Henry Holt, 1991 (*Else-Marie och småpapporna*,1990).

Lindgren, Astrid. *Jag vill inte gå och lägga mig*. Stockholm: Rabén & Sjögren, 1947. ("I Don't Want to Go to Bed").

——. *Pippi Longstocking*. Tr. Florence Lamborn. New York: Viking, 1950. (*Pippi Långstrump*. Stockholm: Rabén & Sjögren, 1945)—The first of three books about Pippi.

——. *Bill Bergson Master Detective*. Tr. Herbert Antione. New York: Viking, 1952. (*Mästerdetekriven Blomkvist*, 1946)—The first of three books about Bill Bergson.

——. *Mio, My Son*. Tr. Marianne Turner. New York: Viking, 1956. (*Mio, min Mio*, 1954).

——. *Rasmus and the Vagabond*. Tr. Gerry Bothmer. New York: Viking, 1960. (*Rasmus på luffen* 1956).

——. *The Children of Noisy Village*. Tr. Florence Lamborn. New York: Viking, 1962. (*Alla vi barn i Bullerbyn*,1947)—The first of the three Noisy Village books.

——. *Emil in the Soup Tureen*. Tr. Michael Heron. Chicago: Folett, 1970. (*Emil i Lönneberga*,1963)—The first of the three books about Emil.

——. *Karlsson-on-the-Roof*. Tr. Marianne Turner. New York: Viking, 1971. (*Lillebror och Karlsson på taket*, 1955)—The first of three books about Karlsson.

——. *The Brothers Lionheart*. Tr. Joan Tate. New York: Viking, 1975. (*Bröderna Lejonhjärta*, 1973).

——. *Ronia, the Robber's Daughter*. Tr. Patricia Crampton. New York: Viking, 1983. (*Ronja Rövardotter*, 1981).

——. *Jag vill inte gå och lägga mig*. Stockholm: Rabén & Sjögren, 1988. ("I Don't Want to Go to Bed").

Lindgren, Barbro. *Hilding's Summer*. Tr. Annabelle MacMillan. New York: Macmillan, 1967. (*Mathias sommar* 1965).

——. *Jättehemligt*. Stockholm: Rabén & Sjögren, 1971. ("Top Secret")—The first book of three in a diary suite.

——. *Lilla Sparvel*. Stockholm: Rabén & Sjögren, 1976. ("Little Sparvel")—The first book of three about Sparvel.

——. *The Wild Baby*. Tr. Jack Prilutsky. New York: Greenwillow, 1981. (*Mamman och den vilda bebin*, 1980)—The first of three Wild Baby picturebooks. Also tr. Alison Winn. London: Hodder & Stoughton, 1981.

——. *A Worm's Tale*. Tr. Dianne Jonasson. Stockholm: R&S Books, 1988. (*Sagan om Karlknut*, 1985).

Lunn, Janet. *The Root Cellar*. Toronto: Lester and Orpen, 1980.

MacDonald, George. *Phantastes* (1858). New York: Ballantine, 1970.

———. *At the Back of the North Wind* (1871). New York: Macmillan, 1964.

———. *The Princess and the Goblin* (1872). Harmondsworth, England: Penguin, 1964.

———. *The Princess and Curdie* (1883). Harmondsworth, England: Penguin, 1966.

MacLachlan, Patricia. *Arthur, For the Very First Time*. New York: HarperCollins, 1980, Collins.

———. *Cassie Binegar*. New York: Harper & Row, 1982.

———. *Unclaimed Treasures*. New York: Harper Collins, 1984.

———. *Sarah Plain and Tall*. New York: Harper Collins, 1985.

———. *The Facts and Fictions of Minna Pratt*. New York: Harper Collins, 1988.

Magorian, Michelle. *Back Home*. New York: Harper, 1984.

Mählqvist, Stefan. *I'll Take Care of the Crocodiles*. New York: Atheneum, 1978. (*Inte farligt pappa, krokodilerna klarar jag*. 1977).

———. *Come into My Night, Come into My Dream*. London: Pepper Press, 1981. (*Kom in i min natt, kom in i min dröm*, 1978).

Malot, Hector. *The Adventures of Remi*. Tr. Philip Schuyler Allen. Chicago: Rand, McNally, 1925. (*Sans famille*, 1878).

Marshak, Samuil. *The Ice Cream Man*. Tr. Dora Lawson. London: Transatlantic Art, 1943.

Mayne, William, ed. *William Mayne's Book of Giants*. New York: Dutton, 1969.

McCauffrey, Anne. *Dragonsong*. New York: Atheneum, 1976—The first book in a suite about the land of Pern.

McCaughrean, Geraldine. *A Pack of Lies*. London: Oxford University Press, 1988.

McCloskey, Robert. *Homer Price*. New York: Viking, 1943.

McCullers, Carson. *The Member of the Wedding*. Boston: Houghton Mifflin, 1946.

McKinley, Robin. *The Hero and the Crown*. New York: Greenwillow, 1984.

Mikkola, Marja-Leena. *Anni Maninen*. Helsinki: Otava, 1977. ("Anni Maninen").

Milne, A.A. *Winnie-the-Pooh*. New York: Dutton, 1926.

Molesworth, Mary. *The Cuckoo Clock* (1877). New York: Garland, 1976.

Montgomery, L.M. *Anne of Green Gables*. Boston: Page, 1908—The first of many books about Anne.

———. *Emily of the New Moon*. New York: Stokes, 1923—The first of three books about Emily.

Nesbit, Edith. *The Book of Dragons*. New York: Harper and Brothers, 1901.

———. *Nine Unlikely Tales for Children*. New York: Dutton, 1901.

———. *Five Children and It*. London: Unwin, 1902; New York: Dodd Mead, 1905.

———. *The Phoenix and the Carpet*. New York: Macmillan, 1904.

———. *The Story of the Amulet*. London: Unwin, 1906; New York: Dutton, 1907.

———. *The Enchanted Castle*. London: Unwin, 1907; New York: Harper, 1908.

———. *The House of Arden*. London: Unwin, 1908; New York: Dutton, 1909.

———. *Harding's Luck*. London: Hodder & Stoughton, 1909; New York: Stokes, 1910.

———. *The Magic City*. London: Macmillan, 1910; New York: Gregg, 1981.

———. *The Wonderful Garden*. London: Macmillan, 1911; New York: Coward McCann, 1935.

———. *The Magic World*. New York: Macmillan, 1912.

———. *Fairy Stories*. Ed. Naomi Lewis. London: Benn, 1977.

———. 'The Town in the Library.' In her *Fairy Stories*. Ed. Naomi Lewis. London: Benn, 1977: 79–98.

Newman, Lesléa, *Heather Has Two Mommies*. Boston: Alyson, 1989.

Nilsson, Per. *Mellan vakna och somna*. Stockholm: Bonnier, 1986. ("Between Waking Up and Going to Sleep").

———. *Viktiga saker*. Stockholm: Alfabeta, 1987. ("Important Things").

———. *Baklängeslivet*. Stockholm: Alfabeta, 1990. ("The Backwards Life").

Nordqvist, Sven. *Pancake Pie*. New York: Morrow, 1985. (*Pannkakstårtan*, 1984)— The first of many picturebooks about Festus and Mercury.

Norton, Mary. *The Magic Bed-Knob*. London: Dent, 1945.

———. *Bonfires and Broomsticks*. London: Dent, 1947.

Nöstlinger, Christine. *Konrad*. Tr. Anthea Bell. New York: Avon, 1982. (*Konrad oder das Kind aus der Konservenbüchse*, 1975).

———. *The Cucumber King*. Tr. Anthea Bell. New York: Avon, 1984 (*Wir pfeifen auf den Gurkekönig*, 1972).

Nuñes, Lygia Bojunga. *The Companions*. Tr. Ellen Watson. New York: Farrar Straus, 1989. (*Os colegas*, 1984).

Oakley, Graham. *The Church Mice and the Moon*. New York: Atheneum, 1974.

O'Dell, Scott. *Island of the Blue Dolphins*. Boston: Houghton Mifflin, 1960.

Opie, Iona & Peter Opie. *The Classic Fairy Tales*. London: Oxford University Press, 1974.

Ormerod, Jan. *Sunshine*. London: Lothrop, 1981.

———. *Moonlight*. London: Lothrop, 1982.

Orzcy, Emmuska. *The Scarlet Pimpernel* (1905). New York: Hall, 1980 and other editions.

Pascal, Francine. *Double Love*. New York: Bantam, 1984—The first book in the Sweet Valley High series.

———. *Best Friends*. New York: Bantam, 1986—The first book in the Sweet Valley twins series.

Park, Ruth. *Playing Beatie Bow*. Sydney, Australia: Thomas Nelson, 1980; New York: Atheneum, 1982.

Paterson, Katherine. *Bridge to Terabithia*. New York: Crowell, 1977.

———. *The Great Gilly Hopkins*. New York: Crowell, 1978.

———. *Jacob Have I Loved*. New York: Crowell, 1980.

———. *Lyddie*. New York: Dutton, 1991.

Paton Walsh, Jill. *Fireweed*. London: Macmillan, 1969; New York: Farrar Straus, 1970.

Paulsen, Gary. *Hatchet*. Scarsdale, NY: Bradbury, 1987.

———. *The Island*. New York: Dell, 1988.

Pearce, Philippa. *Tom's Midnight Garden*. Philadelphia: Lippincott, 1958.

Peck, Richard. *Secrets of the Shopping Mall*. New York: Delacorte, 1979.

Perrault, Charles. *The Fairy Tales*. Tr. Angela Carter. New York: Avon, 1977.

Peterson, Hans. *Pelle Jansson, en kille mitt i stan*. Stockholm: Rabén & Sjögren, 1971. ("Pelle Jansson—a Boy in the Middle of the City").

Picard, Barbara Leonie. *Stories of King Arthur and His Knights*. London: Oxford University Press, 1955.

Pierce, Meredith Ann. *The Darkangel*. New York: Atlantic Monthly Press, 1982.

Pohl, Peter. *Regnbågen har bara åtta fårger*. Stockholm: AWG, 1986. ("The Rainbow Only Has Eight Colors").

———. *Vi kallar honom Anna*. Stockholm: AWG, 1987. ("Let's Call Him Anna").

———. *Alltid den där Anette!*. Stockholm: Alfabeta, 1988. ("Always That Anette").

———. *Medan regnbågen bleknar*. Stockholm: Alfabeta, 1989. ("While the Rainbow Fades").

———. *Kan ingen hjälpa Anette?* Stockholm: Alfabeta 1990. ("Can No One Help Anette?").

———. *Johnny My Friend*. Tr. Laurie Thompson. London: Turton & Chambers, 1991. (*Janne min vän*, 1985).

Potter, Beatrix. *The Tale of Peter Rabbit*. New York: Warne, 1902.

Pratchett, Terry. *Truckers*. New York: Doubleday, 1989.

———. *Diggers*. New York: Doubleday, 1990.

———. *Wings*. New York: Doubleday, 1990.

Preussler, Ottfried. *The Little Witch*. Tr. Anthea Bell. New York: Abelard-Schuman, 1961. (*Die kleine Hexe*, 1957).

———. *The Little Ghost*. Tr. Anthea Bell. New York: Abelard-Schuman, 1967. (*Das kleine Gespenst*, 1968).

———. *The Satanic Mill*. Tr. Anthea Bell. New York: Macmillan, 1976 (*Krabat*, 1971).

Price, Moe. *The Incredible Mungwort Quest*. Toronto: McClelland & Stewart, 1990.

Prochazka, Jan. *Long Live the Republic*. Tr. Peter Kussi. New York: Doubleday, 1973.

Prøysen, Alf. *Little Old Mrs. Pepperpot and Other Stories*. Tr. Marianne Helwig. New York: Astor-Honor, 1960. (*Kjerringa som ble så lita som ei teskje*, 1957)—The first of many books about Mrs. Pepperpot.

Rabelais, François. *Gargantua and Pantagruel*. New York: Dutton, 1932–33 and many other editions. (*Gargantua et Pantagruel*, 1535).

Rawlings, Marjorie Kinnan. *The Yearling*. New York: Scribner, 1938.

Reggiani, Renée. *The Adventures of Five Children and a Dog*. Tr. Mary Lambert & Anne Chisholm. New York: Coward McCann, 1963. (*Le avventure di cinque ragazzi e un cane*, 1960).

Reuterswärd, Maud. *A Way from Home*. Tr. Joan Tate. London: Turton & Chambers, 1990. (*Flickan och dockskåpet*, 1979).

Richler, Mordechai. *Jacob Two-Two Meets the Hooded Fang*. New York: Knopf, 1975.

Riordan, James. *A World of Folk Tales*. London: Hamlyn, 1981.

Rodari, Gianni. *Telephone Tales*. Tr. Patric Craig. London: Harrap, 1965. (*Favole al telefono*, 1962).

———. *The Befana's Toy Shop*. Tr. Patric Craig. London: Benn, 1970. (*La freccia azzura*, 1954).

———. *A Pie in the Sky*. Tr. Patric Craig. London: Dent, 1971. (*La torta in cielo*, 1966).

Rodgers, Mary. *Freaky Friday*. New York: Harper, 1972.

Rushdie, Salman. *Haroun and the Sea of Stories*. London: Granta, 1990.

Ruskin, Ellen. *The Westing Game*. New York: Dutton, 1978.

Saint-Exupéry, Antoine de. *The Little Prince*. Tr. Katherine Woods. New York: Reynal & Hitchcock, 1943. (*Le petit prince*, 1943).

Salinger, J.D. *The Catcher in the Rye*. Boston: Little, Brown, 1951.

Sandberg, Inger. *What Anne Saw*. New York: Lothrope, Lee & Shepard, 1964. (*Vad Anna fick se*, 1964)—The first of many picturebooks about little Anne.

———. *Daniel and the Coconut Cakes*. London: Black, 1973. (*Mathias bakar kakor*, 1968)—The first picturebook about Daniel.

———. *Nicholas' Red Day*. New York: Delacorte, 1967. (*Niklas röda dag*, 1964)—The first picturebook about Nicholas.

———. *The Boy With 100 Cars*. New York: Delacorte, 1967. (*Pojken med de hundra bilarna*, 1966)—The first picturebook in "The Boy With" series.

———. *Dusty Wants to Help*. Tr. Judy Abbot Mauer. Stockholm: R&S Books, 1987. (*Hjälpa till, sa Pulvret*, 1983)—The first picturebook about Dusty.

———. *ABCD*. Stockholm: Rabén & Sjögren, 1986.

Sandburg, Carl. *Rootabaga Stories*. New York: Harcourt Brace, 1922.

Saroyan, William. *Little Children*. New York: Harcourt Brace, 1937.

———. *My Name is Aram*. New York: Harcourt Brace, 1940.

Schmidt, Annie G.M. *Wiplala*. Tr. Henrietta Anthony. New York: Abelard-Schuman, 1962. (*Wiplala*, 1960).

———. *Dusty and Smudge and the Bride*. Tr. Lance Salway. London: Methuen, 1977. (*Floddertje en de bruid*, 1973)—First book in a series.

Scott, Walter. *Ivanhoe* (1820). New York: Hart, 1976 and other editions.

———. *Kenilworth* (1821). New York: Dutton, 1972 and other editions.

Sendak, Maurice. *Where the Wild Things Are*. New York: Harper & Row, 1963.

———. *In the Night Kitchen*. New York: Harper & Row, 1970.

Seuss, Dr. *The Cat in the Hat*. New York: Random House, 1957.

Sinclair, Upton. *Gnomobile*. New York: Farrar & Rinehart, 1936.

Sleigh, Barbara. *The Kingdom of Carbonel*. Indianapolis: Bobbs Merrill, 1960.

———. *Jessamy*. Indianapolis: Bobbs Merrill, 1967.

Spinelli, Jerry. *Maniac Magee*. Boston: Little, Brown, 1990.

Stark, Ulf. *Dårfinkar och dönickar*. Stockholm: Bonnier 1984. ("The Nuts and the No-Goods").

Steinbeck, John. *The Red Pony*. New York: Covici-Friede, 1937.

Stevenson, Robert Louis. *Treasure Island* (1883). New York: Doubleday, 1954 and other editions.

―――. *Kidnapped* (1886). London: Penguin, 1975 and other editions.

Stowe, Harriet Beecher. *Uncle Tom's Cabin* (1852). New York: Dodd Mead, 1972.

Sundvall, Viveca. *En ettas dagbok*. Stockholm: Rabén & Sjögren, 1982. ("The Diary of a First-Grader")―The first book in the series about Mimmi.

―――. *Mimi and the Biscuit Factory*. Tr. Eric Bibb. Stockholm: R&S Books, 1989. (*Mimmi och kexfabriken*, 1988).

Sutcliff, Rosemary. *The Eagle of the Ninth*. London: Oxford University Press, 1954; New York: Walck, 1961.

Swados, Harvey. *On the Line*. Boston: Little, Brown, 1957.

―――. *A Story for Teddy*. New York: Simon & Schuster, 1965.

Swift, Jonathan. *Gulliver's Travels into Several Remote Nations of the World* (1726). New York: Dent, 1978 and other editions.

Thorval, Kerstin. *And Leffe Was Instead of a Dad*. Tr. Francine L. Mirro. Scarsdale, NY: Bradbury, 1974. (*Istället för en pappa*, 1971).

Tolkien, J.R.R. *The Hobbit*. London: Allen & Unwin, 1937; Boston: Houghton Mifflin, 1938.

―――. *The Fellowship of the Ring*. Boston: Houghton Mifflin, 1954―The first book in "The Lord of the Rings" trilogy.

Tournier, Michel. *Friday and Robinson*. Tr. Ralf Manheim. New York: Knopf, 1972. (*Vendredi ou la vie sauvage*, 1971).

Townsend, Sue. *The Secret Diary of Adrian Mole, Aged 13 1/4*. London: Methuen, 1982―The first book in a series.

Travers, Pamela. *Mary Poppins*. New York: Reynal & Hitchcock, 1934―The first book about Mary Poppins.

―――. *Mary Poppins in the Park*. New York: Harcourt Brace, 1952.

Turner, Ann. *Grasshopper Summer*. New York: Macmillan, 1989.

Twain, Mark (pseud). *The Adventures of Tom Sawyer* (1876). New York: Bobbs-Merrill, 1972 and other editions.

Uttley, Alison. *A Traveller in Time*. London: Faber, 1939; New York: Merrimack, 1981.

Vestly, Ann-Cath. *Eight Children and a Truck*. Tr. Patricia Crampton. London: Methuen, 1973. (*Åtte små, to store og en lastebil*, 1957).

―――. *Hello Aurora*. Tr. Eileen Amos. New York: Crowell, 1974. (*Aurora i blokk Z*, 1966).

Verne, Jules. *Around the World in Eighty Days*. Tr. George M. Towle. New York: Simon & Schuster, 1957 and other editions. (*Le tour du monde en quatre-vingt jours*, 1872).

―――. *Captain Grant's Children*. New York: Associated Booksellers, 1964 and other editions. (*Les enfants des capitaine Grant*, 1868).

―――. *Twenty Thousand Leagues Under the Sea*. Tr. Anthony Bonner. New York: Bantam, 1964 and other editions. (*Vingt mille lieues sur les mers*, 1870).

―――. *The Giant Raft*. Tr. W.J. Gordon. New York: Associated Booksellers, 1967 and other editions; also as *The Jangada, or 800 Leagues over the Amazon*. (*La Jangada: Huit cents lieues sur l'Amazone*, 1881).

―――. *From the Earth to the Moon*. Tr. Louis Mercier. New York: Aeonian Press, 1974 and other editions. (*De la terre à la lune*, 1865).

Voigt, Cynthia. *Homecoming*. New York: Atheneum, 1981.

Wahl, Mats. *Husbonden*. Stockholm: Bonnier, 1985. ("The Master").

―――. *Anna-Carolinas krig*. Stockholm: Bonnier, 1986. ("Anna-Carolina's War").

―――. *Den lakerade apan*. Stockholm: Rabén & Sjögren, 1986. ("The Lacquered Ape").

―――. *Maj Darlin*. Stockholm: Bonnier 1988. ("Maj Darlin").

Wells, H.G. *The Time Machine* (1895). Chicago: Folett, 1969.

―――. *The Invisible Man* (1897). Chicago: Folett, 1969.

Westall, Robert. *Blitzcat*. New York: Scholastic, 1989.
———. *The Kingdom by the Sea*. New York: Farrar, 1991.
White, E.B. *Charlotte's Web*. New York: Harper, 1952.
Widerberg, Siv. *Hasse*. Stockholm: Rabén & Sjögren, 1983. ("Hasse")—The first of the three books about Hasse.
Wilder, Laura Ingalls. *Little House in the Big Woods*. New York: Harper, 1932—The first book in a series.
Williams, Jay. *The Practical Princess and Other Liberating Fairy Tales*. New York: Parents, 1978.
Winthrop, Elisabeth. *The Castle in the Attic*. New York: Holiday, 1985.
Wolde, Gunilla. *Thomas Goes Out*. New York: Random House, 1971 (*Totte går ut*, 1969)—One of many picturebooks about Thomas.
———. *Betsy's First Day at Nursery School*. New York: Random House, 1976. (*Emmas första dag på dagis*, 1976)—One of many picturebooks about Betsy.
Wrightson, Patricia. *The Ice Is Coming*. New York: Atheneum, 1977—The first book in the Wirrun trilogy.
Yep, Lawrence. *Dragonwings*. New York: Harper & Row, 1975.
———. *Child of the Owl*. New York: Harper & Row, 1977.
Yolen, Jane. *Dragon's Blood*. New York: Doubleday, 1982—The first book in a fantasy trilogy.
———. *Favorite Folktales from Around the World*. New York: Pantheon, 1986.

SECONDARY SOURCES

The list contains sources that are quoted in the study and also those that have been consulted and found indispensable. I do not, however, include articles and essays from *Signal*, *ChLA Quarterly*, *Children's Literature*, and other sources which do not have a direct significance for my own arguments. Some English-language sources on Swedish writers discussed in my study are included for further reading.

Aers, Lesley. "The Treatment of Time in Four Children's Books." *Children's Literature in Education* 2 (1970): 69–81.
Åhmansson, Gabriella. *A Life and its Mirrors. A Feminist Reading of L. M. Montgomery's Fiction*. Uppsala, Sweden: Acta Universitatis Upsaliensis, 1991.
———. "Är det bara pojkar som kan rädda världen?" *Opsis kalopsis* 1 (1992): 24-27.
Algulin, Ingemar. *A History of Swedish Literature*. Stockholm: Swedish Institute, 1989.
Applebee, Arthur N. *The Child's Concept of Story: Age Two to Seventeen*. Chicago: University of Chicago Press, 1978.
Appleyard, J.A. *Becoming a Reader: The Experience of Fiction from Childhood to Adulthood*. Cambridge: Cambridge University Press, 1990.
Arbuthnot, May Hill, Margaret Mary Clark & Harriet G. Long. *Children's Books Too Good to Miss*. Cleveland: Case Western Reserve University Press, 1966.
Ariès, Philippe. *Centuries of Childhood: A Social History of Family Life*. Tr. Robert Baldick. New York: Vintage-Random House, 1962.
Attebery, Brian. *The Fantasy Tradition in American Literature. From Irwing to Le Guin*. Bloomington: Indiana University Press, 1980.
Auerbach, Erich. *Mimesis. The Represenation of Reality in Western Literature*. 4th ed. Princeton: Princeton University Press, 1974.
Avery, Gillian. *Nineteenth Century Children. Heroes and Heroines in English Children's Stories, 1780-1900*. London: Hodder & Stoughton, 1965.
Bakhtin, Michail. *Rabelais and His World*. Cambridge: MIT Press, 1968.

—————. *The Dialogic Imagination.* Austin: University of Texas Press, 1981.

—————. *Problems of Dostoyevsky's Poetics.* Minneapolis: University of Minnesota Press, 1984.

Bamberger, Richard. "Astrid Lindgren and a New Kind of Book for Children." *Bookbird* 3 (1967): 3-12.

Baran, Henryk, ed. *Semiotics and Structuralism. Readings from the Soviet Union.* White Plains, NY: International Arts and Sciences Press, 1976.

Barron, Neil. *Anatomy of Wonder. Science Fiction.* New York: Bowker, 1976.

Bator, Robert, ed. *Signposts to Criticism of Children's Literature.* Chicago: American Library Association, 1988.

Bell, Anthea. *E. Nesbit.* London: Bodley Head, 1960.

—————. "Children's books in translation." *Signal* 28 (1979):47-53.

Bergsten, Staffan. *Mary Poppins and Myth.* Stockholm: Almqvist & Wiksell International, 1978. (Studies Published by the Swedish Institute for Children's Books; 8).

Bergstrand, Ulla. "Elsa Beskow and Children's Picture Books in Sweden, 1900-1940." *Swedish Book Review* (1990 suppl.) 9-14.

Bettelheim, Bruno. *The Uses of Enchantment: The Meaning and Importance of Fairy Tales.* New York: Knopf, 1976.

Blishen, Edward, ed. *The Thorny Paradise. Writers on Writing for Children.* Harmondsworth, England: Kestrel, 1975.

Bloom, Harold. *The Anxiety of Influence.* New York: Oxford University Press, 1973.

Bloomingdale, Judith. "Alice as Anima. The Image of the Woman in Carroll's Classic." In *Aspects of Alice,* ed. Robert Phillips. New York: Vanguard Press, 1971, 378-390.

Booth, Wayne C. *The Rhetoric of Fiction.* Chicago: University of Chicago Press, 1961.

Bolin, Greta, Eva von Zweigbergk & Mary Ørvig. *Barn och böcker. En orientering.* Stockholm: Rabén & Sjögren, 1972.

Bottigheimer, Ruth. *Grimm's Bad Girls and Bold Boys: The Moral and Social Vision of the Tales.* New Haven: Yale University Press, 1987.

Brostrøm, Torben. *Folkeeventyrets moderne genbrug, eller Hvad forfatteren gør.* Copenhagen: Gyldendal, 1987.

Buckley, Mary F. *Words of Power: Language and Reality in the Fantasy Novels of E. Nesbit and P.L.Travers.* Ann Arbor, MI: University Microfilms, 1979. Dissertation, East Texas State University, 1977.

Butts, Dennis. *Good Writers for Young Readers.* St. Albans: Hart-Davis, 1977.

Cadogan, Mary & Patricia Craig. *You're a Brick, Angela! A New Look at Girls' Fiction from 1839 to 1975.* London: Gollantz, 1976.

Cameron, Eleanor. *The Green and Burning Tree. On the Writing and Enjoyment of Children's Books.* Boston: Little, Brown, 1969.

Campbell, Joseph. *The Hero with a Thousand Faces.* New York: Pantheon, 1949.

Carpenter, Humfrey & Mari Prichard. *The Oxford Companion to Children's Literature.* London: Oxford University Press, 1984.

Cawelty, John G. *Adventure, Mystery and Romance: Formula Stories as Art and Popular Culture.* Chicago: University of Chicago Press, 1976.

Chambers, Aidan. "Literary . . . Crossword Puzzle . . . or Masterpiece?" *Horn Book Magazine* 49 (1973): 494-497.

—————. *Introducing Books to Children.* London: Heinemann, 1973.

—————. *Booktalk. Occasional Writing on Literature and Children.* London: Bodley Head, 1985.

—————. *Tell Me: Children, Reading and Talk.* Stroud, Gloucester, England: Thimble Press, 1993.

Chambers, Nancy, ed. *The Signal Approach to Children's Books.* Harmondsworth, England: Kestrel, 1980.

Chatman, Seymour. *Story and Discourse.* Ithaca, NY: Cornell University Press, 1978.

Chernyavskaya, Irina, ed. *Zarubezhnaya detskaya literatura.* 2nd ed. Moscow: Prosveshcheniye, 1982.

Children's Literature Association Quarterly. Special issue: "Narrative theory." 15:2 (1990) 46-57.

Chukovsky, Kornei. *From Two to Five.* Berkeley and Los Angeles: University of California Press, 1963.

Cohen, J.A. *An Examination of Four Key Motifs in High Fantasy for Children.* Ann Arbor: University Microfilms, 1980—Dissertation, Ohio State University, 1975.

Cooper, Susan. "Escaping into Ourselves." In *Fantasists on Fantasy,* eds. Robert H. Boyer & Kenneth J. Zahorski. New York: Avon, 1984: 280-287.

Cott, Jonathan. *Pipers at the Gate of Dawn: The Wisdom of Children's Literature.* New York: Random House, 1983.

Cresswell, Helen. "If it's Someone from Porlock, Don't Answer the Door." *Children's Literature in Education* 4 (1971): 32-39.

Crouch, Marcus. *Treasure Seekers and Borrowers. Children's Books in Britain, 1900-1960.* London: Library Association, 1962.

———. *The Nesbit Tradition. The Children's Novel, 1945-1970.* London: Benn, 1972.

Culler, Jonathan. *On Deconstruction.* Ithaca, NY: Cornell University Press, 1982.

Curtius, Ernst Robert. *Europäische Literatur und lateinische Mittelalter.* 2 Aufg., Bern, Switzerland: A. Franke, 1954.

De skriver för barn och ungdom. Svenska nutidsförfattare. Vol 1–2. Lund, Sweden: Bubliotekstjänst, 1990.

Derrida, Jacques. *Of Grammatology.* Baltimore: Johns Hopkins University Press, 1976.

Doderer, Klaus. "Von der Solidarität der guten Menschen in der desolaten Welt." In *Gebt uns Bücher, gebt uns Flügel.* Hamburg: Oetinger, 1978: 25-31.

Dusinberre, Juliet. *Alice to the Lighthouse. Children's Books and Radical Experiments in Art.* London: Macmillan, 1987.

Eager, Edward. "Daily Magic." In *Horn Book Reflections,* ed. Elinor Whitney Field. Boston: Horn Book, 1969: 211-127.

Eco, Umberto. *A Theory of Semiotics.* Bloomington: Indiana University Press, 1976.

Edström, Vivi. *Barnbokens form. En studie i konsten att berätta.* 2nd ed. Göteborg, Sweden: Gothia, 1982. (Studies Published by the Swedish Institute for Children's Books; 11, with a summary in English: "Form in Children's Books. A Study in Narrative Art."

——— & Kristin Hallberg, eds. *Ungdomsboken. Värderingar och mönster.* Stockholm: Liber, 1984.

———. *Selma Lagerlöf.* Boston: Twayne, 1984.

———. *Astrid Lindgren.* Stockholm: The Swedish Institute, 1987.

———. "Pippi Longstocking: Chaos and Postmodernism." *Swedish Book Review* (1990) suppl.: 22-29.

———. *Astrid Lindgren—vildtoring och lägereld.* Stockholm: Rabén & Sjögren, 1992. Studies published by the Swedish Institute for Children's Books; 43, with a summary in English: "Astrid Lindgren—Campfire Rebel" (a).

———. "Den barnlitterära texten." In *Modern litteraturteori och metod i barnlitteraturforskningen,* ed. Maria Nikolajeva. Stockholm: Centrum för barnkulturforskning, 1992: 13-22, with a summary in English: "The children's text" (b).

Egoff, Sheila. *The Republic of Childhood. A Critical Guide to Canadian Children's literature.* 2nd ed. Toronto: Oxford University Press, 1975.

———, et al., eds. *Only Connect. Readings on Children's Literature.* 2nd ed. Toronto: Oxford University Press, 1980.

Epstein, Michail. *Paradoksy novizny.* Moscow: Sovetskij pisatel, 1988.

Escarpit, Denise. *La littérature d'enfance et de jeunesse en Europe. Panorame historique.* Paris: Presses Universitaires de France, 1981.

Espmark, Kjell. *Dialoger.* Stockholm: Norstedts, 1985.

Ewers, Hans-Heino, et al., eds. *Kinderlitteratur und Moderne.* Weinheim-Munich: Juventa, 1990.

———, ed. *Komik im Kinderbuch. Erscheinungsformen des Komischen in der Kinder- und Jugendliteratur.* Weinheim-Munich: Juventa, 1992.

Eyre, Frank. *British Children's Books in the Twentieth Century.* London: Longman, 1971.

Fagerström, Gudrun. *Maria Gripe, hennes verk och hennes läsare.* Stockholm: Bonnier, 1977. Studies published by the Swedish Institute for Children's Books; 6, with a summary in English: "Maria Gripe, Her Work and Her Readers."

Fawcett, Robin P., et al., eds. *The Semiotics of Culture and Language.* Vol 1-2. London: Frances Pinter, 1984.

Fenwich, Sara, ed. *A Critical Approach to Children's Literature.* Chicago: University of Chicago Press, 1967.

Field, Elinor Whitney, ed. *Horn Book Reflections. On Children's Books and Reading.* Boston: Horn Book, 1969.

Fisher, Margery. *Intent Upon Reading. A Critical Appraisal of Modern Fiction for Children.* Leicester, England: Brockhampton Press, 1964.

———. *The Who is Who in Children's Books. A Treasury of the Familiar Characters of Childhood.* London: Weidenfeld & Nicholson, 1975.

———. *The Bright Face of Danger: An Exploration of the Adventure Story.* London: Hodder & Stoughton, 1986.

Flaker, Aleksander. *Modelle der Jeans Prosa.* Kronberg, West Germany: Scriptor, 1975.

Fox, Geoff, ed. *Writers, Critics and Children.* New York: Agaton, 1976.

——— & Graham Hammond, eds. *Responses to Children's Literature. Proceedings of the Fourth Symposium of the International Research Society for Children's Literature.* Munich: Saur, 1980.

Franz, Marie-Louise von. *Shadow and Evil in Fairy Tales.* New York: Spring, 1974.

———. *Interpretation of Fairy Tales.* New York: Spring, 1970.

Fraser, James H., ed. *Society and Children's Literature.* Boston: Godine, 1978.

Fridell, Lena, ed. *Barnbok och barnboksforskning.* Stockholm: Almqvist & Wiksell, 1972.

Fryatt, Norma R., ed. *A Horn Book Sampler. On Children's Books and Reading.* Boston: Horn Book, 1969.

Frye, Northrop. *Anatomy of Criticism. Four Essays.* Princeton: Princeton University Press, 1957.

Furuland, Lars & Mary Ørvig. *Utblick över barn- och ungdomslitteraturen.* Stockholm: Rabén & Sjögren, 1986.

Garner, Alan. "Coming to Terms." *Children's Literature in Education* 2 (1970): 15-29.

———. "A Bit More Practice." In *The Cool Web,* ed. Margaret Meek. New York: Atheneum, 1978: 196-200.

Gilbert, Sandra M. & Susan Gubar. *The Madwoman in the Attic. The Woman Writer and the Nineteenth Century Literary Imagination.* New Haven: Yale University Press, 1977.

Gillis, Caroline. "Possession and Structure in the Novels of Alan Garner." *Children's Literature in Education* 18 (1975): 107-117.

Golden, Joanne M. *The Narrative Symbol in Childhood Literature. Exploration in the Construction of Text.* Berlin: Mouton, 1990.

Gormsen, Jakob. *Elleve nordiske børne bogsforfattere.* Copenhagen: Gyldendal, 1979.

Granlund-Lind, Rigmor. "Ungdomsboken i DDR—en översikt." In *Ungomsboken. Värderingar och mönster,* eds. Vivi Edström & Kristin Hallberg. Stockholm: Liber, 1984: 176-194.

Green, Roger Lancelyn. *C.S. Lewis.* London: Bodley Head, 1957.

———. *Tellers of Tales. British Authors of Children's Books from 1800 to 1964.* London: Ward, 1965.

Greimas, Algirdas Julien. *Sémantique structurale: recherche de méthode.* Paris:

Larousse, 1966.

Grønbech, Bo. *H. C. Andersens eventyrverden*. Copenhagen: Branner, 1945.

Haas, Gerhard, ed. *Kinder- und Jugendliteratur. Zur Typologie und Funktion einer literarischen Gattung*. Stuttgart, Germany: Reclam, 1974.

Hallberg, Kristin. "Litteraturvetenskap och bilderboksforskningen." *Tidskrift för litteraturvetenskap* 3/4 (1982): 163-168.

—— & Boel Westin, eds. *I bilderbokens värld*. Stockholm: Liber, 1985.

——. "Swedish Illustrated Children's Books." *Swedish Book Review* (1990 suppl.): 15-21.

Halle, Morris, et al., eds. *Semiosis. Semiotics and the History of Culture. In honorem Georgii Lotman*. Ann Arbor: University of Michigan Press, 1984. (Michigan Slavic Contributions; 10).

Harker, Mary J. "Textual Capers: Carnival in the Novels of Brian Doyle." *Canadian Children's Literature* 63 (1991): 41-52.

Haviland, Virginia. *Children and Literature. Views and Reviews*. London: Bodley Head, 1974.

Hawking, Stephen. *A Brief History of Time. From Big Bang to Black Holes*. New York: Bantam, 1988.

Hearne, Betsy & Marilyn Kaye, eds. *Celebrating Children's Books. Essays on Children's Literature in Honor of Zena Sutherland*. New York: Lothrop, Lee & Shepard, 1981.

——. *Choosing Books for Children. A Commonsense Guide*. 2nd revised ed. New York: Delacorte, 1990.

Holub, Robert C. *Reception Theory. A Critical Introduction*. London: Methuen, 1984.

Hume, Kathryn. *Fantasy and Mimesis. Responses to Reality in Western Literature*. New York: Methuen, 1984.

Hunt, Peter. "Childist Criticism: The Subculture of the Child, the Book and the Critic." *Signal* 43 (1984): 42-59 (a).

——. "Questions of Method and Methods of Questioning: Childist Criticism in Action." *Signal* 45 (1984): 180-200 (b).

——. "Necessary Misreadings: Directions in Narrative Theory for Children's Literature." *Studies in the Literary Imagination* 18:2 (1985): 107-121.

——, ed. *Children's Literature. The Development of Criticism*. New York: Routledge, 1990.

——. *Criticism, Theory and Children's Literature*. London: Blackwell, 1991 (a).

——. "The Decline and Decline of the Children's Book? The Problems of Adults Reading Children's Books and What Can Be Done About Them." In *Children's Literature and Contemporary Theory*, ed. Michael Stone. Wollongong, Australia: University of Wollongong Press, 1991: 1-14 (b).

Hurwitz, Johanna. *Astrid Lindgren: Storyteller of the World*. Harmondsworth, England: Puffin, 1989.

Iser, Wolfgang. *The Implied Reader*. Baltimore: Johns Hopkins University Press, 1974.

——. *The Act of Reading: A Theory of Aesthetic Response*. Baltimore: Johns Hopkins University Press, 1974.

Jackson, Rosemary. *Fantasy: the Literature of Subversion*. New York: Methuen, 1981.

Johansson, Jane. "Vägen till Fantasien: Receptionsforskningens metoder och mål." In *Modern litteraturteori och metod i barnlitteraturforskningen*, ed. Maria Nikolajeva. Stockholm: Centrum för barnkulturforskning 1992: 151-166. With a summary in English: "The Road to Fantastica: Goals and Methods of Reception Studies."

Jones, W. Glyn. *Tove Jansson*. Boston: Twayne, 1984.

Klingberg, Göte. *Barn- och ungdomslitteraturen*. Stockholm: Natur och Kultur, 1970.

——. *Barnlitteraturforskning. En introduktion*. Stockholm: Almqvist & Wiksell, 1972.

——, et al., eds. *Children's Books in Translation. The Situation and the Problems*.

Stockholm: Almqvist & Wiksell International, 1978. (Studies Published by the Swedish Institute for Children's Books; 9).

———. *De främmande världarna i barn- och ungdomslitteraturen.* Stockholm: Rabén & Sjögren, 1980. With a summary in English: "The Strange Worlds in Children's Fiction."

——— *Adaptation av en text till barns egenskaper: en lägesrapport om ett begrepp.* Lund, Sweden: University of Lund Press, 1981.

———. "Barthomleys smärta och Mow Cops frid," *Barnboken* 3 (1982): 21-26.

———. *Children's Fiction in the Hands of the Translators.* Lund, Sweden: Gleerup, 1986.

———. *Besök i brittiska barnbokslandskap.* Stockholm: Sjöstrands, 1987. (Studies Published by the Swedish Institute for Children's Books; 22).With a summary in English: "Visits to British Children's Book Landscapes."

———. *Till gagn och nöje—svensk barnbok 400 år.* Stockholm: Rabén & Sjögren, 1991. (Studies Published by the Swedish Institute for Children's Books; 38).With a summary in English: "For Instruction and Delight. The Swedish Children's Book—400 Years."

Kondrup, Jonny. *Levned og tolkninger. Studier i nordisk selvbiografi.* Odense, Denmark: Odense University Press, 1982.

Kristeva, Julia. "Word, dialogue and novel." In *The Kristeva Reader,* ed. Toril Moi. London: Blackwell, 1986: 34-61.

———. "The Adolescent Novel." In her *Abjection, Melancholia and Love,* ed. J. Fletcher. London; Routledge, 1990: 8-23.

Krüger, Anna. *Die erzählende Kinder- und Jugendliteratur im Wandel. Neue Inhalte und Formen im Kommunikations- und Sozialisationsmittel Jugendliteratur.* Frankfurt am Main: Diesterweg, 1980.

Landsberg, Michele. *The World of Children's Books. A Guide of Choosing the Best.* London: Simon & Schuster, 1988.

Lane, Selma G. *Down the Rabbit Hole. Adventures and Misadventures in the Realm of Children's Literature.* New York: Atheneum, 1972.

Laughlin, Jeannine & Sherry Laughlin, eds. *Children's Authors Speak.* Englewood, CO: Libraries Unlimited, 1993.

Le Guin, Ursula. *The Language of the Night. Essays on Fantasy and Science Fiction.* New York: Berkley Books, 1979.

Leeson, Robert. *Children's Books and Class Society. Past and Present.* London: Writers and Readers Publishing Cooperative, 1977.

Lehtonen, Maija & Marita Rajalin. *Barnboken i Finland förr och nu.* Stockholm: Rabén & Sjögren, 1984. With a summary in English: "Children's Books in Finland."

Lévi-Strauss, Claude. *Structural Anthropology.* Garden City, NY: Doubleday, 1967.

Lewis, C.S. "On Three Ways of Writing for Children." In *Only Connect,* eds. Sheila Egoff et al. Toronto: Oxford University Press, 1980: 207-220.

Lochhead, Marion. *The Renaissance of Wonder in Children's Literature.* Edinburgh: Canongate, 1977.

Löfgren, Eva M. "Kalle Blomkvist och draken. Arketypstudier i Astrid Lindgrens barndeckare." In *Modern litteraturteori och metod i barnlitteraturforskningen,* ed. Maria Nikolajeva. Stockholm: Centrum för barnkulturforskning, 1992: 47-74.With a summary in English: "Bill Bergson and the Dragon: Archetypal Studies of Astrid Lindgren's Detective Stories for Children."

———. *Schoolmates of the Long-Ago. Motifs and Archetypes in Dorita Fairlie Bruce's Boarding School Stories.* Stockholm: Symposion, 1993.

Lotman, Yuri. "Kanonicheskoye iskusstvo kak informatsionny paradoks." In *Problemy kanona.* Moscow: Nauka, 1973: 16-22.

———. *The Structure of the Artistic Text.* Ann Arbor: University of Michigan Press, 1977.

———. *Universe of the Mind: A Semiotic Theory of Culture.* London: Tauris, 1990.

————. *Izbrannye stat'i*, vol 1-3. Tallinn, Estonia: Alexandra, 1992-93.

Lucid, Daniel P., ed. *Soviet Semiotics*. Baltimore: Johns Hopkins University Press, 1977.

Lukens, Rebecca J. *A Critical Handbook of Children's Literature*. 4th ed. New York: Harper Collins, 1990.

Lundqvist, Ulla & Sonja Svensson, eds. *Kring den svenska ungdomsboken*. Stockholm: Natur och Kultur, 1977.

————. *Århundradets barn. Fenomenet Pippi Långstrump och dess förutsättningar*. Stockholm: Rabén & Sjögren, 1979.With a summary in English: "The Child of the Century."

————. "Some portraits of teenagers in modern junior novels in Sweden." In *The Portrayal of the Child in Children's Literature*, ed. Denise Escarpit. Munich: Saur, 1985, pp. 117-124.

————. *Tradition och förnyelse. Svensk ungdomsbok från sextiotal till nittiotal*. Stockholm: Rabén & Sjögren, 1994. (Studies Published by the Swedish Institute for Children's Books; 51).With a summary in English: "Traditional Patterns and New Ones. Swedish Books for Young Adults from the Sixties to the Nineties."

Lynch-Brown, Carol & Carl M. Tomlinson. *Essentials of Children's Literature*. Boston: Allyn and Bacon, 1993.

Lynn, Ruth Nadelman. *Fantasy for Children. An Annotated Checklist and Reference Guide*. 2nd ed. New York: Bowker, 1983.

McGillis, Roderick. "The Embrace: Narrative Voice and Children's Books". *Canadian Children's Literature* 63 (1991): 24-40.

McVitty, Walter. "Response to *Red Shift*." *Labrys* 7 (1981): 133-138.

Mählqvist, Stefan. "Harry Kullman." *Bookbird* 2 (1980): 7-10.

————. *Kaos i tiden. En läsning av Alan Garners Red Shift*. Uppsala, Sweden: Aber, 1992. (Studies Published by the Swedish Institute for Children's Books; 42). With a summary in English: "Chaos in Time. Reading Alan Garner's *Red Shift*."

Manlove, C.N. *Modern Fantasy. Five Studies*. Cambridge: Cambridge University Press, 1975.

Mannheimer, Carin. "Maria Gripe." *Bookbird* 2 (1973): 24-34.

Matejka, Ladislaw, et al., eds. *Readings in Soviet Semiotics*. Ann Arbor: University of Michigan Press, 1977. (Michigan Slavic Publications; 15).

Meek, Margaret, et al., eds. *The Cool Web. The Patterns of Children's Reading*. London: Bodley Head, 1977.

Meigs, Cornelia, et al. *A Critical History of Children's Literature*. New York: Macmillan, 1969.

Metcalf, Eva Maria. "The Invisible Child in the Works of Tormod Haugen." *Barnboken* 1 (1992): 15-23.

Moebius, William. "Introduction to Picturebook Codes." In *Children's Literature. The Development of Criticism*, ed. Peter Hunt. London: Routledge, 1990: 131-147.

Moi, Toril. *Sexual/textual Politics. Feminist Literary Theory*. London: Methuen, 1985.

Molson, Francis J. *Children's Fantasy*. San Bernardino, CA: Borgo, 1989.

Niall, Brenda. *Australia Through the Looking-Glass. Children's Fiction 1830-1980*. Melbourne, Australia: Melbourne University Press, 1984.

Nieuwenhuizen, Agnes. *Good Books for Teenagers. A Comprehensive Reading Guide*. Port Melbourne, Australia: Mandarin, 1992.

Nikolajeva, Maria. "The Function of the Charm." *Labrys* 7 (1981): 141-145.

————. "Bilderboken som försvann." In *I bilderbokens värld*, eds. Kristin Hallberg & Boel Westin. Stockholm: Liber, 1985: 127-142.

————. "Edith Nesbit—the Maker of Modern Fairy-Tales." *Merveilles & contes* 1:1 (1987): 31-44.

————. *The Magic Code. The Use of Magical Patterns in Fantasy for Children*. Stockholm: Almqvist & Wiksell International, 1988. (Studies Published by the Swedish Institute for Children's Books; 31).

———. "The Insignificance of Time: *Red Shift*." *Children's Literature Association Quarterly* 14:3 (1989): 128-131.

———. "How Fantasy is Made: Patterns and Structures in *The Neverending Story* by Michael Ende." *Merveilles & contes* 4:1 (1990): 34-42.

———, ed. *Modern litteraturteori och metod i barnlitteraturforskningen.* Stockholm: Centrum för barnkulturforskning, 1992. With a summary in English: "Modern Literary Theory in Children's Literature Research."

———. "Fantasy: The Evolution of a Pattern." In *Fantasy and Feminism*, ed. Rhonda Bunbury. Geelong, Australia: Deakin University Press, 1992: 3-39.

———. "Stages of Transformation: Folklore Elements in Children's Novels." *Canadian Children's Literature* 73 (1994): 48-54.

Nodelman, Perry. "Interpretation and the Apparent Sameness of Children's Literature." *Studies in the Literary Imagination* 18:2 (1985): 5–20.

———, ed. *Touchstones: Reflections on the Best in Children's Literature.* vol. 1-3. West Lafayette, IN: ChLA Publications, 1985-89.

———. *Words About Pictures: The Narrative Art of Children's Picture Books.* Athens, Georgia: University of Georgia Press, 1988.

———. *The Pleasures of Children's Literature.* New York: Longman, 1992.

Nordlinder, Eva. *Sekelskiftets svenska konstsaga och sagodiktaren Helena Nyblom.* Stockholm: Bonnier, 1991. With a summary in English: "The Kunstmärchen in Turn-of-the-century Sweden: Helena Nyblom and Her Tales."

Norton, Donna E. *Through the Eyes of a Child. An Introduction to Children's Literature.* 3rd ed. New York: Macmillan, 1991.

Oittinen, Riitta. *I Am Me—I Am Other. On the Dialogics of Translating for Children.* Tampere, Finland: University of Tampere, 1993. (Acta Univeritatis Tamperensis ser A vol 386).

Ong, Walter J. *Orality and Literacy: The Technologizing of the Word.* London: Methuen, 1982.

Opie, Iona & Peter Opie. *The Classic Fairy Tales.* Oxford: Oxford University Press, 1974.

Ørjasæter, Tordis, et al. *Den norske barnelitteraturen gjennom 200 år.* Oslo: Cappelen, 1981.

Ørvig, Mary, ed. *En bok om Astrid Lindgren.* Stockholm: Rabén & Sjögren, 1977. (Studies Published by the Swedish Institute for Children's Books; 3).—With a summary in English: "A Book about Astrid Lindgren."

———, ed. *Barnboken i Tjechoslovakien.* Stockholm: Rabén & Sjögren, 1981. With a summary in English: "Children's Books in Czechoslovakia."

———, Marianne Eriksson & Birgitta Sjöstedt, eds. *Duvdrottningen. En bok till Astrid Lindgren.* Stockholm: Rabén & Sjögren, 1987. (Studies Published by the Swedish Institute for Children's Books; 27). With a summary in English: "To Astrid Lindgren: Queen of the Doves."

Pellowski, Anne. *The World of Children's Literature.* New York: Bowker, 1968.

———. *Made to Measure: Children's Books in Developing Countries.* Paris: UNESCO, 1980.

Perrot, Jean, ed. *Culture, texte et jeune lecteure.* Nancy, France: Presses Universitaires de Nancy, 1992.

Philip, Neil. *A Fine Anger: A Critical Introduction to the Work of Alan Garner.* London: Collins, 1981.

———. "Michael Ende, *The Neverending Story*." *Times Literary Supplement* (London) 1984, 6 January.

Posner, Roland. "What is Culture? Toward a Semiotic Explication of Anthropological Concepts." In *The Nature of Culture*, ed. Walter A Koch. Bochum, Germany: Brockmeyer, 1989: 240–295.

Prigogine, Ilya & Isabelle Stengers. *Order Out of Chaos: Man's New Dialogue with Nature.* London: Heinemann, 1984.

Propp, Vladimir. *Morphology of the Folktale.* Austin: University of Texas Press, 1968.

————. *Theory and History of Folklore*. Manchester, England: Manchester University Press, 1984.

Reeder, Kik. "Pippi Longstocking—Feminist or Anti-feminist?" *Interracial Books for Children* 4 (1974): 1-2.

Rees, David. *The Marble in the Water. Essays on Contemporary Writers of Fiction for Children and Young Adults*. Boston: Horn Book, 1980.

Rönnerstrand, Torsten. "Barn- och ungdomslitteraturen ur jungianskt perspektiv." In *Modern litteraturteori och metod i barnlitteraturforskningen*, ed. Maria Nikolajeva. Stockholm: Centrum för barnkulturforskning, 1992: 75-112. With a summary in English: "Children's and Youth Literature in a Jungian Perspective."

Rose, Jacqueline. *The Case of Peter Pan, or The Impossibility of Children's Fiction*. London: Macmillan, 1984.

Roxburgh, Stephen. "A Picture Equals How Many Words? Narrative Theory and Picture Books for Children." *The Lion and the Unicorn* 7/8 (1983): 20–33.

Rudman, Masha Kabakow. *Children's Literature: An Issues Approach*. 2nd ed. New York: Longman, 1984.

Rustin, Margaret & Michael. *Narratives of Love and Loss. Studies in Modern Children's Fiction*. London: Verso, 1987.

Sale, Roger. *Fairy Tales and After*. Cambridge: Cambridge University Press, 1978.

Saltman, Judith. *Modern Canadian Children's Books*. Toronto: Oxford University Press, 1987.

Sammonds, Martha C. *A Guide Through Narnia*. London: Hodder & Stoughton, 1979.

————. *"A Better Country." The Worlds of Religious Fantasy and Science Fiction*. New York: Greenwood, 1988.

Saxby, Maurice. *A History of Australian Children's Literature 1841-1941*. Sydney, Australia: Wentworth, 1969.

————. *A History of Australian Children's Literature 1941-1970*. Sydney, Australia: Wentworth, 1971.

————. *First Choice. A Guide to the Best Books for Australian Children*. Melbourne, Australia: Oxford University Press, 1991.

————. *The Proof of the Puddin'. Australian Children's Literature 1970-1990*. Sydney, Australia: Ashton Scholastic, 1993.

Schaffer, Barbro. "Solen som lingonbröd. Bilden i den moderna bilderboken." In *Vår moderna bilderbok*, ed Vivi Edström. Stockholm: Rabén & Sjögren, 1991. (Studies Published by the Swedish Institute for Children's Books: 40: 104-154.) With a summary in English: "The Modern Swedish Picturebook."

Schakel, Peter J. *Reading with the Heart: The Way Into Narnia*. Grand Rapids, MI: William B. Eerdman, 1979.

Scherf, Walter. *Strukturanalyse der Kinder- und Jugendliteratur*. Bad Heilbrunn/Obb, Germany: Klinghardt, 1978.

Scholes, Robert. *Structuralism in Literature: An Introduction*. New Haven: Yale University Press, 1974.

————. *Semiotics and Interpretation*. New Haven: Yale University Press, 1982.

Schwarcz, Joseph H. *Ways of the Illustrator: Visual Communication in Children's Literature*. Chicago: American Library Association, 1982.

Shavit, Zohar. "The Ambivalent Status of Texts. The Case of Children's Literature." *Poetics Today* 173 (1980): 75-86.

————. *Poetics of Children's Literature*. Athens, Georgia: University of Georgia Press, 1986.

Skjønsberg, Kari. *Hvem forteller? Om adaptasjoner i barnelitteratur*. Oslo: Tiden, 1979.

————. "Lesere og forfattere i barne- og ungdomslitteratur." In *Mer enn bøker. SBIH 50 år. Jubileumsskrift*, ed. Hans Eirik Aarek. Oslo: Statens bibliotek- och informasjonshøgskole, 1990: 65-76.

Smith, James Steel. *A Critical Approach to Children's Literature*. New York: McGraw-Hill, 1967.

Smith, Lilian H. *The Unreluctant Years: A Critical Approach to Children's Literature*. New York: Viking, 1967.

Stephens, John. *Language and Ideology in Children's Fiction*. London: Longman, 1992.

Stone, Michael, ed. *Children's Literature and Contemporary Theory*. Wollongong, Australia: University of Wollongong Press, 1991.

Streatfeild, Noel. *Magic and the Magician. Edith Nesbit and Her Children's Books*. London: Benn, 1958.

Studies in the Literary Imagination. Special issue: "Narrative Theory and Children's Literature." ed. R.T.H. Keenan, 18:2 (1985).

Suleiman, Susan & Inge Crossman, eds. *The Reader in the Text: Essays on Audience and Participation*. Princeton: Princeton University Press, 1980.

Sutherland, Zena, Dianne L. Monson & May Hill Arbuthnot. *Children and Books*. 6th ed. Glenview, IL: Scott, Foresman, 1981.

Svensson, Sonja. *Läsning för folkets barn. Folkskolans Barntidning och dess förlag, 1892-1914*. Stockholm: Rabén & Sjögren, 1983. (Studies Published by the Swedish Institute for Children's Books; 16). With a summary in English: "Reading Matter for Working Class Children. 'The Elementary School Child's Magazine' and Its Publishing House 1892-1914."

———. "Barn- och ungdomslitteraturen—fram till 1920." In *Den svenska litteraturen*, eds. Lars Lönnroth & Sven Delblanc. Vol. 4. Stockholm: Bonnier, 1989: 207-228.

———. "Så skulle världen bli som ny—barn- och ungdomslitteraturen efter andra världskriget." In *Den svenska litteraturen*, eds. Lars Lönnroth & Sven Delblanc. Vol. 6. Stockholm: Bonnier, 1990: 221-241.

Swinfen, Ann. *In Defence of Fantasy. A Study of the Genre in English and American Literature Since 1945*. London: Rutledge & Kegan Paul, 1984.

Tabbert, Reinbert. "The Impact of Children's Books—Cases and Concepts." In *Responses to Children's Literature*, eds. Geoff Fox & Graham Hammond. Munich: Saur, 1980: 34-58.

———. *Kinderbuchanalysen. Autoren-Themen-Gattungen*. Frankfurt-am-Main: Dipa, 1990.

———. *Kinderbuchanalysen II. Wirkung—kultureller Kontext—Unterricht*. Frankfurt-am-Main: Dipa, 1991.

Tatar, Maria. *The Hard Facts of the Grimms' Fairy Tales*. Princeton: Princeton University Press, 1987.

———. *Off With Their Heads! Fairy Tales and the Cultures of Childhood*. Princeton: Princeton University Press, 1992.

Taylor, Gordon O. *Studies in Modern American Autobiography*. London: Macmillan, 1983.

Timenchik, R. "K simvolike telefona v russkoj poezii." In *Trudy po znakovym sistemam 22*. Tartu, Estonia: Acta et commentationes universitatis Tartuensis, 1988: 155-163.

Timofeyeva, Inessa. *Sto knig vashemu rebyonku*. Moscow: Kniga, 1987.

Todorov, Tsvetan. *The Fantastic: A Structural Approach to a Literary Genre*. Cleveland: Case Western Reserve University Press, 1973.

———. *Mikhail Bakhtin: The Dialogical Principle*. Manchester, England: Manchester University Press, 1984.

Toijer-Nilsson, Ying. *Berättelser för fria barn. Könsroller i barnboken*. Göteborg, Sweden: Stegeland, 1978. (Studies Published by the Swedish Institute for Children's Books; 10). With a summary in English: "Stories for Free Children. Sex Roles in Children's Books."

———. *Fantasins underland. Myt och idé i den fantastiska berättelsen*. Stockholm: EFS-förlag, 1981. With a summary in English: "The Wonderland of Fantasy. Myth and Ideology in Fantasy Literature."

————. *Minnet av det förflutna. Motiv i den moderna historiska ungdomsromanen.* Stockholm: Rabén & Sjögren 1987. (Studies Published by the Swedish Institute for Children's Books; 24). With a summary in English: "Re-living the Past. Themes of Modern Historical Novels for Young Readers."

————. *77 svenskspråkiga barnboksförfattare.* Stockholm: Rabén & Sjögren, 1989.

————. *Minnet av igår.* Stockholm: Rabén & Sjögren, 1990. (Studies Published by the Swedish Institute for Children's Books; 36). With a summary in English: "Calling Back Yesterday."

————. "Tormod Haugen." In *De skriver för barn och ungdomar. Översatta nutidsförfattare.* Lund, Sweden: Bibliotekstjänst, 1991: 169-178.

Toivonen, Pirjo-Maija. "Semiotics and the Cognitive Theories of Reading." In *Ämnesdidaktisk forkning och dess framtid,* ed. Katri Sarmavuori & Veijo Meisalo. Helsinki, University of Helsinki Press, 1990: 33-41.

Tolkien, J.R.R. "On Fairy Stories." In his: *Tree and Leaf.* London: Allen & Unwin, 1968: 11-70.

Törnqvist, Egil. "Astrid Lindgrens halvsaga. Berättartekniken i *Bröderna Lejonhjärta.*" *Svensk litteraturtidskrift* 2 (1975): 17-34.

Townsend, John Rowe. *A Sense of Story. Essays on Contemporary Writers for Children.* London: Longman, 1971.

————. *Written for Children. An Outline of English-language Children's Literature.* 2nd ed. Harmondsworth, England: Kestrel, 1983.

Tucker, Nickolas, ed. *Suitable for Children? Controversies in Children's Literature.* Berkeley and Los Angeles: University of California Press, 1976.

Veglahn, Nancy. "Images of Evil: Male and Female Monsters in Heroic Fantasy." *Children's literature* 15 (1987): 106-119.

Wall, Barbara. *The Narrator's Voice. The Dilemma of Children's Fiction.* London: Macmillan, 1991.

Watson, Victor. "In Defence of Jan." *Signal* 41 (1983): 77-87.

Waugh, Patricia. *Metafiction. The Theory and Practice of Self-Conscious Fiction.* London: Methuen, 1984.

Westin, Boel. "Resan till mumindalen. Om Tove Janssons bilderboksestetik." In *I bilderbokens värld,* ed. Kristin Hallberg & Boel Westin. Stockholm: Liber, 1985: 235-253.

————. *Familjen i dalen. Tove Janssons muminvärld.* Stockholm: Bonnier, 1988. With a summary in English: "The Family in the Valley. The Moomin World of Tove Jansson" (a).

————, ed. *Böcker ska blänka som solar. En bok till Vivi Edström.* Stockholm: Rabén & Sjögren, 1988. (Studies Published by the Swedish Institute for Children's Books; 32). With a summary in English: "Let Books Shine Like Suns" (b).

————. "Creating a Zest for Life: Feminine, Masculine and Human in Tove Jansson's Moomin World." *Swedish Book Review* (1990): 30-35.

————. *Children's Literature in Sweden.* Stockholm: Swedish Institute, 1991 (a).

————. "Konsten som äventyr. Tove Jansson och bilderboken." In *Vår moderna bilderbok,* ed. Vivi Edström. Stockholm: Rabén & Sjögren, 1991. (Studies Published by the Swedish Institute for Children's Books; 40: 51–70). With a summary in English: "The Modern Swedish Picturebook."

Winqvist, Margareta. *Den engelske Robinson Crusoes sällsamma öden och äventyr genom svenska sprøket.* Stockholm: Bonnier, 1973. (Studies Published by the Swedish Institute for Children's Books; 2). With a summary in English: "The Strange Suprising Adventures of Robinson Crusoe of York Through the Swedish Translations."

Whitrow, Gerald James. *The Natural Philosophy of Time.* London: Oxford University Press, 1980.

Wolf, Virginia L. "Paradise Lost? The Displacement of Myth in Children's Novels."

Studies in the Literary Imagination 18:2 (1985): 47-64.

Zadworna-Fjellestad, Danuta. *Alice's Adventures in Wonderland and Gravity's Rainbow: A Study in Duplex Fiction.* Stockholm: Almqvist & Wiksell International, 1986.

Zipes, Jack. *Breaking the Magic Spell: Radical Theories of Folk and Fairy Tales.* Austin: University of Texas Press, 1979.

———. *Fairy Tales and the Art of Subversion: The Classical Genre for Children and the Process of Civilisation.* London: Heinemann, 1982.

———, ed. *Don't Bet on the Prince: Contemporary Feminist Fairy Tales in North America and England.* New York: Methuen, 1986.

———. "Critical Observations on Recent Psychoanalytical Approaches to the Tales of Brothers Grimm." *Merveilles & Contes* 1:1 (1987): 19-30.

———. *The Brothers Grimm: From Enchanted Forests to the Modern World.* New York: Routledge, 1988.

Zweigbergk, Eva von. *Barnboken i Sverige, 1750-1950.* Stockholm: Rabén & Sjögren, 1965.

Index